PRAISE FOR *THE SAVVY CONSUMER:*

"Boy do we need this book now! It's not preachy, it's a good, fun read and it WILL save you money. But more importantly, it will also save you the hassle of having to fix something gone wrong . . . and it's all organized so you can whip it out before the guy on the other end of the phone talks you into something."
—Lea Thompson, Chief Consumer Correspondent for Dateline NBC

"Breezy, conversational and informative. Ms. Leamy has taken the arcane and made it understandable. Her book helps consumers navigate the often foreboding world of refinancing a home, buying a car or deciding what charity to contribute to, and she has done it with the trained eye of someone who has spent years as a consumer advocate. Her book is a real contribution to the often befuddled consumer."
—Terence McElroy, Communications Director,
Florida Department of Agriculture and Consumer Services

"Elisabeth Leamy's hard-hitting book, *The Savvy Consumer*, is packed with practical advice and insights, delivered in a lively style. It will help consumers avoid wasting time and money on scams, rip-offs, and just plain lousy deals—with lots of guidance on how to do the job of consuming up front before the damage is done."
—Robert Krughoff, President, Consumers' CHECKBOOK magazine

"Leamy doesn't force readers to take on the entire text, but makes it easy for them to pick and choose the relevant areas as their needs arise. In reading the automotive sections, I was very surprised how much Leamy taught me—and I have dealt with consumer automobile issues daily for almost a decade at AAA Mid-Atlantic. Since issues relating to auto purchase and repair are the top generator of consumer complaints in America, Elisabeth Leamy provides an important reference—and critical information—that will aid motorists in navigating the minefields of automobile rip-offs!"
—Lon Anderson, AAA Mid-Atlantic

"Bravo! *The Savvy Consumer* is indeed an exceptional piece and Leamy has certainly provided a tremendous amount of information on each of the consumer topics covered. This book will definitely be added to my arsenal. The info it gives is on target, presented in easy to understand everyday language, and shows some terrific insight as well.

Recommended reading for anyone involved in consumer education, consumer affairs issues, and even those who just want to avoid the pain, hassle, and expense of being a victim."
—Bob E. Harris, North American Consumer Protection Investigators

"For an easy-to-read and even easier to digest road map to beating the odds of consumer traps, get *The Savvy Consumer*. From 'Cars' to 'Credit,' each chapter gives shoppers, whether beginners or vets, the essentials for avoiding mishaps and better yet, how to deal with them when they do happen. It's a unique source, all in one place, of information consumers can use every day."
—Jodie Bernstein, Former Director of Consumer Education, Federal Trade Commission

"Consumers face a confusing world of challenges, choices, and traps. Elisabeth Leamy offers valuable tips for avoiding scams, preventing heartache, and getting the most bang for the buck. With personal anecdotes, no-nonsense advice, and coverage of a wide variety of marketplace issues, Leamy offers any consumer the chance to become a 'Savvy Consumer.' "
—Carol McKay, Vice President of Communications, National Consumers League

"*The Savvy Consumer* is the must have book for consumers. Whether its buying a car, fixing up a home, or dealing with credit issues, Leamy's book presents the information consumers need in a very organized and informative fashion. Anyone reading this book is going to be a smarter consumer. Down to earth, very readable, and chock full of excellent information, it should be in everyone's library."
—Shirley Rooker, President, Call For Action

"Consumers work just as hard for the dollars they give to charity as for the dollars they spend on goods and services. We applaud *The Savvy Consumer's* practical advice on making informed giving decisions. Our experience in charity evaluation shows it's important to be a 'Savvy Donor' as well."
—Art Taylor, President and CEO, BBB Wise Giving Alliance

THE SAVVY CONSUMER

FROM CAPITAL IDEAS—
Practical books that offer expert advice
on key personal and professional aspects of life.
Other titles include:

"Just Sign Here, Honey":
Women's 10 Biggest Legal Mistakes
and How to Avoid Them
by Marilyn Barrett

"Honey, I've Shrunk the Bills!":
Save from $5,000 to $10,000 Every Year
by Jack Weber

Our Money Ourselves for Couples:
A New Way of Relating to Money and Each Other
by C. Diane Ealy and Kay Lesh

Use Your Fingers, Use Your Toes:
Quick and Easy Step-by-Step Solutions
to Your Everyday Math Problems
by Beth Norcross

The R.A.T. (Real-World Aptitude Test):
Preparing Yourself for Leaving Home
by Homer E. Moyer, Jr.

Safe Living in a Dangerous World:
An Expert Answers Your Every Question
from Homeland Security to Home Safety
by Nancy Harvey Steorts

UPI Stylebook and Guide to Newswriting
by Harold Martin, Bruce Cook and the Editors at UPI

A Grammar Book for You and I...Oops, Me!: All the
Grammar You Need to Succeed in Life
by C. Edward Good

THE SAVVY CONSUMER

How to Avoid Scams and Rip-Offs That Cost You Time and Money

ELISABETH LEAMY

A Capital Ideas Book

CAPITAL
BOOKS, INC.
Sterling, Virginia

Capital Books, Inc.
P.O. Box 605
Herndon, Virginia 20172-0605

ISBN 1-931868-57-3 (alk.paper)

Library of Congress Cataloging-in-Publication Data

Leamy, Elisabeth.
  The savvy consumer : how to avoid scams and ripoffs that cost you time and money / Elisabeth Leamy.— 1st ed.
       p.   cm.—(A capital ideas book)
     ISBN 1-931868-57-3
       1. Consumer protection—United States.   2. Consumer education—United States.   3. Fraud—United States—Prevention.   I. Title.   II. Series.
     HC110.C63L43   2004
     332.024—dc22

                                                    2003017342

Printed in the United States of America on acid-free paper that meets the American National Standards Institute Z39-48 Standard.

First Edition

10 9 8 7 6 5 4 3 2

For Daddy and Jeanne,
who gave me a great start in life.
And Kris, who keeps me going strong.
I love you.

CONTENTS

FOREWORD

The concept of *caveat emptor*—let the buyer beware—is as relevant today as when the term was coined more than a thousand years ago. Old adages exist for good reason. It seems some things never change.

Most businesses are customer-focused and care about matters of integrity. Indeed, smart businesspeople build their companies on a foundation of satisfied, repeat customers. However, this does not mean the public should automatically assume all businesses are motivated by honest dealings. This assumption is inherently problematic, and the problem is magnified when consumers perform little to no due diligence in their decision-making process. Unfortunately, the reality is that some businesses lack principles and treat ethics as an unaffordable luxury.

Today's marketplace is competitive and complex. This does not make for easy buying decisions, but experience shows that an overwhelming number of disputes can be prevented through knowledge and vigilance. Arming yourself with prepurchase information about the reliability of a business is paramount. Educating yourself about the product or service and the industry as a whole is also critical. Without such information, your likelihood of becoming the target of unscrupulous business practices increases dramatically. Consoling yourself by saying, "I should have known better," *after* you have fallen victim to a scam is not an enviable position.

Full of sage advice, this book serves as an excellent resource for developing a prudent approach to consumer matters. The book provides useful information on what you need to know before you make a buying decision. Each chapter offers important tips on how to perform the all-important due diligence. It is wise to be a savvy consumer. Elisabeth Leamy's book will show you how to achieve this aim.

Edward Johnson
President and CEO
Better Business Bureau, Washington, D.C.

INTRODUCTION

I'm not gonna lie to you.

Being a savvy consumer is hard work. But I would argue that being a *lazy* consumer is even *harder* work. The proverb, "a stitch in time saves nine," was tailor-made for consumers. Since hardly anybody sews anymore, let me explain what I mean. Getting a mechanic to check out a used car before you buy it takes work. Getting that car towed off the freeway where it has stalled; getting it fixed only to learn it's a salvage vehicle that's actually two other cars welded together; getting a lawyer; suing the used car dealer; selling the used car that you now know is worth next to nothing; earning enough money to pay the lawyer; earning enough money to buy another used car; hiring a mechanic now that you know better; and buying your replacement car—now *that's* work!

Think I'm exaggerating? Then I invite you to come answer my phone sometime. I could use the help. You see, I'm the consumer and investigative reporter at a television station in Washington, D.C. I hear horror stories like the one above all the time. In fact, years ago I was forced to install a second phone line at my desk to take in all the hard luck stories. If I answered all the calls live, I would never get any work done. All day the tip line rings. Every morning my voice mail is full. There's always a new scam, always a new story. I will never go out of business. I would gladly retire if consumers suddenly wised up and learned how to avoid scams and rip-offs.

So here's your first lesson. To be a savvy consumer you need to be a hunter. Huh? That's right, you need to *be the hunter, not the hunted.* In other words, avoid the telemarketer who calls with a vacation offer, the contractor who goes door to door claiming to be working on other houses in the neighborhood, and the carpet cleaner who sends you a coupon offering to clean five rooms for five bucks. Don't do business with the companies that come looking for *you*. When you need something, conduct your own search and do business with the companies you *seek out*.

Let me give you the knowledge you need to save time and money as a consumer. Don't think of it as drudgery. Actually, it's exciting! After all, one way to *make* money is not to waste it. And putting a crooked business in its place feels good. Very good. This is not a mind-numbing "A" through "Z" guide listing every step you need to take. More like steps "I" through "Q"—your consumer "intelligence quotient." For example, I'm not going to tell you how to buy a used car. I'm going to tell you how *not* to buy a used car. I'll get to the heart of the matter, warning you about the very worst pitfalls and blunders.

You can read the book cover to cover and become one tough customer. Or you can read chapters when you need them as you go about your life. Each chapter covers a consumer category. Within that category, topics are organized alphabetically for easy reference. At the end of each subchapter, I tell you the signs to look out for, the questions to ask, how to do your homework, and where to complain. I also list related subchapters, with the really, really relevant ones in bold.

Congratulations! This book is your first purchase as a savvy consumer.

CHAPTER 1

BEFORE YOU BUY

Checking Out a Company

Here's how so many of the calls to my tip line sound: "Ms. Leamy, I'm calling because I want you to do a story about CCC Carpet Cleaners. I had a coupon and they told me it was only going to cost eighty dollars. Then they refused to leave my house until I paid them three hundred fifty dollars. They didn't even clean under the furniture, and they soaked my carpets so badly that now they're all rippled. I just called the Better Business Bureau, and CCC Carpet Cleaners has an unsatisfactory record. So, I think you should do a story about this. I need your help."

What's wrong with this picture? My tipster called the BBB *after* having a bad experience. Don't think I'm exaggerating. *Most* of my messages sound like this. People want me to help them, even though they've done nothing to help themselves. Callers want me to expose crooked companies and get their money back *after* the fact. Trust me. It's much easier to *research* a crooked company and not pay them any money in the *first* place.

Word of mouth is still one of the best ways to find a good business. Ask friends and family if they can recommend a good carpenter, contractor, car dealer, carpet cleaner. Approach neighbors whose landscaping or paint job you admire and ask who did it. Get referrals from other professionals. If you know a good plumber, chances are he or she knows a good electrician. But don't rely completely on your initial source. I once used a hardwood floor guy just because a neighbor recommended him. He turned out to be lousy, and my neighbor turned out to be an airhead.

Another source? Clip out admiring articles about businesses from local newspapers and magazines. *Not* advertisements, but articles! Just because a company advertises in a reputable newspaper or on a big TV or radio station does not mean it's reputable. Media companies have no legal obligation to check the reputations of their advertisers. I once prepared a devastating story about a local mortgage broker. In an attempt to block the story from airing, the broker bought advertising time on my station. If viewers paid more attention to the commercials than to my story, they certainly received the wrong message.

The easiest way to take your search to the next level is by contacting the **Better Business Bureau.** You can call or go online to **www.bbb.org**, where you'll be linked to your local BBB. The Better Business Bureau is a great place to check the reputation of a company, because it's the first place most consumers call when they want to complain. The BBB has incredible name recognition, even though a lot of people don't fully understand what it is or what it does. The Better Business Bureau is not a government entity. It's a private, nonprofit organization that serves consumers and businesses.

The complaint records the Better Business Bureau keeps form a sort of trail of bread crumbs for you to follow. The Better Business Bureau will tell you whether a business is a member, and whether it has a satisfactory or unsatisfactory record. The latter is based on the number of complaints and whether those complaints were resolved satisfactorily. You'll also get a broad idea of *what* consumers have complained about. When the BBB is aware of a government action against a company, you'll find that listed, too.

It's crucial that you contact the BBB yourself, rather than relying on plaques or signs in a company's lobby. I can't tell you how many shady companies I've investigated that had those BBB plaques on display. It's not the BBB's fault. Often a questionable company will join the Bureau for one year, then get kicked out but keep displaying the shiny plaques.

If you're researching a substantial purchase, I suggest you dig even deeper. That means calling one of the government watchdogs that records consumer complaints. Large cities and counties have their own consumer protection offices. The trick is finding them because they all have different names. Your local agency may be under consumer affairs, consumer protection, consumer services, etc. Or it may be lumped in with fair housing, housing, licensing, regulation, and on and on. Look in the blue pages of the phone book or call the county information line for guidance. If you live in a county that, (a) has a consumer protection office and (b) has a well-staffed one, you're luckier than you know. In my experience, these local agencies do the most to help consumers directly.

You can also access complaint records at the state level. Again, the trick is finding the right agency to help you. Many state consumer divisions are run by the state's attorney general. Others fall under the state department of agriculture (for reasons that boggle the mind). I'm sure there are other variations that I haven't even heard of. If you're stuck, call the governor's office for help. Once you find the main state consumer protection office, ask about other, more specialized state agencies that may have additional information on the company you're researching. For example, if the company is required to be licensed, the department that handles licensing may track consumer complaints as well.

Whether you check out a company through your county or state, you should be able to get pretty decent details about it. I've been able to obtain the exact number of complaints and how those complaints break down by year. I've also gotten reasonably detailed descriptions of the nature of those complaints—especially at the county level. If you're vetting an incredibly expensive service, like home building, you could even try filing a Freedom of Information Act request to get a copy of the actual letters of complaint written by consumers. (The consumers' names will be whited out.) You can also go to the courthouse to see if the business has ever been sued.

I suggest you ramp up your research in direct proportion to the size of the purchase. For example, if you're buying something for less than $200, maybe you can afford to just go for it without checking out the company. If you're prepared to spend $500, maybe you contact the BBB. If you're looking at a $1,000 investment, check with your county or state consumer protection office. And for major investments, involving thousands of dollars, tap into every possible resource.

DO YOUR HOMEWORK:

1. Check the company's complaint record with the BBB and government watchdogs. Consider checking for lawsuits at the courthouse.
2. Check under the company name and the owner's name. Often bad businesses change names when they rack up too many consumer complaints.

SEE ALSO:

FIGHTING BACK: Better Business Bureau, Government Watchdogs

Contracts

Admit it!

You don't actually read all that legalese, gobbledygook, mumbo jumbo, teeny tiny, premature-use-of-reading-glasses, &*$% fine print, do you? Most people don't, and that's a big mistake. In my job as a consumer and investigative reporter, I have to. Ugh. I don't enjoy reading contracts, but it's very enlightening. You wouldn't believe the self-serving clauses contained in the fine print of companies' contracts. So many consumers call me and insist they've been ripped off. But then I read their contracts and learn the company did nothing wrong because the consumers signed away their rights. Keep in mind, not all contracts have the word, "CONTRACT," helpfully typed across the top. Receipts, sales slips, tickets, guarantees, and more can all serve as contracts.

When I bought my home, the closing took three times as long as the settlement attorney expected, because I actually *read* that pile of paperwork they shove under your nose. He was huffing and puffing because I made him late for his next appointment. But I didn't care. You see, reading the "contract" turned out to be more than just an academic exercise. I discovered the mortgage company and the title company had both overcharged me. I demanded an adjustment and got more than $600 back.

Here's what I suggest: Whenever you're making a major purchase, insist on seeing the contract well in advance of when you have to sign. Don't rely on the salesperson's summary of what the contract means. If possible, take a copy somewhere else so you won't have to read it under the manager's sharklike gaze. Take a coffee or lunch break and bring the contract with you. Better yet, take it home overnight. Once you have some privacy, not only should you *read* the entire contract but you should also make sure you *understand* it. If you have trouble with the legal mumbo jumbo, get a friend to help. Maybe you know somebody who's knowledgeable about cars, diamonds, time-shares, or whatever. Maybe there's a lawyer in the family.

A government bureaucrat who constantly has to read codes, rules, and laws, once taught me a neat trick that works for contracts, too. Make a copy and underline only the important words. Leave out all the extraneous stuff the lawyers always add in. Suddenly the mysterious meaning begins to come into focus. Here's an example from a law about towing. Read the entire paragraph, then read only the underlined words:

Whenever any motor vehicle, trailer or semi-trailer is found on the public streets or public grounds, unattended by the owner or operator and constitutes a hazard to traffic or is parked in such a manner as to be in violation of law, or whenever any motor vehicle, trailer or semi-trailer is left unattended for more than ten days upon any public property <u>or privately owned property</u> other than the property of the owner of said motor vehicle, trailer or semi-trailer, <u>any</u> <u>such</u> motor <u>vehicle,</u> trailer or semi-trailer <u>may be removed</u> for safekeeping <u>by</u> or under the direction of <u>a police officer to a storage</u> garage or <u>area.</u>

Better? In addition to understanding the prewritten language of your contract, study it to make sure the terms you and the seller agreed on are included. Never sign a contract that contains blanks. Cross them out before you sign. If there are any clauses you don't like, ask the company to delete them.

Arbitration clauses are one thing you may want to try to strike from some contracts you sign. On the up side, arbitration allows you to resolve your problem without expensive legal costs. If it's done by a reputable, unbiased arbitrator, it can be a blessing. On the down side, legally binding arbitration denies you the right to sue the company in court. Consumer lawyers warn that many people come to them after suffering some terrible fraud or injury, and there's nothing they can do to help. Forward-thinking companies make their arbitration clauses obvious and give you a chance to opt out if you prefer. Other companies bury them. It's up to you to find the clause, read it, and decide whether you can live with it.

Oral promises are not enough. If you want a clause added or deleted for your protection, write it in or ask for an addendum and get a company representative to sign or initial it. If a low-level employee says he or she can't do that, ask for a manager. If the manager refuses, come up with a compromise or consider taking your business elsewhere.

I once ordered a teal leather chair. The contract stated that if I wanted to return it, I'd owe a 50 percent restocking fee. I didn't think that was fair. I was concerned that the color wouldn't be true to the tiny swatch I'd seen in the store. Teal was risky enough, but what if I ended up with turquoise? So I asked the manager to cross out the restocking clause. She said she couldn't do that because of company policy, but she gave me a great alternative. She added an approval clause. The furniture factory set aside the actual leather for my chair and sent the store a large piece of it. Once I approved the color, the purchase went forward. Reasonable contract, fabulous chair!

You should know that normally contracts *cannot* be canceled. The buyer and the seller are the two parties to the contract and each is bound to uphold the terms of the deal. Neither one can break the contract without the permission of the other. This means that if you change your mind, the seller can legally refuse to let you out of the contract. Your signature on a contract indicates that you have read and understood it—even if you haven't.

BEFORE YOU BUY

Here's an offbeat tip: make your signature BIG when you sign a contract. I've seen crooks cut nice neat signatures off the bottom of paperwork and paste them onto less favorable contracts. Scrawl your name large enough that it overlaps the lines above it, so it's hard for the company to cut and paste. And NEVER, EVER leave the business without a signed copy of your contract in hand.

The Cooling-Off Rule

I hesitate to even call this section, "The Cooling-Off Rule," because in most cases there is NO SUCH THING. Many consumers are under the unfortunate impression that you have three days to return anything you buy. IT'S NOT TRUE! I'm not sure why this consumer myth lives on, but I do know where it came from. The Federal Trade Commission has a helpful regulation, called, you guessed it, The Cooling-Off Rule, but it *only* applies to sales made away from the seller's place of business.

It's sort of a quaint regulation, really, from the days when women spent their days at home and overbearing salesmen hawked their wares door to door. The Cooling-Off Rule gives you three days to cancel your purchase. It applies to purchases of $25 or more made at your home or workplace or at short-term facilities rented by the seller, like hotel rooms, convention centers, and fairgrounds.

Some products are exempt from The Cooling-Off Rule, including real estate, insurance, and securities. Vehicles sold at temporary locations (like auto shows) are exempt from the three-day rule as long as the seller *does* have a permanent place of business. (Now hear this: Once you sign a contract for a *car*, YOU CANNOT RETURN IT! This is one of the most damaging consumer myths!)

Salespeople who sell you something from a temporary location are required to inform you of your three-day cancellation rights and give you a cancellation form. To cancel, you fill out the form or write a letter of your own and mail it to the seller. You must make sure it's postmarked by midnight of the third business day after you made the purchase. The seller then has ten days to give you a refund and twenty days to pick up the items you purchased.

I mention all this because if you purchase something that does not fall into the narrow scope of the FTC's Cooling-Off Rule, the company has the right to set its own return policy. In other words, before you buy, you need to check the seller's policy and make sure you really want the merchandise.

SEE ALSO:

CARS: Buying New, Buying Used; SHOPPING: **Returns**, Warranties

How to Pay

If after checking out the business, scrutinizing the contract, and inquiring about the return policy, you *still* feel squeamish about a purchase, then you'll want to choose the best way to pay. Of course, cash is the worst, because if you have a problem, you'll never see your money again. You could write a check (if anybody does that anymore), but if you're so skeptical of the business, why would you want them to have your bank account number? Everything a crook needs to plunder your account is right at the bottom of your check.

That leaves credit cards. As long as you're not a revolving debt junkie, paying by credit card is a wise and wonderful choice. Why? When you use a credit card, if a company does you wrong, you can dispute the charges through your credit card company, then withhold payment until the matter is resolved. This privilege is guaranteed by the Fair Credit Billing Act. The act protects you against wrongdoing by your credit card company and against bad businesses where you've *used* your credit card. Say you purchased unsatisfactory goods or services. Or maybe the seller mischarged you. Perhaps the items were not delivered as agreed. All these cases are covered.

Technically, according to the Federal Trade Commission, the Fair Credit Billing Act only applies to purchases of more than $50 made in your own state or within a hundred miles of your home. But in my experience, credit card companies typically expand the protection to include the entire United States. You're supposed to make a good faith effort to settle the dispute with the seller first, but you're not required to prove that you've done so.

So, all you have to do is write a letter to your credit card company within sixty days of receiving the bill with the disputed charge on it. Describe why you think the charge is unfair. Your credit card company then has two billing cycles (but no more than ninety days) to correspond with the seller and try to resolve the matter. If your claim is reasonable, chances are the credit card company will successfully fight for you. Be prepared, though, because sometimes credit card companies do side with the seller. If that happens, at least you'll have avoided paying for a couple months, giving you enough time to research other avenues of dispute.

I once purchased theater tickets from a Dallas-based company for a trip to London. My trip was only a day away, and the tickets hadn't arrived. I called the company and the owner swore she'd sent the tickets long ago and refused to give me a refund. She practically accused me of trying to get the tickets for free! With time running out before my trip, I decided to buy a second set of tickets from a different company and have them held at the box office. It was a great trip and a stellar show. When I returned home, I disputed the charge for the original tickets, which never had arrived. Even though the seller had been incredibly rude to *me,* she knuckled under and gave in to American Express.

CHAPTER 2

Cars

Accidents

Every two seconds someone is injured in a traffic accident. Being involved in an accident can be traumatic even if you're *not* injured. A drowsy driver ran into my car once when it was parked by the side of the road. I was miles away when it happened, but I was still flustered when I found out about it. Because you may be shaky, it's a good idea to keep a checklist in your car of everything you should do after an accident. That way you can just go down the list without worrying that you're forgetting a step.

DO YOUR HOMEWORK:

1. Most jurisdictions want you to move your car out of traffic after a collision. A few require you to leave your car where it came to rest after the crash. Find out what the law is in your area and keep that in mind, but if you feel unsafe, move regardless.

CARS

2. If you are not badly hurt, your first responsibility is to keep it that way. Don't venture into traffic unless it's safe. If it is, your next responsibility is to help those who are hurt. Try to make injured people feel comfortable without moving them.

3. Next, approach witnesses and ask what they saw. Take notes, including their names and contact numbers.

4. Most car crashes are just fender benders, so your main concern is exchanging information with the other driver. Many people fail to get all the details they need. Write down the other driver's name, address, phone number, and driver's license number as well as the name and phone number of the other driver's insurance company and the policy number. For good measure, get the license plate number of the other car and its vehicle identification number (VIN).

5. If police arrive at the accident scene, get their names and badge numbers and press them to make a formal report. Some insurance companies will hassle you about processing your claim if there's no police report.

6. Some states also require people involved in significant accidents to file a written report of their own with state or local authorities. This must be done soon after the accident or you could risk having your license suspended.

7. If your car needs to be towed, tow trucks often just show up or police will call them. Find out if the truck is required to honor a rate set by the authorities. If not, don't feel pressured to use the tow truck just because it's there. Call a towing company you trust or an auto club if you belong to one.

8. Definitely don't feel pressured to let a tow truck driver take you to the auto body shop of his choice. Some shops pay drivers a bounty to bring them business. Have the car towed to your home or to your mechanic if you need more time to choose a body shop.

9. Although it may seem awkward, experts say you shouldn't admit fault at the scene of the accident. They say there's a time and a place to take responsibility after the initial accident investigation is over.

10. Notify your insurance company of the accident within twenty-four hours. Delaying could result in a denied claim. If you sense

the other driver is irresponsible, notify his or her insurance company, too.

11. If it's determined that the accident was not your fault, you'll have to choose whether to make your claim through your own insurance company or the other driver's company. If you make the claim through your own company, you'll have to pay the deductible up front. Your insurance company will then pay for the repairs and go after the other insurance company for reimbursement. You'll get your deductible back when the process is completed. Contrary to popular belief, it is okay to make a claim when the *other* driver is at fault. Your insurance company should not raise your rate. If it *does,* complain to your state insurance commissioner. I prefer to do it this way because I believe your own insurance company is more likely to have your best interests in mind and be generous. After all, *your* company isn't the one that will pay in the end. Of course, if cash for the deductible is a problem, then make your claim through the other driver's insurance company.

SEE ALSO:

CARS: **Auto Body,** Towing; INSURANCE: Car Insurance

Auto Body

Getting in a car accident is bad enough. But some consumers feel like fate comes crashing down on them a second time when they go to get their car repaired. Shoddy work. Junkyard parts. Insurance company influence. But even if your car is a tangle of metal, like something from a bad dream, getting it fixed doesn't have to be a nightmare. The key is choosing the right auto body shop. It's an important choice because, for most of us, our car is our second-biggest investment after our home.

Start with your insurance company. Most insurers keep a list of approved shops they've worked with in the past. You don't have to use a company from this list, but it's a way of narrowing down

CARS

your choices. Also ask friends and colleagues if they have any recommendations or if they've had any experience with the shops on the list.

Do a background check of the shops on the list by calling or going online. Contact the Better Business Bureau and your county and state consumer protection offices. You should be able to find out the number of complaints, the nature of those complaints, and how they were resolved.

Some insurance companies allow certain shops to do their own adjusting work, in place of the insurance company's adjuster. This could save you time. Plus, since the people at the auto body shop want to make money and want to do a thorough job, if they do their own adjusting you may get the better benefit of the doubt. Ask about programs like this.

Find out whether the body shop belongs to any professional organizations. For example, shops that belong to the **Automotive Service Association** (ASA) pledge to uphold that organization's code of ethics. Call **(800) ASA-SHOP** for a referral. Some auto body shops also belong to America's Collision Repair Association (ACRA). See if the actual technicians are certified to do body work by Automotive Service Excellence (ASE).

Once you go to the shop, make sure it has a professional appearance and works on newer, nicer cars. Ask the shop if it regularly works on your make and model and has the equipment recommended by your vehicle manufacturer.

Some insurance companies pressure customers to accept generic parts. Auto body experts say most of these parts are lighter in weight than the originals. If you must use generic body parts, ask about the Certified Automotive Parts Association (CAPA) seal of approval. CAPA tests auto parts. You may also run into junkyard parts. If your car is fairly new, don't accept these parts. If you have an older car, it's not as much of an issue.

When it's time to pick up your car, study it carefully. Test every single button, switch, and lock in the car to make sure it works. Check the stereo! Make sure the doors, hood, and trunk open and close smoothly. Examine the paint in bright sunlight to make sure the color matches. I once had to have major body work done on my car and, for three months afterward, I discovered additional problems because I didn't test every last thing before I left the body shop.

DO YOUR HOMEWORK:

1. Carefully choose which collision repair facility will work on your car.
2. Don't feel pressured to accept generic parts or junkyard parts. Remember, the body shop works for you, not your insurance company.
3. Put your car through its paces before you take it home.

WHERE TO COMPLAIN:

If you're unhappy with an auto body shop, report it to any professional organizations it belongs to and file a complaint with your county or state consumer protection office. File a complaint with the BBB as well.

SEE ALSO:

CARS: **Accidents, Mechanics;** INSURANCE: Car Insurance

Buying New

A car is the second-biggest thing most of us purchase in our life times, yet most of us aren't very good at it. After all, we only do it a few times in our life, and the back and forth rituals of new-car dealerships are pretty baffling. I get dozens of calls a week from people complaining about their miserable experiences buying new cars. Let me see if I can help.

Once you've chosen the make and model car you want, learn the reputations of all the dealers in your area that sell that car. Check with the BBB and/or your county and state consumer protection agencies. Determine the number of complaints against each dealer, the nature of those complaints, and whether they were resolved satisfactorily. Cross complaint-ridden dealers off your list.

Next, look in the newspaper and see if the dealerships you're interested in are offering any specials. Call and get the details of these deals. Often you'll find the ad in the paper only refers to a single car. It's usually a stripped-down model with a manual transmission. If that's what you're looking for, you could do very well. But beware, some dealers advertise a breathtakingly cheap car, but when you call first thing in the morning, they say it's already gone. They may be playing a game of bait and switch to lure customers to their lot. Call them on it. Dealers are not allowed to advertise a car unless they have it in stock.

Now, consult a car-pricing resource like **www.edmunds.com** to find out how much the manufacturer charges dealers for the car you want. These guides are incredibly detailed. They give the invoice price for the basic model and break down prices for every optional upgrade. You can also look up any rebates the manufacturer is currently offering its dealers. Say Toyota is offering dealers a $1,000 bonus for every new Camry they sell. That means if the dealership sells you the car "at invoice," it's still making a $1,000 profit. It also means you've got another $1,000 worth of wiggle room when you start haggling.

Here are a couple of key terms you'll need to know when you visit a dealership. The invoice price is the amount the manufacturer charges the dealer for the car—the rock-bottom price. The MSRP is the price at the top of the scale. (Many people believe MSRP stands for "manufacturers suggested retail price," but according to the Federal Trade Commission, it stands for "Monroney Sticker Price.") Anyway, you want to negotiate from the invoice price *up*, rather than from the MSRP *down*.

When you bargain, make it clear that you're talking about what you'll pay to take the car "out the door." In other words, your offer should include tax, tag, and licensing fees. I once made what I thought was a decent deal, but then the dealer added in another $1,500 worth of tax and tag fees, because I had not made my intentions clear.

If you reach an impasse in your haggling, I HIGHLY RECOMMEND WALKING OFF THE LOT. If there are plenty of similar cars in stock ... if it's the end of the month when salesmen must make their quotas ... chances are you'll get a call offering to drop the price further. New-car dealerships use a bit of psychological warfare to make sales, so you should, too!

Speaking of psychology, a colleague of mine once investigated a dealership that routinely took the keys of little old ladies' trade-ins and refused to give them back. Sleazy! Before you visit the dealer, find out how much your trade-in is worth. Use guides like the **Kelly Blue Book** and the **National Automobile Dealers Association** (NADA) book. Also look at similar cars in the classifieds. You can probably make more money by selling your old car yourself. Another option is to take it to a used car superstore where you can get an estimate and/or sell it on the spot. If you do want to trade in your old car, don't discuss that transaction until *after* you've negotiated the price of your new car. The value of your trade-in is another variable the dealership can use to bamboozle you. Keep the transactions separate.

If you are uncomfortable doing the dealership dance where you bargain back and forth, you may be tempted to get somebody else to do it for you. Be aware that some online services that offer to get you price quotes from dealerships in your area are *owned* by the dealers. You'd be better off using an online car shopping service run by a consumer group instead. Credit unions often negotiate with car dealers to get fixed prices for their members. You could also try a "no haggle" dealership. In my experience, the prices at these dealerships are somewhere in between the MSRP and the invoice price.

However you do it, once your contract is drawn up, DON'T SIGN IT until you've scrutinized it carefully. Ask for some privacy and take your time. Make sure the dealer has not added a freight or destination and delivery charge, both of which should be included in the invoice price. Balk at "conveyance fees," a made-up charge for processing the paperwork for the sale. Look for add-ons that you didn't ask for and delete them. For example, extended warranties are often unnecessary because today's manufacturer warranties are so good. Undercoating and protective coating are also obsolete. Credit life insurance, which pays off the car if you die, is a real rip-off. Your standard life insurance should provide plenty of money for that.

If you want any additions to the contract, get them in writing. Verbal promises carry no weight. One guarantee you should *always* get is that the car has never been damaged. That's right. New cars sometimes get wrecked coming off the truck or during test drives. Dealers are not required to disclose the damage to you if it's only a small percentage of the vehicle's value. Outrageous! I always ask the dealer to write a letter stating that the car has never been damaged.

Okay. Ready to sign on the dotted line? WAIT! Once you do, the deal is final and that car is yours. CONTRARY TO POPULAR BELIEF, YOU CANNOT RETURN A CAR! Many people believe you have three days in which to change your mind. It's one of the most pervasive consumer myths and drives me absolutely crazy. A few rare and noble dealerships have begun allowing limited returns, but that's NOT the norm. So take a deep breath. Consider the price. Consider the financing. And then, *if* you're comfortable, sign your life away. Did I mention that YOU CANNOT RETURN A CAR?!

DO YOUR HOMEWORK:

1. Check dealers' reputations.
2. Scan the classified ads and call to see what's actually being advertised.
3. Read pricing guides to determine the "invoice" price of the car you want.
4. Bargain from the bottom price up.
5. Research the value of your trade-in and make it a separate transaction.
6. Scrutinize the contract and ask for a letter guaranteeing the car's never been damaged.

WHERE TO COMPLAIN:

If you've made a bad deal, and you want to return your new car, don't expect any sympathy or help from the authorities. Overcharging somebody is not a crime. If you believe the dealer did something illegal or unethical, contact the Department of Motor Vehicles (DMV) or Motor Vehicle Dealer Board as well as your county and state consumer protection offices. Also complain to the Better Business Bureau, so the next person who checks a dealership's reputation can take your complaint into account.

SEE ALSO:

CARS: Extended Warranties, **Financing,** Leasing, **Lemon Law, Spot Delivery**

CARS

Buying Used

Americans buy more used cars each year than they do new ones. When you buy a used car, very often you're the one who feels used. I hear sob stories about crummy used cars day in and day out. My sympathy is wearing thin because most people make no effort to check out a used car before they seal the deal. Guess what, folks? YOU CANNOT RETURN A USED CAR. Let me say that again: YOU CANNOT RETURN A USED CAR. Federal laws guarantee refunds for certain products sold in certain places, but CARS ARE NOT ONE OF THEM. A car is an incredibly expensive piece of machinery and, once you sign on the dotted line, it's YOURS.

Sheri R. bought a sleek Toyota Celica. Of course, she didn't find out until three months later that the car had been in a wreck so bad that the front end was in the front seat. If Sheri had had the car checked out in the first place, she would have learned that there were still price tags on her rebuilt engine, and her hood was hopelessly crooked. The purchase hurt her pocketbook and could have hurt her. The car was too dangerous to drive.

So where should you shop for a used car? New-car dealers have advantages because they get so many trade-in vehicles. Most new-car dealers have their own shops so they can tune up the trade-in and offer a warranty. Typically, dealers sell the cleanest trade-ins themselves and dump the dirtier ones at auctions. But these days, used cars are in such high demand that new-car dealers themselves may supplement their supply by buying at an auction. By law, a dealer must post a "buyer's guide" on each used car that tells you whether the car is being sold "as is" or with a warranty. The buyer's guide becomes a part of your sales contract, so hang onto it. If the used car was serviced at the dealership, you may be able to get copies of the service records. If the dealer is offering a basic warranty on the car, you may be able to negotiate to get more things covered.

Used-car dealers get most of their cars at wholesale auctions, which are not open to the general public. Keep in mind, even reputable used-car dealers get mostly the leftovers new-car dealers didn't want. Be wary of used-car dealerships that are brand new, change names often, or move around a lot. Used-car dealers must also post the "buyer's guide" telling you whether a car comes with a warranty. If the guide is missing, that's illegal.

Some used-car dealerships call *themselves* "auctions" to generate excitement and make people think they're getting a deal. These make-believe auctions don't allow test-drives. One customer called me to complain that she bought a car at an "auction" and later learned the car couldn't drive in reverse! The auctioneer had driven the car forward when it came up for a bid, and the customer had driven it forward—right off the lot.

Used-car superstores, like CarMax®, are a handy place to test-drive all different kinds of cars. If you're a master bargainer, you can probably get a better price somewhere else, but if you're allergic to haggling, this could be a good choice for you. Just remember, even though the salespeople are low-key and the showroom is sleek, a used car superstore still sells USED cars. You need to scrutinize the car, same as always. One rare exception: some used car superstores have actually begun allowing returns. There's a time limit of three to seven days, but it *is* progress. Why shouldn't cars be sold just like other products? If you buy a used car someplace that accepts returns, count your lucky stars and use the grace period to have the car checked out by a mechanic.

You can get a good deal buying from a private owner, because there's no dealer markup. To protect yourself, insist on seeing copies of service records as well as records of the original purchase. Scrutinize the car carefully, because you're not dealing with a business that has a reputation to uphold. Private-owner sales are assumed to be "as is" unless you draw up a written contract with the seller.

These days, computer databases are a godsend for used-car buyers. CARFAX is probably the best known. You just go to **www.carfax.com** and provide the vehicle identification number, or VIN, of the car you're interested in—then pay a nominal fee. Within minutes you can find out whether that car is a problem— or a peach! You'll get a vehicle history report, which can reveal salvage cars, odometer fraud, flood titles, and more. You can even find out whether the car was once a taxi or rental car. There is one weakness: These databases rely on government records. If the car was in a fender bender that wasn't big enough to warrant a police report, there will be no record of the accident. That's where a physical inspection becomes important.

You can inspect a used car yourself to get a feel for whether it's ever been in an accident big enough to require body work. Scrutinize the paint in bright sunlight. Today's paints are extremely difficult to match, so you may see subtle color contrasts. Also look for paint lines; shoddy shops leave paint lines underneath the hood where they've taped. Look at the underside of door handles and you may see more paint lines. Sometimes you can detect overspray on a car's weather stripping, too. If there is a tiny crack in the paint around the bolts that hold the doors on, it may mean those doors were removed for bodywork.

Open the hood and look for the factory stickers on the underside. If the hood has been replaced, the stickers will be missing or handwritten. Make sure the gaps along the sides of the hood are the same width from side to side and from top to bottom. You're looking for symmetry. Test to see whether all the doors open and close smoothly. Accidents can also damage electrical systems. Try out every single button, bell, and whistle to make sure it's working. When I got out of college, I bought a used car without testing the stereo. It didn't work, and as a twenty-something, music seemed all-important to me at the time.

If the car passes your own inspection, next have a trusted mechanic inspect it for you. THIS IS AN INCREDIBLY IMPORTANT

CARS

STEP AND ONE THAT TOO MANY PEOPLE SKIP! If the seller won't let you take the car to a mechanic, walk away from the deal. If you're looking for convenience, there *are* mobile mechanics who specialize in used-car inspections and will bring their diagnostic tools to *you* instead. If you don't have your mechanic check for flaws before you buy the car, don't be upset when he starts pointing out those flaws the first time you take it in for an oil change.

CARS

DO YOUR HOMEWORK:

1. Check the reputation of every new-car dealer, used-car dealer, "auction," or used-car superstore before you buy a car there. In some states, the DMV keeps a file on dealers. In other states, those records are held by the Motor Vehicle Dealer Board. You should be able to learn the number and nature of complaints and how those complaints were handled. Also check with your local Better Business Bureau and your county and state consumer protection offices.

2. To get a feel for a fair price, check online resources like **www.edmunds.com** and **Kelly Blue Book**, **www.kbb.com.**

3. Once you've spotted a car you like, go to **www.carfax.com** or another database and pay for a vehicle history report.

4. Perform a visual inspection of the car yourself. If you don't feel confident doing this, take the car to an auto body shop for an inspection.

5. Pay a mechanic to check out the car's innards and make sure everything is running smoothly. If it isn't, you can either walk away from the car or use that information to bargain for a better deal.

6. If you want the dealer to make repairs as part of the deal, get any and all promises in writing. Oral contracts are nearly impossible to enforce. Do *not* sign the contract or pay for the car until the repairs have been made.

7. REMEMBER THAT DEALERSHIPS HAVE NO OBLIGATION TO TAKE BACK USED CARS (unless they offer refunds, in writing, as part of their contract).

WHERE TO COMPLAIN:

If you feel a car dealer has defrauded you, file a formal complaint with the DMV or Motor Vehicle Dealer Board and the authorities will investigate. Also complain to the Better Business Bureau and your county and state consumer protection offices to leave a paper trail for other consumers.

CARS

SEE ALSO:

CARS: Auto Body, Buying New, **Curbstoning,** Financing, Lemon Law, **Odometer Fraud, Salvaged, Spot Delivery**

Curbstoning

Experts estimate that 80 percent of the used cars in the classifieds are not being advertised by individual owners. Cars parked by the side of the road with "For Sale" signs are even more suspect. Chances are they're being sold by "curbstoners." Curbstoners are illegal, unlicensed used-car dealers who sell cars from the curb instead of from a dealership. They usually pretend the cars are their personal vehicles. Many curbstoner cars are salvage vehicles, others are too dangerous to drive, and some might even be stolen. By the time you figure out you've been duped, the curbstoner is long gone.

Reese F. got two trucks for the price of one—but they were no bargain. The Ford truck he bought for $15,000 was actually two totaled trucks welded together. The seller told him he was helping his brother sell the truck and that his brother bought it new from a Ford dealership. When Reese found out the frame was hopelessly twisted, he couldn't exactly go back to the Taco Bell parking lot to find the curbstoner. And when Reese went to sell the truck, by law he had to disclose to the next buyer that the vehicle was a mess. Needless to say, he lost thousands of dollars on the deal.

When I investigated curbstoning, I easily found odometer rollbacks, salt and rust damage, flood vehicles, and salvage vehicles. All my team did was scan the classifieds for duplicate phone numbers and look for cars for sale by the side of the road. Some strip mall parking lots have come to look like used-car dealerships. We spotted one with dozens of cars lined up, all for sale. The malls are so inundated with curbstoners that they've started posting signs that say "no car sales allowed." One day we spotted a car for sale right next to one of those signs! If you have any doubt that curbstoning can be big business, listen to this. I went undercover and found one curbstoner with a fifty-car inventory. That's expensive to maintain. He had been at it for years and lived in a mansion in one of the most exclusive counties in the country.

Curbstoning is infuriating to legitimate, licensed used-car dealers. After all, they pay taxes and pay for the property where they display their cars. They can't compete with illegal dealers who don't follow the rules. Occasionally a *licensed* car salesman crosses the line and becomes a curbstoner, selling cars on the side and taking business away from the dealership where he's employed. Most states have laws that make it illegal to sell more than five or six cars a year without a dealer's license.

KNOW THE SIGNS:

1. Cars for sale by the side of the road, in driveways, or at shopping centers often belong to curbstoners.
2. If you see the same contact phone number listed for more than one car in the paper or on the street, watch out; it could be a curbstoner selling multiple cars.
3. Tags are telltale: Be wary if there are no license tags, if they're from out of state, or if they're temporary tags or dealer plates. (Sometimes curbstoners borrow license plates from unscrupulous licensed dealers.)
4. If the seller gives you only a pager or cell phone number, proceed with caution. He or she may be preparing to disappear after selling you the car.
5. Curbstoners sometimes admit they sell cars for a living but claim *this* is their personal car. Yeah, right.
6. Beware of sellers who refuse to show you the title before you

buy the car. Title paperwork lists the correct odometer reading and often reveals whether a car is considered salvage.

7. If you *do* see the title and it's not in the seller's name, that's a tip-off that this is not the seller's personal car. Most curbstoners never transfer title into their own names. It could be the name of the previous owner or the name of an auction house.

8. If the seller offers to do your DMV paperwork for you, he or she may have plans to doctor that paperwork.

9. Also beware of recently issued titles. Most individual owners would not sell a car so soon. Ask how long the seller has owned the car.

10. And, finally, if the seller insists on cash instead of a bank check, you could be dealing with an unlicensed dealer.

DO YOUR HOMEWORK:

1. Look for a dealer's license. If it's a legitimate used-car operation, the dealer is required to display the license on the premises.

2. Ask the seller to show you both the title and his or her driver's license. Make sure the names match.

3. Make sure the vehicle identification number (VIN), make, model, and year of the vehicle match the information on the title.

4. Check the odometer reading against the reading listed on the title to make sure they correspond. Rule of thumb: cars usually accumulate 10,000–12,000 miles a year.

5. Ask if there are any service records for the vehicle. A real owner may have them; a curbstoner won't

6. Have the vehicle checked out by a mechanic you trust. If the seller refuses, walk away from the deal.

7. Use research tools like www.carfax.com to look up the history of any vehicle you are interested in buying.

WHERE TO COMPLAIN:

If you have already been victimized by a curbstoner, contact your state and county consumer protection agencies and the Department of Motor Vehicles to file a complaint. If you're lucky, government watchdogs will investigate, but the chances of recovering your money are slim.

SEE ALSO:

CARS

CARS: Buying Used, **Odometer Fraud**, **Salvaged**

Donations

A vehicle is likely to be the biggest charitable donation many of us will ever make. So even if you're just in it for the tax deduction, make sure your donation dollars count. In recent years you may have noticed these ads everywhere: Donate your car! Free towing! There are two reasons for this, one understandable, the other more sinister. Charities are searching for new ways to put money in their coffers. And third-party brokers are searching for new ways to put money in their *pockets*. Many car donation programs are run by these brokers. The broker approaches a charity and offers to give it donations in exchange for use of the charity's name and tax-exempt status. Often the donations are minuscule, $25 a car or a tiny percentage of its value. The charities go along with it because it's money they wouldn't have otherwise. Believe it or not, there is no law mandating that any particular percentage of the proceeds must go to the charity.

David A. spotted a vehicle donation ad in his church newspaper. The ad said secondhand vehicles would be used to raise money for a home for teenage mothers. David liked the idea of giving to a cause he believed in, and he *didn't* like the idea of having to sell his two used cars on his own. So he donated a Mercedes and a Jeep Grand Cherokee—nice, clean cars—but it was a dirty deal. David didn't find that out until I conducted an investigation.

I spotted David's cars and about sixty others at a used-car dealership a couple of counties away. What a business model! Get people to *give* you their cars and then . . . sell them. It's brilliant! Pure profit. The tow truck driver who picked up the cars claimed he worked for the teen mothers' home, but he didn't. And a used car salesman at the dealership claimed it was a nonprofit. But it wasn't. Turns out, the dealership owner offered to make a donation to the teen mothers' home and asked for the home's tax ID number. The director had no idea her name was being used in newspaper ads and her tax ID number was being used on Internal Revenue Service (IRS) receipts given to donors. We discovered the dealership was owned by a convicted felon and former drug dealer.

There *are* honorable car donation programs out there. The best are those that fix up the cars and give them to people in need. That way, 100 percent of your donation goes to the actual cause. Some ambitious charities run their own car donation programs, cutting out the middleman and keeping more cash for the cause. And, of course, some third-party brokers truly want to help charities too. The point is, THERE'S NO MINIMUM AMOUNT THEY'RE OBLIGATED TO GIVE TO THE CHARITY, and there's no easy way for you to know how much they give because they're not required to report it.

The IRS has started taking a closer look at vehicle donation programs because they've multiplied so quickly. Make sure the *program* is legitimate or your *tax deduction* won't be. Many states require companies that solicit on behalf of charities to register with the state—including vehicle brokers who place ads. Some states require charities to get certified through the DMV before they can participate in vehicle donation programs. Others require the broker and charity to sign written sales contracts for each donated car so the charity has an idea how much money is coming in.

KNOW THE SIGNS:

1. If the car donation program uses an 800 number, it may be run by an out-of-state broker rather than a local charity. Call the number and ask the person who answers where the program is located.
2. If the charity uses a familiar-sounding name that's a bit "off," trust your instincts. Many unscrupulous groups use copycat names that sound similar to real charity names.

DO YOUR HOMEWORK:

1. Consider donating to a charity that gives cars directly to needy families or choose a charity that runs its own car donation program. Check the charity's reputation.

2. If you want to donate to a charity that uses a third-party broker, ask the charity (not the broker) how much money it gets for each car.
3. For tax purposes, make sure the organization is tax-exempt—a bona fide 501(c)(3). You can check by going to the IRS Web site, **www.irs.gov**, and looking for publication number 78. Or call the IRS customer service number, **(877) 829-5500**.
4. Also, make sure your vehicle title will be transferred to the charity's name. The IRS requires that for the donation to be legitimate. One way to make sure it happens is to take your license plates off the car. Whoever buys it can't drive around very long without plates.
5. To protect yourself further, some DMVs have a form you can fill out notifying the state that you no longer own the car. That way if the next owner gets a ticket, you will not be held responsible for it.
6. Don't believe ads that say you can deduct the full "Blue Book" value of your car. The IRS allows you to deduct the fair market value only. So determine the Blue Book value and adjust down from there if your car is in poor condition If you claim the car is worth more than $5,000, the IRS requires you to get it appraised.

WHERE TO COMPLAIN:

If you suspect a car donation program is crooked, alert the DMV and whatever agency handles charities in your state. It varies from state to state, but it could be the Secretary of State's office, the Attorney General, or the Department of Agriculture and Consumer Services. You can also file a complaint with the IRS. The government takes this sort of violation pretty seriously, so you could see results.

SEE ALSO:

CARS: Titles; FINANCES: **Charity**

Extended Warranties

There's no such thing as an "extended warranty." Oh, that's what they're *called,* but they're really breakdown insurance policies. The companies that offer them just don't like to call them "insurance" because then they'd have to comply with insurance regulations. Today's manufacturer warranties are so generous that it's harder and harder to justify spending money on an extended warranty, or service contract. These packages typically cost anywhere from a few hundred dollars to more than a thousand dollars. And then you may have to pay a deductible whenever you need repairs. If you're buying a new car, the extended warranty often duplicates items already covered by the manufacturer's warranty. If you *are* going to purchase an extended warranty, get it when your manufacturer's warranty expires.

It's important for you to know that most extended warranties are offered by third parties, not by the dealer or manufacturer. So that's one more entity whose reputation you need to check out. Plenty of consumers have been left with worthless warranties when the companies offering them went out of business. Contact the Better Business Bureau to determine the company's complaint record. Some states *do* regulate warranty companies as insurance providers, so you may be able to check with your state insurance commissioner, too. Test the company's toll-free number to see how hard it is to get through to make a claim.

Learn what is and isn't covered by the extended warranty. Often you are required to pay for routine maintenance yourself. Used-car extended warranties usually don't offer bumper-to-bumper coverage; only items on the list are included. Ask whether repairs must be made at the dealership where you bought the car or another designated shop. This may not be convenient for you. And find out what happens if your car breaks down on a road trip. Here's a hot tip: Often two-year coverage costs just a few dollars more than a one-year policy.

You're probably better off buying an extended warranty directly

CARS

from the warranty company or through a credit union rather than through the dealer, because dealers usually mark up the price of extended warranties by 100 percent or more. Another option is to negotiate the price of the service contract with the dealer. Some dealers try to claim that you *must* buy an extended warranty or your financing will not be approved. Check with the finance company to see if this is true. Other dealers have been known to sell you an extended warranty, then keep your payment and never forward it to the warranty company. Ask for written confirmation that your payment has been received.

Another little-known tip: if you sell your car before the extended warranty expires, you may be entitled to a refund for the remaining coverage. Kathy B. paid $795 for an extended warranty on her Dodge minivan, but traded it in before her three years were up. A friend encouraged her to ask about a refund, and, sure enough, she got $356 back. The same principle applies if you get rid of your car for some other reason, such as if it's totaled in an accident.

DO YOUR HOMEWORK:

1. Make sure the extended warranty or service contract doesn't duplicate your manufacturer's warranty.
2. Make sure your service contract begins when your manufacturer's warranty expires. Sometimes the contract kicks in right away, and that duplication is wasteful.
3. Check out the warranty company.
4. Find out exactly what your extended warranty covers and how you make a claim.
5. Consider buying an extended warranty from someone other than the dealer.
6. Make sure the dealer forwards your payment to the warranty company.
7. Keep all your extended warranty paperwork, so you can get a refund if you get rid of your car early.
8. Better yet, create your own service contract by setting aside money each month to use if your car ever needs major repairs.

WHERE TO COMPLAIN:

If your state regulates extended warranties, complain to your insurance commissioner. If not, complain to your county and state consumer protection offices and the BBB.

SEE ALSO:

CARS: Buying New, Buying Used

Financing

Car companies sell two things: cars and financing. Depending on the market, it's a toss-up which one is the bigger moneymaker. Everybody knows that to get the best deal on a car, you need to hustle and haggle. But many people don't think about how to get the best deal on their financing. It's important to keep the two transactions separate: First negotiate the purchase price, *then* the financing package.

Kathy W. had shaky credit, so she thought her only option was to purchase a car at a "Buy Here, Pay Here" lot. The dealer charged her 29 percent interest on a $5,000 loan—and then disappeared! When I investigated, it turned out the general manager was quadruple-dipping: stealing from customers, stealing from the dealership, stealing from the dealership's finance company, and stealing from the customers' finance companies.

Here's how it worked: The general manager would buy a car dirt cheap at auction. But he would tell his own bank that the car cost much more—and keep the extra money the bank extended him. Next, he sold the car to a customer and pocketed the down payment. He arranged financing for each customer, and when the check came in, he kept that, too. And, finally, the general manager would sell the customer an extended warranty, but instead of forwarding the payment to the warranty company, he kept that as well! Even if Kathy had finished paying off the car at the outrageous 29 percent interest rate, chances are she never would have gotten legal title to it, because the two banks had also paid in full for the car and had a legal claim to it.

That was an incredibly complex case. Most bad financing deals are more basic: You pay too much for financing because you fail to shop around. Buying a car is complicated enough. Avoid letting the financing package become yet another variable for the dealership to manipulate.

NEVER GO INTO A DEALERSHIP WITHOUT FIRST GETTING OUTSIDE FINANCING QUOTES! Check with the bank where you have your checking account and with the bank that holds the mortgage on your house. Some car insurance companies now offer car financing. And credit unions may be the best bet of all. Compare those outside offers with the dealer's financing plan. Sometimes dealers offer specials that are hard to beat. But chances are you'll get a better deal somewhere else.

When dealerships advertise low-interest or no-interest financing, it sounds really enticing. That's the point. They get you in the door. Once you're there, you may learn that the loan is for such a short term—such as a single year—that you can't afford the monthly payments. Sometimes these "hot" deals are only for certain models and require an enormous down payment.

On the flip side, some car salesmen emphasize how much your monthly payment is going to be, instead of talking about the total cost of the car. Don't fall for it! If the total cost is high, but the monthly payments are low, you're going to be paying off that loan for years and years to come. Cars depreciate so fast that you could end up owing more on the car than it is later worth.

If you do go with the dealer's financing, don't drive off the lot until you have a copy of the contract signed by both you and the dealer. And make sure all the blanks on the contract are filled in. Unscrupulous dealers have been known to change the terms of a contract after you drive off into the sunset.

DO YOUR HOMEWORK:

1. Get quotes from outside banks before you go shopping at a dealership.

2. Never tell the car salesman how much you're looking to spend per month.
3. If you *are* interested in the dealership's financing, check the dealer's complaint record with the DMV and/or Motor Vehicle Dealer Board to see if any past complaints dealt with financing.
3. Read and understand everything about your financing package: the total sales price, the amount you're financing, how much the credit will cost you over the years, the interest rate, the amount of the monthly payment, and the number of monthly payments.

CARS

WHERE TO COMPLAIN:

If a car dealer does you wrong on your financing, complain to the DMV and/or the Motor Vehicle Dealer Board. Also, because it's a financing issue, your state department of banking or finance may have jurisdiction. As always, send copies of your complaint letter to the BBB and your county and state consumer protection offices for good measure. Sounds like a lot of legwork, but once you've written a letter, it's pretty easy to send out multiple copies.

SEE ALSO:

CARS: Buying Used, Buying New, **Spot Delivery**; SHOPPING: "No, No, No" Deals

Gasoline

We are a car culture. The amount we spend on gasoline over our lifetimes is ludicrous. And we don't have to burn so much *or* spend so much. The American Automobile Association (AAA) says that only 5 percent of the cars sold in the United States require premium gasoline. But premium accounts for 20 percent of all gasoline sold. What a waste. Say you use 20 gallons of gas per week. Regular costs an average of 20 cents less per gallon, so you'll save $4 per week, or $208 per year, by using regular!

Using a higher-octane gas than the manufacturer recommends

offers no benefit at all. But people remain convinced that premium gas will make their cars go faster or get better mileage. IT'S JUST NOT TRUE. All the term *octane* refers to is a fuel's ability to help your car resist "engine knock." This knocking, rattling, or pinging sound comes from premature ignition of fuel in your engine. Your car is built to run on whatever grade of gasoline is recommended in your owner's manual. If the manual says premium is *required*, use it, but the vast majority of cars are designed to run on regular octane. The only reason you would need to switch to a higher octane is in the rare instance that your engine might be knocking when you use the recommended fuel. Light knocking is not harmful to your car, but heavy, persistent knocking can cause engine damage.

Most gas stations offer regular (usually 87 octane), mid-grade (usually 89 octane), and premium (usually 92 or 93). These levels vary from state to state. For example, one state may require all premium gasoline to have an octane of 92 or above, while another state may allow 90 octane to be labeled premium. When you read your owner's manual, be sure to note the precise octane level your car requires. Then look for that level rather than relying on a generic term like "regular" or "premium."

There are other ways to save money on gas, too. Here's a novel idea! Try driving the speed limit. AAA says that driving sixty-five miles an hour instead of fifty-five increases your fuel consumption by 20 percent. Going seventy-five miles an hour instead of sixty-five increases consumption by *another* 25 percent! Erratic acceleration and braking burn up fuel, too—up to fifty cents a gallon. Keeping your car tuned up is another way to economize. And properly inflated tires save you money too; they cause less road resistance. You can also take heavy items out of your trunk to lighten the load.

Now here are a few more ideas. Several gasoline companies now offer discounts if you buy their gas and pay with their credit card. Shell offers 5 percent off. Exxon/Mobil and Amoco offer a 3 percent discount. AAA now has a Visa card that gets you 5 percent off, too. If you're taking a trip, keep in mind that some hotels and theme parks provide gas vouchers to encourage people to visit. You can go online or inquire when you check in. Finally, the calendar could

CARS

determine whether it's your lucky day. Prices at the pump supposedly creep higher toward the end of the week when more people are traveling. Prices start coming down on Sunday, and experts say the best day to buy is typically Wednesday.

Now a caution: when gas prices go up, so does hype about "gas-saving" products. The Federal Trade Commission warns that very few devices, oils, or additives actually improve gas mileage, and the ones that *do* work provide very small savings. The manufacturers claim these products will save you 12 to 25 percent, but the Environmental Protection Agency conducted several tests and found the claims to be false. In fact, some of these products can even damage your engine.

CARS

DO YOUR HOMEWORK:

1. Read your owner's manual and use the level of octane recommended.
2. Know what level of octane constitutes "regular" or "premium" in your state.
3. Slow down! Accelerate and brake gradually.
4. Keep your car well tuned, your tires properly inflated, and your trunk empty.
5. If you drive a lot, try a gas station credit card that offers a discount.
6. Ask about gas vouchers.
7. Note whether gas prices in your area fluctuate depending on the day of the week.
8. Be skeptical of "gas-saving" products. Go to **www.ftc.gov** for more information.

Leasing

What if you had to learn a foreign language to get a new car? That's exactly what it can feel like to *lease* a car. The process is baffling. Experts say between a quarter and a half of all new cars are leased. Leases often require a smaller down payment and lower monthly

CARS

payments than buying, but that's not enough reason to lease. If you like to change vehicles every few years, and you don't mind having a car payment at all times, then leasing could be suitable for you. If you prefer to own your car and keep driving it for a number of years after it's paid off, you should buy.

You see the ads all the time: "Lease the sleek new sporty speedster for just $299 a month for 36 months!" A lot of people go for these deals, then get the car home and realize they have no idea how much they've actually agreed to pay. Car dealers often emphasize the monthly payment instead of the total cost because it sounds more manageable to buyers. But some leases are so bad that if they were purchases, it would be like paying 30 percent interest on your car loan—then not getting to keep the car once you've paid it off!

If you learn nothing else about car leases, learn this: *BEFORE YOU LEASE, YOU SHOULD NEGOTIATE A PRICE FOR THE CAR*, the same way you would if you were buying it. The monthly lease payment is then based on this price. It's not some random number the dealer dreams up! If you hate haggling, this may not be welcome news. But think of it this way: you could end up paying *less* than the $299 a month advertised. Monthly lease payments are calculated lots of different ways, but here's a simplified formula: You take the car's purchase price, minus what it will be worth at the end of the lease, and divide by the number of months.

Before you sign on the dotted line, here's a lesson in leasing lingo.

Up-front costs: Lease deals don't include anything called a down payment. Instead it has the catchy name, "capitalized cost reduction"—either cash or a trade-in. Other up-front costs include first and last month's payment and a security deposit.

Monthly costs: Lease payments are usually lower than purchase payments because you only have to pay for the "part" of the car you "use" during the years of the lease. You will also have to pay something called the "rent charge," "lease charge," or "money factor." This is similar to an interest rate when you're financing a car.

Maintenance costs: Keep in mind, you are responsible for maintaining and repairing the car, even though after two to five years it won't be yours anymore. Some lease deals include maintenance, but may charge you a deductible each time you go to the shop.

Penalties: You may have to pay fines for moving away from the area where you leased the car or turning the car in early, among others.

End-of-lease costs: Many leases contain yearly mileage caps of 12,000–15,000. Exceed the cap and you could be forced to pay up to twenty-five cents for every extra mile you've traveled. You may also owe for extra wear and tear to the vehicle. If you want to buy the car at the end of the lease, you'll have to pay for the car *and* pay a *fee* for that privilege. Well, isn't that special? If you *don't* want to buy the car, you may have to pay a "vehicle disposition charge" for the dealer to prepare your car for sale.

CARS

DO YOUR HOMEWORK:

1. Decide whether leasing or buying is best for you.
2. Check to see how much it will cost to insure the car. When you lease, dealerships often make you purchase a pricey insurance policy to protect *them*. If you *purchase* the same car, the insurance could be hundreds less per year.
3. Negotiate the price of the car before you negotiate the terms of the lease.
4. Negotiate the mileage cap. It's often cheaper to ask for a higher cap in advance rather than to pay penalties later.
5. Read and understand the handy one-page leasing form required by federal law—*and* the pages and pages of details—before agreeing to the deal. Ask the car dealer if you can take the paperwork home and study it. If the dealer says no, march right off the lot.

WHERE TO COMPLAIN:

Oddly enough, the Federal Reserve regulates vehicle leases and all lease transactions that last more than four months. You may not get personal help from the Fed, but complain anyway. The big guys need to know how their rules are working in the real world. Also complain to the DMV, the Motor Vehicle Dealer Board, the BBB, and your state and county consumer protection offices.

SEE ALSO:

CARS: Buying New, Buying Used

CARS

Lemon Law

To the general public, a "lemon" is slang for a crummy car—one that gives you a sour feeling and makes your face pucker up. To the government, a lemon is a crummy *new* car. This distinction causes a lot of confusion. Plenty of consumers call me to complain about the lemons they've bought. The first thing I ask is, "new or used?" The callers always seem surprised. I guess they're wondering what could be wrong with a new car. The answer is, plenty.

Each state's lemon law is a little different. Generally, you must have purchased or leased the car brand new. In some cases you can make a claim if the previous owner bought the car a short time ago and then quickly sold it to you. Some state lemon laws only cover vehicles used primarily for personal use. Others include cars and SUVs but exclude motorcycles. Each state sets a time and mileage limit. For example, you may be required to make a lemon law claim within fifteen months or 15,000 miles of buying the vehicle. Explore the lemon law in your state for details.

Each state also defines what *counts* as a lemon. For example, in one state if the dealer can't correct critical brake or steering problems in *one* try, the car's considered a lemon. In another, a car is defined as a lemon if the dealer has tried and failed *three* times to repair a repeat flaw. In a third state, the lemon law covers new cars that have been in the shop for a cumulative total of more than thirty days.

If you believe your car is a lemon, it's your responsibility to notify the manufacturer. Let the dealer know, too. I recommend doing so in writing, by certified mail. Once all of the dealer's repair attempts have been exhausted, the manufacturer is required to repair or replace your car. Of course, many manufacturers fight this, and you may have to get help. Your state consumer protection office can give you guidance. Many manufacturers participate in arbitration, like the BBB's AUTO LINE program. If all else fails, you'll have to sue in court. Lemon law procedures should be outlined in your vehicle's warranty manual.

Back to you *used*-car buyers. Some states now require vehicles that were returned as lemons to carry a permanent "brand" on the title. This lemon alert lets subsequent buyers know they may be purchasing a problem car.

CARS

DO YOUR HOMEWORK:

1. Learn the lemon law in your state.
2. If you believe your car may qualify, immediately send the dealer and manufacturer a certified letter putting them on notice that you may act under the lemon law. Don't wait. You don't want to miss the deadline.
3. Mark your calendar each day your new car spends in the shop.
4. Keep detailed records of every repair and write down the names and numbers of everybody you speak with in connection with your claim.
5. You can check to see if cars of your make and model are the subject of any recalls or service bulletins. To obtain a list, contact the **Center for Auto Safety, (202) 328-7700**, and/or the **National Highway Traffic Safety Administration, (800) 424-9393**. Also try going online and typing your make and model into a search engine.

WHERE TO COMPLAIN:

If you have difficulty getting the manufacturer to honor the lemon law, contact your county and state consumer protection offices for help. Complain to the DMV or Motor Vehicle Dealer Board.

SEE ALSO:

CARS: Buying New, Leasing

Mechanics

CARS

If you're prepared, there's no reason to have a *nervous* breakdown when you have a *mechanical* breakdown. The key is to find a good shop before you ever need it. Word of mouth is still a great tool. Ask friends and family for referrals. Make sure the shop you choose has experience with your kind of car. Here's a novel idea: Ask mechanics who *don't* work on your make and model which shop they would recommend. Check out the shop before you commit. Contact the Better Business Bureau and your county and state consumer protection offices to see if the shop has a complaint record and, if so, how those complaints were resolved. Find out whether the mechanic holds any Automotive Service Excellence (ASE) certifications. This means he's passed tests in certain areas of expertise. Some shops belong to a trade organization, called the Automotive Service Association (ASA), whose members pledge to uphold a code of ethics. AAA member mechanics are scrutinized rigorously and agree to submit to arbitration through AAA if a dispute arises. Best of all, you can take advantage of the program, even if you don't belong to AAA. Just go to **www.aaa.com** for a referral.

A recent study showed that dealers typically charge 15 percent more than independent mechanics, but both have their advantages. If your car is still under warranty, you must go to the dealer, but the repairs will be free. Today's cars are amazingly high-tech, and the dealer may be the only one with the specialized computer and computer codes to diagnose your car. On the other hand, at a dealership, you typically communicate with a service representative instead of the actual mechanic. This can lead to miscommunication and frustration. When you *do* find a good mechanic, be faithful. That way you'll develop trust, and the mechanic will know the repair history of your car.

One exception: if your car needs major work, you should seek a second opinion. Mechanics are like doctors. The same symptoms could yield more than one diagnosis. More and more mechanics charge a small fee for their diagnosis. I think that's absolutely fair. It also frees you from feeling obligated to hire somebody just because he gave you a free estimate. If you get a second opinion, you may learn your problem isn't so bad after all. At the very least, you'll feel better spending all that money. Mark L.'s car was pulling to the left. He took it to one shop that insisted his car needed major repairs totaling more than a thousand dollars. Mark was skeptical, so he went to another shop and learned he just needed new tires.

It's your right to get a written estimate, and you always should. That estimate should list the problems to be repaired plus the parts and labor needed to make those repairs. That way the mechanic has committed, in writing, to actually fixing the problems. Beware of estimates that are just long lists of parts.

CARS

Mechanics usually calculate their labor charges using labor tables that estimate the average time it takes to perform a certain repair on a certain type of car. There are three major labor tables, available in books and online. Bill B. was on a Christmas road trip when his Cadillac blew a water pump. He made a beeline for the first shop he saw and agreed to pay the book rate for labor. It was a simple job, so he was shocked when the shop charged him for three and a half hours. Other shops later quoted him anywhere from one hour to four hours. Turns out each shop was using a different labor table, and the tables estimate vastly different times for the same job. Bottom line? If your labor estimate seems high, ask the shop if it has access to another labor table that may be lower. Labor rates can be negotiable.

Once you've signed off on an estimate, THE MECHANIC MUST CONTACT YOU FOR AUTHORIZATION IF THE PRICE IS GOING TO RISE SHARPLY. Details vary from state to state, but the most common rule is that the mechanic must contact you if the price is going to be more than 10 percent higher than the estimate. It's illegal for the mechanic to perform the extra work without your okay, but it happens all the time. When Senia S. learned her car needed a rebuilt engine, she told the shop not to do the work because she couldn't afford it. When she went to pick up her car, the shop had removed her old engine anyway. I got involved and cited the law. The shop ended up installing a brand-new engine for Senia. That's how serious this law is.

In most states, you have a right to get your old parts back after a repair. The idea is that asking for your old parts helps assure that the mechanic will actually install *new* ones. Usually you're required to let the mechanic know ahead of time that you want them. The old parts can help prove your point if a repair turns out to be shoddy.

CARS

On the other hand, if you don't want your parts, some of them have value on the rebuilt parts market. That value is called the "core" value, and you should ask for compensation for it.

Find out if there are any warranties on your new parts and get a written copy of that warranty. Deanna G. was angry when her water hose sprang a leak right after a mechanic rebuilt her engine. When I investigated, I learned the water hose was not part of Deanna's warranty, so the mechanic didn't have to fix it for free. Most mechanics also offer a warranty on their labor. They can set whatever terms they want. For example, in one state, the industry standard is six months or 6,000 miles.

After a major repair, always test-drive your vehicle before you pay. I once had a car that shuddered every time it shifted. I felt sure there was a transmission problem. The car was under warranty for only another week, so I got it to the dealership right away. A couple of days later, the dealer claimed the car was fixed and that it *wasn't* a transmission problem. So I asked the service rep to come along with me on a test-drive. Heh, heh, heh. The car immediately started shaking and shuddering as it changed gears. The dealership grudgingly agreed to give me a new transmission. And all that with just three days left on my warranty. Phew!

If there's a dispute over your repairs, always pay with a credit card. That way you can dispute the charges through your credit card company, and you won't have to lay out any cash until the matter is resolved. If you can't stand the thought of giving your mechanic any money at all, you may be able to go to the local courthouse and post a bond for the price of the repairs. Either you or the mechanic will then have to file a small-claims suit, depending on local law. In some states, if the mechanic doesn't bother to file, you automatically get your money back.

KNOW THE SIGNS:

Common methods of overcharging:

1. Add-on repairs: some shops will fix your problem but will also perform additional work that you don't need.
2. Phantom repairs: other shops charge you for repairs they don't do at all.

3. Bait and switch: it's common for mechanics to advertise great specials, then pressure you into buying more services once you're in the door.
4. Periodic maintenance: dealerships have been known to sell elaborate maintenance packages that go well beyond what the manufacturer recommends.
5. Warranty items: some dealerships will charge you for work that's actually covered by your warranty.
6. Salesman or mechanic? If you deal with a sales rep instead of a mechanic, he may actually earn commissions on your repairs.
7. Parts on commission: some technicians also make commissions on parts they sell.
8. Sabotage: this is a worst-case scenario—garages that actually sabotage your vehicle and then charge you to repair it.

CARS

DO YOUR HOMEWORK:

1. Seek out a great mechanic through referrals and check out the shop's reputation.
2. See if the mechanic holds any ASE certifications, but keep in mind that's no guarantee of good work or honesty.
3. If you'd like to try a mechanic who belongs to the Automotive Service Association, call **(800) ASA-SHOP** for a referral.
4. Try to speak directly to the mechanic who will actually work on your car.
5. Some states offer a sticker you can place on your car that warns mechanics you are an informed consumer and won't tolerate fraud.
6. Always ask for a written estimate and make sure it lists what is to be fixed, not just a series of parts.
7. Check your warranty to see if the repair in question ought to be covered.

WHERE TO COMPLAIN:

Your county and state consumer protection offices handle auto repair complaints. Also alert the BBB to your problem, so other consumers will have a paper trail to follow.

SEE ALSO:

CARS: Auto Body, Extended Warranties

CARS

Odometer Fraud

By making a car appear to have lower mileage than it actually does, the seller can rake in thousands of extra dollars. It's called "rolling back" or "spinning" an odometer. Each year in America, crooks tamper with the odometers on about three million used cars. The typical rollback takes thirty thousand miles off the life of a car. Since mileage is used as a gauge of how much wear and tear a used car has had, that translates into pure profit for the seller and pure misery for the buyer. AAA says the difference in value between a car with forty thousand miles and one with seventy thousand miles is about $3,600. According to the National Highway Traffic Safety Administration, consumers lose $4 billion a year because of odometer fraud.

Janice P. bought a 1989 Toyota with the understanding that it had eighty-seven thousand miles on it. I'm the one who broke it to her: The odometer should have shown 143,000 miles—a fifty-five-thousand–mile difference. Janice wanted a reliable car because she works the graveyard shift. One time, as she drove to work around midnight, the Toyota broke down on a busy stretch of freeway. Janice had to get out of the car and walk two miles to the nearest pay phone.

So how do crooks cover up odometer rollbacks? It's called "title washing." Crooks get the DMV to give them a new title for a vehicle, and they lie about the mileage. In Janice's case, my investigation showed the bad guys did it by posing as tow truck drivers. Some states allow mechanics and tow truck drivers to take possession of a vehicle if the owner fails to claim it. The state then issues a new title in the name of the mechanic or tow truck driver. The "washed" title can be used to cover up odometer fraud and other vehicle crimes. After my investigation aired, the leaders of the title-washing ring went to prison.

These days, computer databases like **www.carfax.com** are making it easier for consumers to catch odometer rollbacks. You should definitely invest in such a service before buying any used car. But keep in mind, these databases are not foolproof. They're based on government records. They can tell you if an odometer reading is lower than it was the last time the car was titled. But some crooks have started carefully rolling odometers back below their *true* mileage but *above* the mileage last recorded by the DMV.

Of course, there are situations where an odometer stops working or reaches its limit and starts over. In these cases, most states require a permanent notice on the title. That notice either explains the situation in detail or states "not actual mileage" or words to that effect.

KNOW THE SIGNS:

1. Twelve thousand miles a year is average for a car. If the mileage is much lower than that, the car could be a peach—or a problem.
2. Original tires generally last up to sixty thousand miles. So if the car is supposed to have low mileage, but it has new tires, that could be a clue.
3. Before you buy a used car, ask to see the title—not a copy. Beware if it's a brand-new title, a duplicate, or from out of state. If so, this could be a case of title washing.
4. Missing screws or other parts on and around the dashboard can be a sign that an odometer was "spun."
5. A badly worn brake pedal or floor mat may also tip you that a car's been on the road longer than the seller claims.
6. If the numbers on the odometer itself are not lined up straight, that may be a sign it's been tampered with.
7. General Motors mechanical odometers have black spaces between the numbers. If these spaces are silver or white, the odometer's been altered.
8. Some manufacturers make electronic odometers that display an asterisk or some other symbol if the odometer's been changed.

DO YOUR HOMEWORK:

1. Obtain a vehicle history report from **www.carfax.com** or another computer database.
2. Look for old oil change stickers, inspection certificates, or service records left in the car. Also *ask* for all service records; they may tell you the true story.
3. Have a trusted mechanic inspect the vehicle. High mileage can cause engine, suspension, and steering wear. Emissions problems also come with more miles.

WHERE TO COMPLAIN:

Odometer fraud is a federal crime. Report it immediately to your DMV and/or Motor Vehicle Dealer Board.

SEE ALSO:

CARS: Buying Used, **Curbstoning,** Salvaged

Parking Garages

When you pay to park, do you get what you paid for? Depends. I'm talking about parking garages where you take a ticket as you enter. Have you ever thought to check your watch as you enter and exit one of those lots? You should. You see, some greedy garages set their "in" clock slow and their "out" clock fast so they can collect a little extra money. Why do a couple of minutes matter? The way most parking garage prices are structured, the cost goes up as you pass each hour mark. In some cases, it even doubles. For example, *up to* one hour may cost $3. But anything *between* one and two hours costs $6. So by adding a couple of minutes to the clocks, a garage can push you into the next hour and dramatically increase its revenue. So next time you park in a garage, keep track of how much time you actually spend, because that's what determines how much *money* you should spend.

I tested twenty parking garages for my investigation. In two of them, the clocks were off—but in the customers' favor! Three garages were absolutely accurate. The other fifteen were tweaked in the companies' favor. That's 75 percent! Hard to believe it's a coincidence. We documented clocks that were off by anywhere from six minutes to fifteen. The really fun ones were those where the entrance and exit are right next to each other, back to back. In those, I was able to walk around the cashier's booth and instantly see that the two clocks showed different times. I even encountered a garage where the entrance and exit clocks were out of order. The cashier's solution? He just charged every driver for parking all day!

CARS

DO YOUR HOMEWORK:

1. Whenever you park at a garage, make a note of the time on your own clock as you enter and exit, then tally up the total and be prepared to fight! (Keep in mind, it doesn't matter whether the garage clocks exactly match yours in terms of time of day. What matters is the time elapsed. In other words, if the garage clock is two minutes slow on the way in, that's fine, as long as it's also two minutes slow on the way out.)
2. If you pull into a garage just to drop someone off, it helps to find out if the garage has a grace period. Many commercial parking garages honor a five-minute grace period. Some let you stay as long as ten minutes for free. But, if the garage clocks are off, the cashier may insist you've stayed longer.
3. Most parking garages don't want a fight. So speak up for yourself and they will probably reduce the charges.

WHERE TO COMPLAIN:

If you want to report a parking garage with crooked clocks, try your county or state consumer protection office.

Salvaged

Every year Americans mangle 2.5 million cars in bad accidents. And every year more than half of those cars are patched up and sold to unsuspecting consumers. It's a deception that endangers

consumers and costs them $4 billion a year. The cars should proba-
bly be sent to junkyards, the graveyards of the automotive industry.
But some of them inevitably come back from the dead.

CARS

Henry M. bought a used Acura Legend for $12,000. The used-car
dealer said it was a great deal and never revealed that the car had a
deep, dark past. So when Henry received his title in the mail, he was
shocked to see a big red stamp across it that said, "rebuilt salvage."
During my investigation, a former employee of the used-car dealer
tipped me off to some shady tactics. She explained that the owner
whited out the salvage brand when he faxed the title to Henry's
finance company for approval.

Sure enough, Henry's dream car quickly deteriorated. The Acura's
brake pedal hit the floor whenever he tried to stop. Faulty fuses
caused the radio, clock, and taillights to flicker on and off. And he
couldn't lock the doors or trunk because the nonfactory keys the
dealer gave him didn't work. I tracked down the Acura's former
owner, who was shocked to hear the car was back on the road.
Turns out his insurance company had declared it to be a total loss
after thieves stripped the car down to its metal shell.

Believe it or not, some states allow salvaged vehicles back on the
road if they pass a safety inspection conducted by a state police officer. Other states have a two-tier law in which the very worst wrecks
must be sent to a junkyard, but those with less damage can be
rebuilt. Many states now require a salvage brand on the title. A few
even require salvage stamps on the body of the car itself. The problem is, since each state is different, a crooked car dealer can just go
to a state that doesn't require branding and get a new title.

Congress keeps considering federal legislation to standardize this
patchwork of laws. But the lobbyists and politicians can't even
agree on what constitutes a car so badly damaged that it shouldn't
be on the road anymore. Say you own a car worth $10,000 and you
get in a wreck. Consumer advocates want that car to be considered
salvaged if repairing it costs more than 50 percent of its value, or
$5,000. The auto and insurance industries would like the threshold
to be 80 percent, in this case $8,000. With no consistent law in
place, it's up to you to protect *yourself* from buying a salvaged car.

DO YOUR HOMEWORK:

1. Before you shop for a used car, learn the law in your state. Are sellers required to disclose that a car has been salvaged? Are salvaged cars allowed to be rebuilt or just sold for parts? Does your state put a salvage brand on its titles?
2. Order a vehicle history report through a database like **www.carfax.com** to see if the car has ever had a salvage title in your state or another.
3. Ask the seller directly whether the car is a salvage car. If the seller assures you it isn't, get that guarantee in writing. If the seller refuses to put it in writing, I would be very suspicious indeed. If the seller does give you a written guarantee, and you later learn the car has been salvaged, you'll have proof of the deception.
4. Have any used car checked out by a mechanic—and possibly a body shop—before agreeing to buy it.

CARS

WHERE TO COMPLAIN:

If your state has a law governing salvaged cars, it is probably enforced by the attorney general's office. You can also contact your county consumer protection office. Making a complaint against the dealer's license could also be effective, and for that you'll need the DMV or Motor Vehicle Dealer Board.

SEE ALSO:

CARS: Buying Used, Curbstoning, Odometer Fraud

Spot Delivery

You're not allowed to return a car just because you don't like it. But dealers *are* allowed to make *you* return the car if the *bank* doesn't like *you*. It's called "spot delivery," meaning the dealer lets you take the car home on the spot. But you may get a call a couple of days or weeks later asking you to give that car back. Why? New- and used-car dealers are always hungry to make a sale. They know their best chance to do that is while you're right there on the lot. So they do a lot of deals without getting the bank's approval. (After all, most car sales happen on weekends when banks are closed.) The dealership looks at your credit and estimates what kind of financing the bank will offer you. That's how your contract is drawn up. Often the dealer guesses wrong, however, and the bank refuses to give you the loan. That's when you get the call demanding that you return the car. It's an obnoxious practice, and it happens all the time.

Bonita C. headed home from a dealership in a sleek red sedan. She drove her dream car for about a month, and then she got the call. It turned out that no bank was willing to finance Bonita with the terms promised by the dealership. To salvage the sale, the dealer first asked Bonita to scrape together a bigger down payment. She did, but it wasn't enough. (Sometimes dealers solve the problem by convincing the customer to accept more expensive financing or a *less* expensive car.) In Bonita's case, the dealer eventually made her return the vehicle. She's one of the lucky ones. The old car she had traded in was still on the lot, and the dealer gave it back to her. Often, when a spot delivery falls through, the dealership has already *sold* the customer's trade-in vehicle.

It's amazing that somebody would let you take home such an expensive piece of equipment without knowing whether you'll be able to pay for it. But since most car sales include financing, it's possible the *majority* of them are spot deliveries. Each state addresses the issue in its own way. For example, in one state, consumers have the right to force the dealership to honor the contract. Unfortunately, dealers get around this by having customers sign an addendum promising to return the car if the financing falls through. Another state has effectively legalized spot delivery by requiring a disclosure statement in the contract explaining that the deal may not be final.

DO YOUR HOMEWORK:

1. Obtain financing offers from banks and credit unions before shopping for a car. That way you won't need the dealer's financing.

2. If you do go with the dealer's financing, ask whether the terms of the loan are guaranteed or this is a spot delivery. (Just by knowing such obscure lingo you'll be sending the salesperson a message not to mess with you!)

3. If the financing is NOT guaranteed, offer to complete the sale when it *is*, and drive home in your own car.

4. Read and understand every word of your sales and financing contract. Look for paragraphs or extra pages that talk about your obligation to return the car if the deal falls through.

5. Beware of promissory notes. Some dealers will try to get you to sign something saying you'll find a way to pay for the car even if the dealer's loan is not approved. These documents *are* enforceable, so don't sign one. You could get yourself into a real mess.

6. Other dealers slip multiple financing deals into the stack of paperwork and get consumers to sign all of them. That way the dealer can easily shift you into a less favorable loan. Don't fall for that either.

WHERE TO COMPLAIN:

Spot delivery is typically governed by the DMV or the Motor Vehicle Dealer Board. Your state department of banking and finance may also have jurisdiction. Send copies of your complaint to the BBB and your county and state consumer protection offices.

SEE ALSO:

CARS: Buying New, Buying Used, **Financing**

Theft

Thieves steal a car every twenty-three seconds. There are two kinds of car thieves: joy riders looking for an easy opportunity and chop shops looking for easy money. You can protect against the first with common sense. You can protect against the second with common gadgets.

I once went to a packed parking lot and walked up and down the rows counting how many people had left their cars unlocked. It was unbelievable! Twelve percent of the cars were wide open. These are the cars teenage joyriders like. They even have a name for it: "car shopping." Young thieves look for unlocked cars, then hop in, hotwire them, and go!

By contrast, chop shops go looking for cars that will bring them the most money on the black market. They're willing to work a little harder to get just what they want. We once did a timed demonstration of just how easy it is to strip down a car. Our team did it in twelve minutes and forty-two seconds. The Acura we used was worth $10,000 when it was all in one piece, but the individual parts were worth twice that. Twenty thousand dollars just for taking a car apart!

So how can you protect yourself? The insurance industry recommends a layered approach. The first few steps are free. Lock your doors every time you leave your car, and don't keep a hidden key in one of those magnetic boxes. They are just as convenient for thieves as they are for you. Park your car in well-lit, well-traveled areas. Never leave your car running when you're not in it. Thefts of running cars seem to be on the rise—often with young children or pets inside. Finally, don't keep your title or registration in your car. Safeguard the title at home and keep the registration in your wallet.

You can ramp up your spending on security devices until you feel protected. Start with a steering wheel lock like the "Club." They typically cost $25 to $100. If you get the traditional style, it's best to attach it to your steering wheel backward, so the lock is behind the wheel near the dash. Some thieves have tools to punch out the lock, and this puts it safely out of reach. You can also buy a steering wheel lock with a large round center that covers up your entire steering wheel. Of course, steering wheel locks have one terrible weakness: *you.* You have to use the device every time for it to work.

Window etching is a nifty tactic. You etch all your windows with your VIN or a code, right where thieves will see it if they try to smash your window to get in. Car thieves don't like the idea of having to replace all those windows. And the code is kept in a central database to help identify your car if it's recovered.

Car alarms are a shrieking, honking part of urban life now. There's a mocking bird in my neighborhood that mimics the entire sequence of a car alarm. I swear! Many of us have learned to tune car alarms out, but that doesn't mean a car thief will. Walking past a car as it beeps and blares is different from breaking into one and driving away in it while it's making all that racket. Insurance companies believe in car alarms and offer a discount if you have one.

Some cars now come with a built-in ignition kill feature so they can't be hot-wired. Only the factory-cut laser key will turn the car on. This is one of the most effective deterrents and it's more common than it used to be. Finally, satellite tracking devices may not deter crooks from *taking* your car, but they are amazingly effective in *recovering* stolen cars.

CARS

DO YOUR HOMEWORK:

1. The cars most popular with consumers are usually the most popular with thieves. Find out if your car is one of those most commonly stolen. If so, take extra care to protect it.
2. Develop commonsense habits to protect your car for free.
3. Consider buying antitheft devices—and USE THEM!
4. Read your owner's manual so you'll know if your car has a built-in ignition kill feature.

WHERE TO COMPLAIN:

If your car is missing, of course you should immediately report it to the police. Your insurance company will probably ask for a police report before you can make a claim. Keep in mind your car may have just been towed. Ask police to check their towing database for you so you won't owe hundreds of dollars in storage fees if it was towed.

SEE ALSO:

INSURANCE: Car Insurance

Titles

When you sell your car, you probably think it's the end of an era. Or maybe you think good riddance! Not so fast. If the title isn't transferred out of your name, you could end up having a retro relationship with that car for years to come. It's the *buyer's* responsibility to transfer the title at the DMV. But if you sell your car to a disorganized individual or a disreputable dealer, he or she may not bother. After all, it takes time and costs money. In fact, some unscrupulous used-car dealers *never* transfer titles because they sell a car to someone with bad credit, then repossess it, then sell it to another bad risk and repo it again and so on. The shadiest used-car lots avoid putting titles in their own name because they don't want the car traced back to them when somebody discovers the odometer's been rolled back.

Tim C. was glad to get a little money for his used van. He sold it to a used-car dealer and went on his way. Three months later, he received a registered letter saying the van had been towed and he owed a couple of hundred dollars to get it back. Turns out the car dealer had sold the van to an inmate in a work-release program and had never bothered to transfer the title.

When I investigated, I discovered the inmate didn't even have a driver's license and may not have been insured. Somehow the used-car dealer got the van *back* and sold it to *another* person. I learned that person then lent the van to a friend who was driving it when she was arrested for shoplifting. At that point Tim heard from the authorities again. It took him months to clear his name.

Individual car buyers are generally required to transfer title right away. In some states, dealers are allowed to leave the title in your name while the car sits on their lot. Other states even allow the dealer to leave it in your name for another month or two *after* they've sold it. And since not all states require dealers to ask the buyer for proof of insurance, that's scary in terms of liability.

CARS

DO YOUR HOMEWORK:

1. If you sell your car to an individual, offer to complete the deal at the DMV. Stand in line with the buyer and transfer the title together before you hand over the keys.
2. If you sell your car to a dealer, sign the back of the title. That's supposed to clear you of liability. Also ask the dealer to sign the title. In some states dealers are required by law to sign it. Make a photocopy of the front and back of the signed title and keep it for several years.
3. Write up a formal bill of sale and keep a copy of that for several years, too.
4. Some DMVs offer a form you can fill out to alert the state that you have sold your car. This is an extra step in case the title doesn't get transferred. Make a copy to keep, then turn in the form.

CARS

WHERE TO COMPLAIN:

If you experience title troubles, you can complain to the DMV about individuals and dealers. Some states also have a motor vehicle dealer board you can contact.

SEE ALSO:

CARS: Donations

Towing

Every time I do a story about tow trucks, viewers flood me with calls. It's a tough industry that helps and hurts a lot of people. I know one tow truck driver who considers himself the "asphalt coast guard," eager to help motorists in trouble. I also know of many others who are unlicensed, unethical thugs.

I got a tip that one of the latter kind was cruising the Capital

CARS

Beltway outside Washington, D.C., preying on people stalled by the side of the road. Police call them "Beltway bandits." Carolyn P. broke down on the Beltway and called AAA. Seconds later, not one, not two, but *three* tow trucks pulled up behind her. She later learned none of them had been sent by AAA. The Beltway bandits listen in on AAA dispatches and swoop in before the authorized tow truck can get there. Some use rickety old trucks that can damage your car. All of them overcharge. Carolyn paid more than $100, and the going rate was more like $25.

We went undercover and parked a car by the side of the freeway ourselves. Tow truck drivers charged us between $80 and $100 every time. And there's more. Every single tow truck driver took us to the same gas station, one that was several miles away. They made U-turns and passed up half a dozen other possible shops to take us to that one. Why? We later learned that particular gas station pays tow truck drivers a *bounty* to bring cars there.

Another moneymaker for any towing company is a contract with a shopping center or apartment complex to tow unauthorized vehicles from the parking lot. Tow truck drivers are not supposed to tow a car unless management calls and asks them to. But they do. In fact, they "cherry-pick," lying in wait until they spot a car to tow. That's actually illegal in some jurisdictions. Of course, they often end up towing cars that belong to customers or residents. Once the towing company gets too many consumer complaints, it just paints a new name on its trucks and starts over. Businesses that contract with towing companies are required to post prominent signs warning that you may be towed. If they don't, you may be able to get your money back.

In one city, the local inspector general discovered that police officers were in cahoots with the towing company that held the police contract. The officers would order illegally parked vehicles towed, but not report the tow to the precinct. When the vehicle owners found their cars missing, they reported them stolen. The towing company would wait a few weeks, rack up thousands of dollars in storage charges, and *then* send the motorist a notice that it had the car.

On the flip side, Michelle B. left her crummy old car parked in her neighborhood until the tags expired and it was towed. Hard up for cash, she ignored all the notices telling her how much she needed to pay to get it out of the impound lot. Eventually, the towing company sold her car at auction and sent collection agents after her for the storage charges. She no longer had her car and she *still* owed the money. Can they do that? *Yes,* they can. I investigated, and found the towing company had a police contract and had done everything by the book.

CARS

There are rules that limit other practices. For example, if you return to your car right *before* it's about to be hooked up, most jurisdictions allow you to drive away for free. If you return and your car is *already* hooked up, some counties make the driver cut you loose for free; others allow him to charge you.

In 1994, Congress stripped the *states* of the right to regulate towing prices. Some *counties* still set rates, however. And police dictate prices when a towing company has a police contract to remove illegally parked cars or clear cars after accidents. Still, it's much more of a free-market system than it used to be, and in most places it's *not* illegal for a towing company to overcharge you.

DO YOUR HOMEWORK:

1. If you belong to an auto club, ask the driver for identification and a confirmation number when he arrives.
2. If you don't belong to an auto club, keep the phone number of a reputable towing company in your car.
3. Get the price, in writing, before the driver hooks you up. In our experiment, whenever we asked for the price up front we were quoted a lower rate.
4. Ask to be towed to your own mechanic.
5. If you see "no parking" signs in a parking lot, read carefully to see if they mention the name and number of a towing company. If so, that company may cruise the lot looking for unauthorized vehicles.
6. If you are towed from a private lot unfairly, take pictures of the "no parking" signs and measure the size of the lettering. If the signage is not up to code, the business may have to reimburse you.

7. Contact your county consumer protection office for help. Some counties regularly review towing cases.
8. If police ordered your car towed, check with them to see if they limit how much the towing company can charge.
9. If a towing company took your car and you don't want to pay, some counties allow you to go to the local courthouse and post a bond for the amount of the charge. You and the towing company then fight it out in small claims court. Whoever wins collects the cash.

WHERE TO COMPLAIN:

Take freeway towing complaints to the state highway patrol or department of transportation. If you're towed off private property, your county consumer protection agency is the best bet. If it was a police tow, contact that police department.

SEE ALSO:

CARS: Accidents

CHAPTER 3

Home Buying and Renting

Buy or Rent?

The question of whether to buy or rent is so simple—and yet so complicated—that it makes my head spin as I sit here trying to write about it. I'm going to give you the simple version. For a more complicated analysis of your individual situation, I highly recom mend the various mortgage-calculating programs available on the Internet. There's a good one at **www.quicken.com**, for example, and it's free. You could also ask a mortgage broker or lender to ana lyze your needs. Just remember, mortgage professionals make money by . . . *selling mortgages, so they're biased.*

The first consideration is how long you plan to stay in one place. Say you buy a house at precisely its current value. On top of that, you have to pay closing costs. So if you sell the home two years later for the same price you paid, you have actually *lost* money. You need to keep the home long enough for it to appreciate so you can make a profit that covers those closing costs. The other key is to keep your closing costs down in the first place. Of course, nobody can precisely predict the future value of real estate. In 2001, a stupendous year for property values, the average rate of real estate appreciation was 5 percent. Assume your rate of appreciation will be less than that.

After all, property values also go *down*. If you overestimate your future property value, you could always rent the place out for a few years to give it more time. There are two disadvantages to that plan. One, being a landlord is often a nasty experience. Two, your money will be tied up in the property, making it harder to buy another place for yourself.

HOME BUYING AND RENTING

On to some more encouraging math. To figure out what size monthly housing payment you can afford, start with your rent. I'm going to give you a grossly oversimplified formula that will give you a rough idea. Let's assume you currently make your monthly rent payments without any strain. You'll actually be able to afford a *higher* monthly payment when you own because of the income tax benefits. Let's say you pay $1,000 in rent each month and your top income tax rate is 20 percent. Take your rent and divide it by the other 80 percent to determine an affordable monthly housing payment: 1,000 divided by .80 = $1,250. The formula is **your rent divided by your tax rate = X.** That's *about* how much you can afford to pay for housing when you own the place.

It's not a perfect formula, because you're not allowed to deduct your entire mortgage payment from your taxes. Only the interest is deductible. Then again, at the beginning of a mortgage loan, *most* of your payment *does* go to interest, so it's a reasonable calculation. Now remember, that amount has to cover the mortgage itself plus property taxes, homeowner's insurance, and homeowner's association fees, if any. You should also set aside money for maintenance, since you won't have a landlord to fix things anymore. Keep in mind your utility bills could also be higher if you're buying a bigger place than you rent.

To have access to the cash for your new, higher housing payments, you will need to reduce the amount of income tax withheld from your paycheck. Ask a tax accountant how many additional allowances you should claim on your W-4 form.

So that's an idea of what size mortgage you can *afford*. Now you need to know what size mortgage you're likely to *get*. Lenders use an old rule of thumb, called the 28 percent and 36 percent rule. They say that your total monthly housing costs (mortgage, property taxes, and homeowner's insurance) should be no more than 28 percent of your gross monthly income. They calculate that your total housing costs *plus* long-term debt (alimony, car loans, student loans, etc.) should be no more than 36 percent of your gross monthly income. The strictest lenders make you meet both of these standards—and sometimes they use even lower percentages.

DO YOUR HOMEWORK:

1. Assess whether your current rent payment is comfortable, too high, or too low.
2. Use the basic formula in this chapter to figure out what an equivalent housing payment would be if you owned your home.
3. Go online or ask mortgage professionals to help you calculate that figure more precisely.
4. Research property values and appreciation rates in neighborhoods you like.
5. Learn how to keep your closing costs down.

SEE ALSO:

HOME BUYING AND RENTING: **Closing Costs, Mortgages;** FINANCES: **Predatory Lending**

Closing Costs

Every year, Americans spend $50 million to buy houses. I'm not talking about how much the homes *themselves* cost. I'm talking about how much the *loans* cost. American home buyers routinely pay abusive closing costs. There are two kinds of abuses: real fees that are inflated and junk fees that are just plain made up. It doesn't have to be that way. If you know what you're doing, you can save thousands of dollars when you go to the settlement table.

Here's the problem. When you apply for a loan, the mortgage company gives you a list of the fees you can expect, called a good faith estimate. What a joke! All too often these estimates aren't given "in good faith" at all. You see, there's no law requiring the mortgage company to stick to its good faith estimate. So when you go to close a month later, often you'll find the fees have risen sharply or new fees have been added. The U.S. Department of Housing and Urban Development (HUD) has been fighting to prevent lenders, brokers, and title agents from padding closing costs. But the current law is weak, so courts keep siding with the mortgage industry. Until Congress passes a better law, it's up to *you* to protect *yourself.*

HOME BUYING AND RENTING

At my own closing, the fees were a whopping $2,000 more than I had expected—even though the mortgage company manager *knew* I was an investigative reporter. I can only imagine how that company treats customers who don't have a title like mine to fling around. Of course, I questioned every single line item, found several junk fees, and got the company to knock several hundred dollars off my closing costs. Let me fill you in on several ways the mortgage industry tries to get you.

Cleo S. wanted to refinance her home. The lender charged her $50 for a so-called funding fee. That's a euphemism for a simple wire transfer. First of all, wire transfers don't cost that much. Second, getting the money *to* the borrower is the lender's *job* and shouldn't cost extra. The lender also charged Cleo $150 for a survey, but when you refinance, normally a survey isn't required. The title company took advantage of Cleo, too, by charging her $125 to record her deed with the county. But the county where Cleo lives only charges $25 for that service. The fee was heavily padded—pure profit for the title company!

A couple of proposals could reform abusive closing costs like these. One is for groups of lenders, title agents, surveyors, and appraisers to band together and offer package deals. The packages would be guaranteed, so consumers could shop and compare. These package deals are already starting to become a reality. The other possibility is a law requiring lenders to stick to their original good faith estimates. That would eliminate the bait and switch tactics so common today.

For now, the best thing you can do is learn the lingo and be ready to fight. Here's a breakdown of the often inflated typical fees you will see on your "settlement statement." I explain what the fees are actually for and how much they typically cost in the nation's capital. Keep in mind that these are *rough* estimates. Lots of factors can make these fees higher or lower (such as where you live, whether you're a first-time home buyer, and if you have poor credit.)

FEES IMPOSED BY THE LENDER

Loan Origination Fee: 1 percent of the purchase price

This is simply a way for the lender to make a bit of money up front. If you deal directly with a mortgage company, rather than with a mortgage broker, this is how the loan officer makes his or her money. The loan origination fee is often referred to as a "point" and is tax deductible.

Loan Discount:

"Loan discount" refers to the "points" you pay to buy down your interest rate. If you choose to pay points, each point will be 1 percent of the loan amount. Take out a loan for $100,000 and one point will equal $1,000. As a general rule, for each point you pay, you buy down the interest rate by .25 percent. So, for example, you could pay zero points and get a 7.75 percent interest rate. Or you could pay three points and get a 7 percent interest rate. If you don't plan to keep the home long, points can be expensive for you. If you plan to stay put for a long time, points begin to pay for themselves. If you're buying a house, points are tax-deductible the year you take out the loan. If you're refinancing your house, you have to deduct the points over the life of the loan.

Underwriting Fee: $150–$325

Some lenders charge a fee to weigh the risk of doing business with you. Critics say this fee shouldn't exist, because underwriting is an integral part of what a lender does. It would be like a carpenter charging an extra fee for carrying his tools into your house. But lenders now routinely charge back-end fees like this, so they can keep their interest rates low, which is how they attract customers. You may be able to negotiate a lower underwriting fee.

HOME BUYING AND RENTING

Document Preparation Fee: $75–$325

Lenders have to prepare several documents when granting you a loan, and some charge for doing so. This is another fee often criticized by consumer advocates. You may be able to negotiate a lower one.

Administrative Fee: $390–$550

This fee covers underwriting *and* document preparation. Some lenders lump the two together and call it their "administrative fee." Again, you may be able to negotiate.

Funding Fee/Wiring Fee: $0–$30

This fee is supposed to cover the cost of wiring your loan money to whoever is conducting your closing. Lenders never used to charge this fee. Critics say they still shouldn't, because getting the money to you is part of their job. Try to get the lender to waive this fee.

Credit Report: $15–$60

Lenders and brokers pull your credit report to see if you have a positive payment history. If they require a full residential mortgage credit report, that's more expensive because the credit reporting agency actually takes the time to call your creditors and verify the items on your credit report. Some lenders are not satisfied with a simpler credit report, called a "tri-merge," that contains information from all three major credit bureaus but is not verified manually. This is a fee that often gets padded. Since an outside company provides this service, ask for a receipt to verify the true cost and don't pay a penny more.

Tax Service Fee/Escrow Fee: $58-$89

Lenders like to make sure you pay your property taxes, because if you don't, the county can seize your home and the lender won't get paid. Most lenders require you to send extra money along with your mortgage payments. The lender collects that money in an escrow account and then pays your property taxes for you. If you make a big down payment, you're allowed to pay your property taxes yourself. But the lender still hires an outside company to monitor whether you're paying your taxes. This fee covers that service. If you plan to pay your property taxes directly yourself, this fee should be at the lower end of the scale.

HOME BUYING
AND RENTING

Appraisal Fee: $100-$500

Lenders require a professional appraisal so they will know if the home you are buying is worth the amount of money they are lending you. If you are refinancing, the lender may be satisfied with a "drive-by" appraisal, which is much less expensive. Either way, ask your broker or lender for a receipt showing which appraiser did the work and how much it actually cost. Don't pay an inflated fee.

Survey Fee: $0-$250

A survey is performed to make sure the boundaries of your property are clean and clear. Surveyors look for things like misplaced fences and shared driveways that may cloud property lines and cause a dispute. Lenders ask you to pay for a survey if you are buying a home. If you are refinancing, they may be willing to "recertify" the existing survey at no cost. Surveys do not apply to condominiums, but watch out, because some lenders tack them on anyway. Once again, surveyors are outside companies. Demand receipts and don't allow upcharges.

Flood Certification Fee: $11-$25

If you are buying a single-family home, the lender will want to have a flood survey done to see if the house is in a flood zone. An outside company will review government charts to find out. If you are buying a condo on an upper floor, you shouldn't have to pay for a flood certification, but beware, some lenders charge for it out of habit. This is another outside service for which you can get a receipt.

Hazard Insurance: $300-$600

Lenders require you to purchase at least fire insurance to protect your new property since it serves as collateral for the loan. Most buyers purchase full homeowner's insurance, which covers fires and other disasters. The lender must approve the insurance company you choose. Some brokers and lenders will try to sign you up for a full year's coverage, which can be difficult to afford at the same time as all these other closing costs. Ask questions. Most lenders are satisfied if you prepay just two to four months of insurance.

Interest:

If you are refinancing, avoid scheduling your closing for the beginning of the month. Why? Because that means you will have to pay several days' worth of interest at closing or roll it into the mortgage. It's hard enough to come up with the cash for closing. And you don't want to raise your mortgage any higher.

FEES IMPOSED BY THE BROKER

Mortgage Broker Fee: 1 percent-5 percent of the loan amount

A mortgage broker is like a professional shopper who shops around at numerous mortgage companies to find you the best deal. Your mortgage broker is entitled to make a commission for the work involved in finding you a loan. The amount of this tax-deductible fee is regulated by the government. In some states the percentage is not capped, but brokers are required to disclose their fees in writing and get the borrower's signature of approval. In one state, mortgage brokers cannot charge more than 8 percent of the loan amount. Find out the rules in your area.

Keep in mind, brokering loans is a competitive business, so most brokers charge well below the legal limit. If you have good credit, you will qualify for a "prime" loan, and you can expect to pay your mortgage broker 1 percent to1.25 percent of the loan amount. If you have poor credit, you will be given a "subprime" loan, and chances are your broker will charge 3 percent to 5 percent because finding you a loan takes more work. If the percentage is any higher, ask hard questions and shop around to see if you can get a better deal.

If you can't afford to pay high closing costs, including the broker's fee, there is an alternative, called a "yield spread premium." In this scenario, the broker pays some or all of your closing costs *for* you. In exchange, you pay a higher interest rate on the loan. The broker makes his or her money by charging the lender a fee. Lenders are willing to pay these broker fees because higher-interest rate loans bring them more money in the long run.

Caution: yield spread premium deals are only legitimate if you pay low or no closing costs in exchange for paying a higher interest rate. IF YOU ARE PAYING A HIGH INTEREST RATE *AND* YOUR CLOSING COSTS ARE STILL HIGH, THAT'S ILLEGAL, and you may be a victim of predatory lending.

FEES IMPOSED BY TITLE AGENTS AND SETTLEMENT ATTORNEYS

Closing Fee: $350 for a purchase (split between buyer and seller). $150–$350 for a refinance

Your closing is the meeting where you sign all the paperwork to finalize your loan and purchase the home. Closings can be conducted by title agents or by real estate attorneys who double as title agents. In some parts of the country, these individuals are called "escrow agents." The government does not regulate the fees these professionals charge. IT'S UP TO YOU TO SHOP AROUND AND FIND THE BEST RATE. Don't automatically hire the title agent recommended by your Realtor or mortgage broker.

Settlement Fee

A "settlement" is the same thing as a "closing." It should not be an additional cost, but unscrupulous operators have been known to add it as a separate line item and double charge.

HOME BUYING AND RENTING

Abstract or Title Search: $150-$225

This fee is charged by the title agent to cover the cost of sending somebody to the courthouse to research the history of the property you want to buy. The person verifies that the seller really owns the property free and clear and has a right to sell it to you. Some title agents have somebody in-house who does this work. Others hire an outside company. If yours hires an outside company, as always, ask for a receipt.

Title Examination: $0-$400

This is the fee some title agents charge to analyze the results of the title search done at the courthouse. They look for liens, judgments, and ownership disputes that may hurt you or the lender later on. Many title professionals consider this to be just an extension of the abstract or title search and charge nothing. Others consider it a separate function. Again, shop around for the best deal.

Title Insurance Binder: $0-$50

Title insurance is provided by big national insurance companies. Title agents are generally small, local firms. The title insurance binder is the insurance company's promise to provide title coverage once the sale is complete. It is prepared by the local title agent, who acts as a broker for that insurance company. Some title agents include it in the cost of the title search or title exam.

(Title) Document Preparation: $0-$100

The lender prepares the bulk of the documents required to close a loan and buy a home, but title agents prepare some, too. Some charge for this; many include it under other line items.

Notary Fees: $7-$20

Title agents must have some documents notarized for you. Most have an in-house notary but still pass along the cost to you. Ask how many pages had to be notarized and the price per page. You may be able to negotiate.

HOME BUYING AND RENTING

Release of Lien Fee: $0-$100

This is the fee for getting the county to change the records so the old homeowner and old lender are no longer listed as owners. Some title agents include this service under another heading; others list it separately so you know exactly what you're getting. Good title agents often complain that the bad apples in their industry charge for this service but never do it. That leaves multiple ownership records in place for the same property.

Attorney's Fee

This should be the same as the fee called "settlement" or "closing" fee. If a settlement attorney performs your closing, they may list this service under "attorney's fees" instead.

Courier Fee: $0-$100

Title agents sometimes hire a courier to transport your documents. However, many "estimate" this fee rather than charging you exactly what they were charged. Others charge for a courier service even though they didn't actually use one. Ask for receipts.

(Title) Administrative Fee

Some title agents lump document preparation and courier fees into one category and call it an "administrative fee."

Title Insurance: *Loan amount* × .0250 for lender's coverage; *loan amount* × .003 for lender's and homeowner's coverage

HOME BUYING AND RENTING

Title insurance protects you and the lender in case something was missed during the title search. For example, if the county misspelled a name, somebody with a claim to your property might not show up during the title search. Lenders require you to buy a "lender's" policy to protect their interests in the property, and many people purchase a homeowner's policy to protect themselves as well. The formulas above are very rough guidelines of what you can expect to pay.

In most states, if you are refinancing or if you are buying a house that the seller purchased less than ten years ago, you can qualify for the "reissue rate" on your title insurance. THIS COULD SAVE YOU HUNDREDS OF DOLLARS! You may have to provide proof that there was a valid title insurance policy in place. The discount ranges from 25 percent to 50 percent. The government does not require lenders to offer you the reissue rate, so you should always ask about it. Some title agents will pretend they don't know what you're talking about because it cuts into their commission. Other title insurance companies require their title agents to offer the reissue rate. Once again, you can save money by shopping around in advance for the best title agent.

FEES IMPOSED BY THE GOVERNMENT

Recording Fees

This is simply the amount the county clerk charges to record the fact that you are purchasing the property. If you're refinancing, you typically still have to pay this fee because the county has to record the new lender's name. Some title agents try to pad this fee. Call your county recorder of deed's office to find out the true cost.

Tax Stamps

This is a tax charged when a property changes hands. The amount is based on the purchase price, sort of like a sales tax. It's just a chance for the county or state to collect a little money. If you're a first time home buyer, the amount may be less. Some jurisdictions do not charge tax stamps when you refinance. Others base the charge on the difference between the amount of your old loan and your new one. Call your county office of taxation and revenue to determine the formula.

Recordation Tax

This is the same as "tax stamps," just another name for it.

Transfer Tax

A percentage of the purchase price, this tax is another opportunity for the government to collect money. Many jurisdictions do not charge this tax if you're refinancing. Call your county office of taxation and revenue to find out how this tax is calculated and whether it even applies to you.

DO YOUR HOMEWORK:

1. Shop for mortgages through several different lenders and compare the closing costs on their good faith estimates. Aggressively question the companies about whether the figures on the estimates could change. Remember, the company with the lowest estimate could pull the biggest bait and switch.
2. Shop around for the title agent or settlement attorney who offers the best overall deal. Get a written quote, and if additional charges appear at closing, dispute them.
3. Forewarn your mortgage company, mortgage broker, and title agent that you will not pay padded closing costs for services performed by outside companies. Let them know you plan to ask for receipts.

4. Scan your good faith estimate for fees that don't apply to you if you're buying a condominium.
5. Scan your good faith estimate for fees that don't apply if you're refinancing.
6. Find out whether there's a cap in your state on the fees mortgage brokers are allowed to charge.
7. Find out whether the seller purchased the property less than ten years ago. If so, ask for a copy of the seller's title insurance policy. Inquire about getting the reissue rate. If the title agent plays dumb, ask which national title insurance company the agent represents, then call that company directly to learn its rules on reissue rates.
8. Call your local government and find out how it calculates real estate taxes. Don't let the title agent pad these government fees.

WHERE TO COMPLAIN:

If a lender does you wrong, try your state banking division. You can contact your state department of licensing to lodge a complaint against a mortgage broker. In some states the insurance commissioner governs title agents. If your title agent is an attorney, you can complain to the bar association.

SEE ALSO:

BEFORE YOU BUY: Contracts; FINANCES: **Predatory Lending, Refinancing;** CREDIT: Credit Reports; INSURANCE: Homeowner's Insurance

For Sale by Owner

When the National Association of Realtors surveyed people who sold their homes themselves, only 25 percent said they would do it again. I'm one of those 25 percent. I would also *buy* a home FSBO-style again. I mean, how many times in your life do you get a chance to save not hundreds, but thousands, of dollars? I wouldn't go so far

HOME BUYING AND RENTING

as to say buying or selling a house without a Realtor is *easy*. It's just that it's not that hard—especially not 6 percent-commission-on-the-sales-price hard. For sale by owner (FSBO) deals work best if the housing market is hot. Don't go this route unless you feel comfortable and confident.

The Realtors' association crows that nine out of ten homeowners end up hiring a Realtor after trying to do a FSBO. My answer is, "so what?" Why not try to sell on your own to save the money? If you succeed, you're a genius. If you don't, you're right back where you started. Obviously, this advice doesn't work if you're in a huge hurry to sell. In that case, hiring a real estate agent probably is the best choice. Another option: you could advertise the house yourself, but allow people who come see it to use a "buyer's agent." That way you'll pay half the commission you normally would.

HOME BUYING AND RENTING

The biggest challenge in selling your house yourself is setting the right price. You won't have easy access to the comparative sales data Realtors use. Instead, scan the classifieds to see what other houses are listing for in your neighborhood. Attend open houses and see how those houses compare with yours. Read the obscure section of the newspaper that lists who sold property to whom—and for how much. Sellers always fear they'll underprice their homes and make less money than they deserve. But overpricing is just as deadly. Realtors believe if a house sits on the market too long there are three possible reasons: price, price, and price.

Assume an air of cool objectivity and detachment when you sell your house yourself. Ask friends to walk through your home and tell you what they would change to give it more instant appeal. Don't be offended by comments potential buyers make. Normally, a Realtor would shield you from those critiques, but for several thousand dollars in savings, you can grin and bear it.

You can either improvise your own sales strategy, or you can sign up with one of the FSBO services that offers Internet ads, for sale signs, real estate forms, etc. Here's a great hint! Every weekend, check the classifieds for open houses in your neighborhood. Then hold your own open houses to coincide with them. Take advantage of the foot traffic. Chances are those buyers are attracted to your neighborhood.

Long before you get an offer, you should hire a good real estate attorney. Not only will that attorney guide *you* through the process, you'll be able to run buyers' questions by him or her as well. One of the hurdles in selling your house yourself is convincing buyers that it's not that hard to *buy* a FSBO house. If your attorney can provide the basic paperwork the buyer needs to make you an offer, that's a start. The buyer probably will want to hire his or her own lawyer as you get further along in the process. Your attorney will be able to advise you on the proper protocol, review offers, and be present at your closing. Whether you pay a lump sum or an hourly fee, it should still be much less than what you'd pay a Realtor.

HOME BUYING AND RENTING

When you get an appealing offer, don't accept it until you know the buyers can make good on it. Ask their bank to provide a pre-approval letter, so you know they have good credit and the ability to secure a mortgage. (A prequalification letter is not as credible.) Also ask for a substantial earnest money deposit up front. This is another test of the buyer's creditworthiness and helps prove his or her seriousness. If you are considering *competing* offers, give more weight to the ones that include the biggest down payments.

In addition to price, the buyer and seller need to agree on several other factors. What items are included in the home, such as chandeliers, curtains, and appliances? Where and when will the closing take place, and when will the property change hands? Is the sale based on any contingencies, like repairs, termite inspection, legal review of the contract, or the buyer's ability to get desirable financing?

If your sales contract is contingent on a home inspection, know the protocol in your area. Generally, the buyer has just twenty-four to forty-eight hours after the home inspection to accept the house as it is, ask you to make changes, or withdraw the offer. If the buyer wants you to make repairs, don't be offended. This issue is negotiable. If you'd rather not mess around with hiring a handyman, offer to drop the price slightly to cover the costs of fixes.

When my husband sold his old house to move in with me, the man and woman buying it had some requests. My husband got annoyed and it showed. The man buying the house got annoyed back. Tensions escalated. Eventually, we women had to take over the negotiations to save the deal. If both sides had had Realtors as buffers, that probably wouldn't have happened.

DO YOUR HOMEWORK:

1. Read the classifieds and attend open houses to help determine your asking price.
2. Ask friends to assess things you need to improve immediately to gain "curb appeal."
3. Research FSBO Web sites and services that can help you through the process.
4. Hire a real estate attorney.
5. Check the buyers' creditworthiness before you accept their offer.
6. Keep your cool if the contract is contingent on a home inspection.

HOME BUYING
AND RENTING

SEE ALSO:

HOME BUYING AND RENTING: Closing Costs, Home Inspectors, **Realtors**

Home Inspectors

Many states do not license home inspectors, so anybody can become one. It's up to you to protect *yourself* from clueless—or even crooked—home inspectors. A *clueless* home inspector could miss flaws in the house you're looking at, costing you thousands of dollars down the road. A *crooked* home inspector could be getting kickbacks from the seller and Realtor or could be performing inspections just to solicit repair work.

On the other hand, a talented, thorough home inspector is the best friend a home buyer can have. To find one, don't automatically go with your Realtor's recommendation. I know, I know, in this book I constantly preach about the value of referrals. But buying a house is such a big, important transaction, I believe it's best to hire each professional independently. That way, the advice of each is constructive—even contradictory—which is better than a series of people who just rubber-stamp each other's work. If, after checking out several inspectors, you find the one recommended by your Realtor is the most qualified, that's a different story.

So what on earth do you ask a home inspector when you interview him or her? First and foremost, find out if the inspector belongs to the American Society of Home Inspectors (ASHI) or the National Association of Home Inspectors (NAHI). ASHI is a respected trade organization that requires inspectors to do 250 professional inspections before they can join. NAHI has minimum standards, too. By contrast, one state that *does* regulate home inspectors requires an applicant to perform just fifteen inspections before becoming licensed. ASHI and NAHI members who don't keep up with their continuing education get kicked out.

Ask home inspector candidates what their inspection includes. For example, ASHI inspectors are required to look at the home's exterior (things like doors, decks, and grading), interior (things like walls, floors, and countertops), structural system, electrical system, heating and air conditioning, insulation and ventilation, plumbing, fireplace, and roof. Make sure the inspection includes a written report. Ask to see samples of the inspector's past reports to see if they are thorough and understandable.

Find out the logistics of the inspection. A thorough inspector will spend about three hours going over an average single-family home. If the inspector spends less time, he or she is less thorough. Cost of the inspection varies dramatically, depending on the geographic location and type of home; $300–$500 is a pretty typical range. It's a darn good investment, considering you're about to spend tens of thousands on a house.

Explore the background of the individual inspector you will be working with, especially if he or she works for a multiperson firm. How long has the inspector been in the business? How many inspections has he or she conducted? Does the inspector have specific experience in residential inspections? Does the inspector do continuing education? Does the inspector offer repair services if he or she finds problems? (This last one is a no-no.)

Make sure you are welcome at the inspection. (Run away from

HOME BUYING AND RENTING

any inspector who does not want you there.) You'll learn all sorts of things about the house you are about to buy. At my home inspection, I learned how to work the self-cleaning oven (the owner's manual was long gone), I learned my stove hood had a hidden carbon filter that should be changed every couple of years (who knew?), and I even picked up a couple of remodeling ideas that I implemented later!

DO YOUR HOMEWORK:

HOME BUYING AND RENTING

1. Avoid buying a home "as is." That means you waive your right to get a home inspection and ask for repairs. Instead, write your offer so that it's contingent on a successful home inspection.
2. Some sellers now get home inspections up front as an additional sales tool. This is nice, but should not be a substitute for an independent inspection conducted by the professional of your choice.
3. Develop a short list of home inspectors by asking your Realtor and checking with friends and family.
4. Check to see if these inspectors belong to ASHI or NAHI. Find out if your state requires licensing. If it does, make sure the inspector you choose is licensed.
5. Interview inspectors, asking them what's covered, how long it will take, how much it will cost, whether you can attend, and how much experience they have.
6. Keep in mind that most real estate contracts require you to act on the inspector's findings within a set time frame. You may have, say, forty-eight hours to ask the seller to make repairs, ask for a price reduction, or back out of the deal. If you wait past this window of time, you may be waiving your rights.

WHERE TO COMPLAIN:

If a home inspector fails you in some way, you should definitely squawk, since the stakes are high in home inspections. If your state licenses home inspectors, complain to the licensing agency. If the inspector is a member of a trade organization, file a complaint with that group. You can also write to your county and state consumer protection offices and the BBB.

SEE ALSO:

HOME BUYING AND RENTING: For Sale by Owner, New Homes, Realtors

Mortgages

HOME BUYING AND RENTING

I am not a mortgage expert and this is not a mortgage book. So my first word of advice, especially for first-time home buyers, is to go buy a mortgage book written by a mortgage expert. (If you're a *really* savvy consumer, *borrow* a mortgage book!) With that disclaimer aside, I can share a few principles and pitfalls of mortgages with you. Here's what matters: *who* provides your loan, *what* loan you get, and *how* you manage that loan later.

First of all, you need to know the difference between a mortgage broker and a mortgage lender. Mortgage *brokers* almost never use the word, "broker," in their business names. In fact, they often use names like "XYZ Home Loans," implying that they *make* home loans. They don't. Mortgage brokers don't have any money to give you. Zero. Zilch. Nada. They are simply professional shoppers who approach lenders for you. There are millions of mortgage brokers nationwide, and they tend to be small, locally based businesses. One caution: if you use a mortgage broker and things go wrong, the broker can blame the lender and the lender can blame the broker. You are dealing with a real two-headed monster.

Mortgage *lenders* are usually giant companies that do business nationwide. Some are full-service banks; others specialize in mortgages. Some mortgage lenders don't really do business with consumers. They are in the field simply to make home loans, then they sell those loans to investors as soon as possible. I prefer mortgage lenders who keep their loans. They have more incentive to be consumer-friendly, since they have long-term relationships with their customers.

If you have tip-top credit and enough cash for a big down payment, I suggest you at least *try* to shop for loans directly through mortgage lenders. This advice comes from the basic principle that it's best to cut out middlemen whenever possible. Every middleman has to be paid, right? Information is so accessible these days that shopping for interest rates on your own is pretty easy. Look in the paper. Call the bank where you have your checking account. Go online. I shopped for my mortgage on the Internet, although my trust broke down when it came time to actually apply. For that, I wanted to speak to a live human. On the down side, since mortgage lenders may not deal directly with customers very often, they can be downright klutzy about processing your paperwork. My mortgage lender was clueless. Check out your mortgage lender's reputation before you do a deal with the company.

If your loan shopping is complicated by a lot of factors, *that's* when a mortgage broker can really be worth the commission. For example, if you have poor credit, a mortgage broker can scour the financial world to find you a loan you might not be able to find on your own. If you have little cash for your down payment, a mortgage broker can advise you on creative ways to keep your costs down. If interest rates are high across the board, a mortgage broker may have some sound coping strategies. Since brokers do nothing but serve customers, they may be better than lenders at streamlining their requests for paperwork. Be sure to do a background check. Almost anybody can become a mortgage broker, so you want to be sure you're dealing with a pro.

After you choose your lender or broker, you have to choose what type of loan you want. *Fixed-rate* mortgages are best when interest rates are low and you plan to stay in the home for a long time. These allow you to lock in a good deal, and your monthly payments stay steady for the life of the loan. When rates are rock-bottom, I see no reason to pay points. A point is a fee equal to 1 percent of the loan amount, and it's used to "buy down" the interest rate. If the rate is already low and fixed, you don't need to make it any lower. Some brokers and lenders will try to get you to pay points anyway, because points generate more up-front profit for them.

Adjustable-rate mortgages, or ARMs, work well when interest rates are high and/or you don't plan to live in the house very long. ARMs typically start with a lower, "teaser" rate, which can help you make your monthly payments. It can also help you qualify for a more expensive home than you would with a fixed-rate loan. It's a bit of a gamble. You're hoping that interest rates will go down before it's time for your adjustable-rate mortgage to adjust. That way you can refinance and get a decent fixed rate. Alternatively, you can sell the home before your rate goes up. Most ARMs have a maximum cap for your protection. To be fair, an ARM should adjust upward *and* downward, depending on market conditions. But some predatory lenders sell adjustable rate mortgages that start high, adjust upward only, and have no cap.

HOME BUYING
AND RENTING

The Federal Trade Commission cautions borrowers against what it calls, "creative financing" packages. Example 1: A loan that starts out below-market, but in which both the interest rate and the monthly payment grow every year for the remainder of the loan, regardless of market conditions. Example 2: Some mortgages have high interest rates but still offer low monthly payments. If the payments are not enough to cover the principal and interest, the difference is added to the principal. You could actually end up owing more at the end of the loan term than you did in the beginning! Example 3: To keep early payments low, some lenders ask borrowers to make a "balloon" payment at the end of the loan. The amount is usually so massive that the borrowers have to refinance. That generates more closing fees for the lender and forces borrowers to go with whatever the going interest rate is, which may not be at all favorable.

Once you've chosen a lender or broker, you need to decide whether to "lock in" today's going interest rate, or gamble that rates will go down between now and your closing. If you'd rather go with the sure thing, get that rate guarantee in writing. Have the lender or broker sign a lock-in document that states the interest rate and number of points you will be paying. That way, even if rates go up, you're set. Most banks will only guarantee an interest rate for sixty days. If you feel strongly that interest rates will go down before you close, you can choose to float your interest rate for awhile. You can also request a deal where the interest rate can *decrease* but not increase while you wait to close. Not all banks offer this service, so you might want to find one that does.

These days some lenders will give you a mortgage without any down payment at all. But if you can put 20 percent down, that's still ideal. That's the threshold for avoiding *private mortgage insurance* (PMI). PMI doesn't benefit you in any way. It's something lenders demand to protect *themselves* in case you stop paying back your loan. In addition to putting down 20 percent, there are other innovative ways to structure a first and second mortgage and avoid PMI. Ask a professional.

HOME BUYING AND RENTING

If you *do* end up paying PMI, you get to stop as soon as you have 20 to 22 percent equity in your home. The Homeowners Protection Act of 1998 says that lenders must terminate your PMI when you reach twenty-two percent, based on the original property value. Keep track of that. Some lenders and insurance companies fail to tell you when your PMI obligation is over, because they want to continue collecting the pricey premiums. If yours is a "high-risk" loan because you have poor credit or if you have made late payments on your mortgage, your lender has a right to keep charging for PMI.

If you can pay off your mortgage in less than the fifteen, twenty, or thirty years you are allowed, you will save thousands of dollars in interest. Just make sure there's no penalty for early repayment. In some states, prepayment penalties are illegal, in others they're quite common. There are a couple of different ways to set up your own early repayment system. One way is to simply send extra money each month when you pay your mortgage. Most mortgage companies provide a blank line for you to write in the extra amount you're sending. Just be sure to note that your extra money is to go toward principal. Paying extra toward your principal reduces how much interest you owe in the long run. This method is flexible, so if you're pinched for cash one month, you can send less extra than usual. If you're flush another month, send more.

If you need a more structured approach, consider this: Most of us pay our mortgage bills once a month. But most of us get *paid* every two weeks. If you set aside half your mortgage money every pay period, you will end up with an extra month's payment by the end of the year. Send that money in, say it's for principal, and you'll get ahead on your mortgage.

Because prepaying is such a great benefit, some companies are trying to cash in. These companies offer mortgage savings plans for a price. The company collects your extra money every two weeks and sets it aside for you. This method certainly provides a dose of discipline, but it comes at a price. Mortgage savings plans typically cost about $500 to set up and $2.50 for each withdrawal. If you experience hard times, you still have to pay, and if you don't pay, you could face late fees. To make matters worse, the company holding your mortgage money makes interest on it. Wouldn't you rather earn that interest yourself?

HOME BUYING AND RENTING

DO YOUR HOMEWORK:

1. If you're a first-time home buyer, get every book and pamphlet you can about mortgages. Also consider taking a home-buying class. Fannie Mae and Freddie Mac offer first-time home-buyer classes. If you complete the class, you prequalify for a loan.
2. Shop for mortgages yourself, if you feel confident and comfortable doing so.
3. Figure out who's who in your area. Let's see, is this company a mortgage *lender* or a mortgage *broker?*
4. Check the reputations of lenders and brokers by contacting the BBB, your county and state consumer protection offices, and, possibly, your state department of banking.
5. Determine what kind of loan you want, based on interest rates, your credit history, the size of your down payment, and the cost of the home.
6. Demand a copy of the terms of your loan before closing. Read and understand the loan terms or have a lawyer read and understand them for you. Comb the contract for signs of "creative financing" deals that could get you in trouble.
7. Avoid private mortgage insurance if you can. If you can't avoid it, keep track of it and stop paying as soon as possible.

8. Figure out if your loan has prepayment penalties and whether they're legal in your area. If not, work out a plan to pay extra each month *without* using an outside company.

WHERE TO COMPLAIN:

To lodge a complaint against a mortgage broker, contact your county and state consumer protection offices and the BBB. Do the same for a mortgage lender, but also find out what agency regulates mortgage lenders in your state. It could be the department of banking. If your loan is insured by the federal government, contact HUD (for FHA loans) or the Department of Veterans Affairs (for VA loans).

HOME BUYING AND RENTING

SEE ALSO:

HOME BUYING AND RENTING: Buy or Rent?, **Closing Costs;** FINANCES, **Predatory Lending, Refinancing;** CREDIT: Credit Reports, Credit Scoring, Credit Rescoring

Moving

So you've hired a mover. Congratulations, you could face the following: Misleading lowball estimates that get jacked up at the end, intentional delays so that you owe for additional hours, belongings held hostage until you agree to cough up more money, missing property, damaged property, stolen property . . . BUT, HEY, NO BIG DEAL. We're only talking about all your worldly possessions here. These are all real-life scenarios reported time and time again to consumer protection agencies across the country. Moving companies are one of the top targets of consumer complaints.

Most of the complaints I receive on my tip line are about small-time local movers. Many states regulate movers that operate only inside that state, but there are still plenty of fly-by-nighters that don't bother getting licensed. These companies hire day laborers and change their names whenever too many customers complain. They routinely hold customers' belongings hostage to extort more money. Some "store" your belongings outdoors in the rain. Many use illegal contracts that blatantly favor the company.

Interstate moves used to be a better bet, but they've gotten worse since 1995, when the government abolished the Interstate Commerce Commission. The ICC used to closely regulate interstate movers. Today, moves across state lines are overseen by the Federal Motor Carrier Safety Administration. There are some minimal consumer protection laws in place, but the FMCSA doesn't have the funds to enforce them. Local police usually won't get involved in moving disputes, and state agencies don't have the authority to help with moves that involve more than one state. So . . . it's up to you.

Don't hire just any mover or base your decision on price alone. Ask friends and family for recommendations and double-check the company's reputation with the Better Business Bureau and your county or state consumer protection office. If possible, look up the owner's name in addition to the company name, in case the moving company has changed names a few times. If you're hiring a big national mover, search the national name and the name of the local affiliate as well. Narrow your search further by crossing off movers with less than five years in the business. Ten years is even better. Ask the moving company whether any partner companies will be involved in your move. If so, check those out, too.

Don't let a moving company tell you it can give you a good estimate over the phone. You're just setting yourself up to be lowballed. Instead, invite three or four movers to come to your home, view your belongings, and give you WRITTEN estimates. For local moves, these estimates are usually based on man-hours. For interstate moves, they are based on weight. Be honest. If you have six boxes of files at the office that also need to be moved, tell the estimator. If you keep them a secret, the mover has the right to throw out your original estimate on moving day.

To compete and get your business, movers have a bad habit of underestimating what it'll cost to do your move. INSIST ON A BINDING ESTIMATE. The price will be higher than those wishy-washy, non-binding estimates, but at least you'll know what you're getting into. The best kind of binding estimate is one that is "guaranteed not to exceed." In other words, the mover promises to move your household

HOME BUYING AND RENTING

for a set rate. If your move involves *more* weight or takes *more* time than the mover thought, you *still* pay the estimated amount. If your move involves *less* weight or *less* time than the mover originally estimated, you pay *less!* Now, that's a good deal. You will probably have to follow up with the mover at your destination to see if the price went down; the company may not volunteer this information.

If you end up with competing estimates that are nearly identical, haggle a little. Many companies provide free moving boxes. If the company has overestimated the packing materials it'll take to move you, haggling should help. Keep in mind, however, that price isn't everything. If a mover can pack your things on the date that's most convenient for you and guarantee a timely delivery, that's worth something, too.

If you make a hideous mistake and accept a nonbinding written estimate for an interstate move (and you happen to be reading this book as you fly to your new home), federal law requires the mover to deliver your belongings for the estimated price plus no more than 10 percent. There's also a rule requiring interstate movers to participate in a dispute resolution process with any consumer who makes a claim for less than a thousand dollars. Just remember, many movers don't give a damn about federal law. Florida just passed a law making it a felony to hold a consumer's goods hostage and demand more money. Hopefully other states will soon follow suit.

DO YOUR HOMEWORK:

1. Check out moving companies before you hire them. THIS IS SO CRUCIAL! Once the company has all your worldly belongings on its truck, you have a lot less leverage.
2. Have movers come to your home, look at your things, and give you written estimates.
3. Insist on binding "guaranteed not to exceed" estimates.

WHERE TO COMPLAIN:

If you moved within one state, complain to your county and state consumer protection offices and file a complaint with the BBB. If yours was an interstate move, complain to your state consumer protection office (although it may not have jurisdiction to help you, it can at least offer advice) and contact the Federal Motor Carrier Safety Administration.

SEE ALSO:

BEFORE YOU BUY: Checking Out a Company

New Homes

HOME BUYING AND RENTING

There's an old joke in the construction industry that if you want to build a home you need an architect, a contractor—and a marriage counselor. Many people think building a brand-new house is a way to avoid buying somebody else's problems. That may be true, but trust me, you're buying plenty of problems of your own. One problem is your own expectations. You may expect a *new* house to be a *perfect* house. Ain't gonna happen. These days, houses are built so fast, and city and county inspectors are so scarce, that quality really suffers. Construction crews really can be the lowest possible life form. I found old food wrappers and beer cans inside the walls when I did some work at my own house. Paying more money doesn't necessarily guarantee that you'll be insulated—or that your house will! Every week, I hear home-building horror stories from people building modest houses and mansions.

John and Vicky R. bought a piece of property with a stunning river view. They chose an upscale modular home for it. The builder graded the property and poured the foundation. The day the house arrived by truck, John and Vicky's world turned upside down—and inside out. You see, the house was built backward. It was the reverse of the floor plan they had ordered. Of course, it didn't fit on the foundation. Even more upsetting, there were no windows on the side of the house facing the river. John and Vicky tried to get the builder to send the house back, but he refused. When they sued the builder, he declared bankruptcy. It gets worse. John and Vicky ended up losing their carefully chosen lot, too. Without telling them, the builder had used it as collateral to get their construction loan.

How could such a basket case of a builder be in business? There were no laws regulating new home builders in John and Vicky's state. Builders didn't have to be licensed, bonded, or insured. The contractor who remodeled your bathroom had to have a license, but the builder who constructed your house from the ground up did not. I did a story about John and Vicky's case, and Vicky was invited to testify before the state legislature. Later that year, the law was changed, but it's still not too tough. Home builders are powerful political players. They pay a lot of taxes and enrich the local economy. Some practically own the towns where they're based—after all, they built them.

HOME BUYING AND RENTING

Charles and Diane F. signed a contract to buy a brand-new house in a new subdivision. Three days after they moved in, a leaky pipe sent water cascading from the second floor bathroom to the first floor dining room and eventually to the basement, which flooded. I arranged for a home inspector who specializes in new homes to do a walk-through. He found that there was little, if any, insulation inside the walls of Charles and Diane's house. The pipe had gotten so cold that it froze and then burst. The inspector also discovered that the builder had cut into the structural trusses to make the roof fit, compromising the integrity of the house and voiding the structural warranty. And he found that the builder never secured the furnace flue to the furnace, which created a carbon monoxide hazard for the family.

Unless you're a construction expert with plenty of time to spend at the job site, you should hire somebody to represent your interests during construction. The home inspector who looked at Charles and Diane's house could only detect flaws visible to the eye, because the walls were already closed in. Imagine what he would have found if he had inspected before the concrete was poured, while the framing was being done, and during the plumbing and electrical phases. Try to find a home inspector who specializes in new homes. Before you sign a contract with the builder, make sure this inspector will be allowed onto the property during construction. Although the builder owns the property until the house is complete, some states may require builders to cooperate with your inspector. Find out.

If you can afford to build a *custom* home, you may have a smoother experience. Custom builders who focus on one house at a time may have more reliable crews. Mass builders sometimes have to hire whomever they can get. If your custom home is designed by an *architect,* that's even better. Good, traditional architects serve as advocates for their clients. They hire the engineers and recommend the contractors needed to build the home, and they coordinate those professionals until the job is complete. Bear in mind, today many *builders* have the first contact with the client and then bring in an architect. In my opinion, it's best if the architect is the team leader. After all, the architect wants his or her design to look great and work well and will push the contractor to do the job right. (Full disclosure: my parents are *both* architects, so I'm a bit biased!)

HOME BUYING AND RENTING

DO YOUR HOMEWORK:

1. Find out if home builders have to be licensed in your state and make sure yours is.
2. Check the builder's complaint record with your county and state consumer protection offices and/or licensing division.
3. Visit homes constructed by the builder and ask the owners if they are satisfied. Visit entire developments and gauge the quality of the community centers, landscaping, and other amenities.
4. Visit your city or county land planner and find out what the plans are for any vacant land near where you are looking to build.
5. Don't just review sales brochures. Be sure to inspect the actual architectural drawings before signing
6. Look for clauses in the contract that allow the builder to substitute alternative materials, and make sure you can live with them.
7. Hire a home inspector or architect to be your advocate during the construction process and visit the job site often.
8. Make sure your home inspector will be allowed onto the property before you sign your contract.
9. Keep your deposit on the property as small as possible. If you feel the need to walk away from the deal, you don't want to lose too much money.

10. Beware of new home builders who promise you all sorts of "free" upgrades if you go with *their* financing package. Trust me, you're paying for the upgrades in the form of hidden fees and a higher interest rate.
11. Verify that payments you make for construction of your home will be held in an escrow account dedicated to your project. If they are not, the builder could use *your* money to build somebody *else's* house, then go belly up before building yours.
12. If you take out a construction loan (which is like a mortgage for a house that is being built), negotiate your contract so that the builder has to get your signature before getting a "progress payment" from the bank. That way, you can make sure the builder really has made progress before tapping into more of *your* money.
13. Keep in mind that it's tougher to lock in a good interest rate when you have a home built. See if your bank will extend the lock-in period if there are construction delays. Alternatively, you can go ahead and close on the loan, but don't let the bank pay the balance of the money to the builder until you're satisfied that construction is complete.
14. Do a detailed walk-through before closing on your new home. Insist that major flaws be fixed before you go to settlement, even if you have a warranty.
15. Understand and exercise your warranty. Don't procrastinate. Document the date of every call for service. Builders are notoriously slow in returning to make repairs. Don't let them claim your warranty time has run out.

HOME BUYING AND RENTING

WHERE TO COMPLAIN:

If you think work was not done to code, contact your city or county building inspector and ask for a repeat inspection. To complain about a bad builder, try your county and state consumer protection offices first. They can advise you if you need to contact specialty departments, too. Who's in charge varies from state to state, but you may need to write to the home improvement commission, the department of licensing and regulation, labor and licensing, the department of professional regulation, or the board of contractors. Whew! Also make your displeasure known to the Better Business Bureau.

SEE ALSO:

HOME BUYING AND RENTING: Closing Costs, Home Inspectors, Mortgages; HOME IMPROVEMENT: **Contractors;** HOUSEHOLD: **Termites**

HOME BUYING AND RENTING

Realtors

The majority of people feel most comfortable buying or selling a house through a Realtor. Since it's the biggest purchase most of us ever make, that guidance is comforting. If you're a first-time home buyer, it can be downright critical. There are a couple things you should know when you hire a Realtor. First of all, note that I used the word "hire." Since no money changes hands until the end of the transaction, people often sort of fall into relationships with Realtors.

I did. I was desperately searching for an apartment that allowed dogs. I was new to town and needed a place fast because the movers were already on their way. I walked into the first real estate office I saw and. . .burst into tears. Ohhhh, gawd, how embarrassing! Anyway, fortunately I tripped over a Realtor who knew her stuff. She listened to my weird criteria about wanting the place to look "old on the outside, but new on the inside, blah, blah, blah." Within twenty-four hours she found me just such a place.

Still, try to choose more carefully than I did. If you know you're interested in one neighborhood, and one neighborhood only, find the Realtor who specializes in that area. If you are buying or selling a modest house, seek out somebody who handles less expensive homes. Check references. And also see whether the Realtor has a complaint record with the real estate licensing board. I'm happy to say I almost never get consumer complaints about Realtors.

But the one complaint that comes to mind is a doozy! Patricia D. met a Realtor through friends. At least, she *thought* he was a Realtor. She didn't have a lot of money to spend, so the man showed her several inexpensive HUD properties. When Patricia picked one, the man said, "Actually, I own that one. I had planned to move into it myself, but as a favor, I'll sell it to you instead." Patricia thought her guardian angel was looking out for her.The man even said she could move into the condominium before closing on it! She gave him $5,200 and he gave her the keys.

It turns out, the keys weren't his to give.The man didn't *own* the condominium. He was still trying to *buy* it from HUD. (HUD doesn't keep very good track of its keys.) The man failed to meet several HUD deadlines, and the deal fell through.The property manager got wind of the mess and made Patricia move out.That was the first she heard that the man didn't own the property and wasn't a Realtor. I investigated and learned he *was* a convicted felon! Local, state, *and* federal authorities looked into the matter, but Patricia never got her money back.

HOME BUYING AND RENTING

I doubt you'll have *that* much trouble when you buy or sell a house, but you may encounter smaller headaches.You should know that Realtors have multiple roles these days.The listing agent has a fiduciary duty to help the sellers get as much money for their house as possible. As a buyer, then, you may not want to deal directly with that same agent.Today you can hire your own "buyer's agent," who has a fiduciary duty to help *you*.

On the other hand, if you feel confident that you're a good negotiator, you could use a "transactional agent" who oversees the deal for both sides. Transactional agents may be willing to negotiate lower commission percentages, since they don't have to share the commission with another broker.A seller's agent can only become a transactional agent with the written permission of the seller.

If two Realtors work for the same firm, and one represents the seller and the other the buyer, they are usually called "dual agents." I don't recommend this arrangement for buyers. Why? Because it's human nature for two agents who know each other to compare notes.The top price you're willing to pay may not remain confidential.After all, the higher the sales price, the higher the commission for *both* agents.

Pay attention to the paperwork you sign when you go on your first house-hunting excursion with a Realtor. It's a contract and it goes both ways. You are obligated to that Realtor. Buyer's agents get upset when their clients attend open houses without them. Of course, you have every right to attend. But if you start negotiating with the listing agent, you could be in violation of the agreement you made with your buyer's agent.

Whether you are buying or selling, using one Realtor or two, you should ask if the commission is negotiable. Six percent of the purchase price is still standard, but now more than ever, Realtors may be willing to cut a deal. After all, the Internet has created another forum for listings, a certain segment of the population is always willing to try a For Sale by Owner deal, and it seems like there are more Realtors than ever. If you don't ask, you won't know. Consider this: 6 percent commission on a $250,000 house is $15,000. If you can talk that commission down to 5 percent, its just $12,500. That's enough savings to buy, say, new curtains and blinds!

DO YOUR HOMEWORK:

1. Find the right Realtor through friends, family, and neighbors.
2. Check that Realtor out with the department that licenses realtors.
3. Ask to see the Realtor's license card the first time you meet.
4. Decide what kind of Realtor you want representing you: a seller's agent, buyer's agent, transactional agent, or dual agent.
5. Read and understand the paperwork the Realtor hands you when you hire him or her.
6. Ask whether the commission is negotiable.

WHERE TO COMPLAIN:

If a Realtor does you wrong, go straight to the Board of Realtors, typically at the state level. This board licenses Realtors and has the power to revoke their licenses. You could also file complaints with the BBB and your county and state consumer protection offices.

SEE ALSO:

HOME BUYING AND RENTING: Closing Costs, **For Sale by Owner,** Home Inspectors

Renters' Rights

There are lousy landlords out there as well as terrible tenants. Both have rights. But since tenants are a much bigger population than landlords are, this section focuses on the *renter's* rights. Keep in mind that landlord/tenant law is typically set at the county or state level, so it's impossible to list every possible variation here. However, I can fill you in on the key issues and how they are typically handled. Renters are some of the most frequent callers to my tip line. Most are angry. Some cry. I can see why. After all, shelter is one of our most basic human needs.

HOME BUYING AND RENTING

Your rights begin even before you move in. Many states have laws limiting how much rental application fees can cost. In one state the cap is $25, and landlords can only use that fee to pay for a credit check. Most states also limit the size of the security deposit. Often it's not allowed to exceed the cost of one or two months' rent. Not all places require the landlord and tenant to enter into a lease, but it's a good idea, because it defines the rights and responsibilities of each side.

When it's time to move in, you have additional rights. All states require that rental apartments and houses be safe, sanitary, and free of pests. Some specify that the unit must be in the same condition on moving day as it was when you first looked at it. As an anti lead precaution, more progressive states require landlords to paint apartments at least once every five years so that the paint is never cracked or chipped. No matter where you live, you should expect at least working windows and sound floors plus functioning electrical outlets, appliances, taps, and toilets.

While you are renting a place, your landlord has to do certain things to maintain it. The core requirements are working electricity, hot and cold plumbing, functioning appliances, and trash service. Fire codes require the landlord to install smoke detectors, but it may be up to you to provide fresh batteries. You are entitled to a functioning heating system. Depending on the climate, the landlord may also have to provide air conditioning. Some states and counties require the landlord to hire an exterminator to eliminate insect or rodent problems.

If your landlord doesn't maintain your building properly, you may not have to pay your rent. Tread carefully, though! To withhold rent and remain in the right, you have to follow the precise laws in your area. For example, in some states you have to give your landlord written notice and plenty of time to correct the problem. After that, you're allowed to pay your rent into a special bank account at the courthouse instead of paying the landlord. A judge then decides whether to give you your money back, give it to your landlord, or use it to pay for repairs. A few states allow you to withhold rent and pay for repairs yourself, but, again, you have to jump through legal hoops first. Unfortunately, some jurisdictions still don't give tenants any legal means of holding back rent from slumlords who let their buildings decay.

HOME BUYING AND RENTING

To avoid violating your lease and giving your landlord an excuse not to do his or her part, you have certain responsibilities. You're supposed to obey housing and health codes. You're not allowed to deliberately damage the place or disturb the peace. In some areas, minor plumbing repairs are your responsibility. Of course, you also have to pay your rent. Many states are amazingly tolerant of "squatters" and make life rough for landlords who want to evict them. But bear in mind, at least one state allows landlords to begin eviction proceedings if your rent payment is just three days past due.

So what happens if you need to move out before your lease is up? Some states regulate this, others say you must simply obey the rules outlined in the lease itself. In stricter states you may be liable for unpaid rent, advertising expenses, and any court costs. Generous states allow you to leave early if you can prove you are doing so for reasons beyond your control, such as a company transfer. If you just *want* to move out early, pushover states allow you to sublet your apartment for the remainder of your lease.

You even have rights after you move out. You have the right to be present for the walk-through. And every jurisdiction I know of sets a deadline for the landlord to either return your security deposit or inform you the money will be used to make repairs. The cutoff is usually fifteen, thirty, or forty-five days. Often, the landlord must provide an itemized list of the damage.

DO YOUR HOMEWORK:

1. Ask current tenants whether they are satisfied.
2. Find out whether there's a dollar limit on application fees and security deposits in your state.
3. When you look at a rental apartment or house, check for holes or cracks in the floor and walls. Look for signs of pests. Test the outlets, appliances, hot water, heat and air conditioning, smoke detectors, and windows.
4. Read and understand your lease before you sign it and don't leave the rental office without a signed copy for your records.
5. Find out where your security deposit will be held and whether the account bears interest.
6. If you still have trouble with a landlord, carefully research the rights allowed you by your state before taking action.
7. When you give notice, do so in writing and hand deliver or send the letter by certified mail.
8. Count the number of days after you move out, so you'll know when your landlord must return your security deposit.

HOME BUYING AND RENTING

WHERE TO COMPLAIN:

The government agencies that handle landlord/tenant disputes vary widely from one locality to another. It could be the department of housing, department of licensing and regulation, rent control board, landlord/tenant court, or your county or state consumer protection office.

SEE ALSO:

BEFORE YOU BUY: Contracts; HOME BUYING AND RENTING: **Buy or Rent?,** Moving; CREDIT: Credit Reports; INSURANCE: **Renter's Insurance**

CHAPTER 4

Household

Appliances

So your dishwasher leaks and the VCR eats tapes. Should you take them to the repair shop or the junkyard? Whether to fix it or trash it is a tough call. The first step is to check your warranty. Many household appliances have long-term manufacturer's warranties. Next, get an estimate. If the repair cost is 50 percent or more of the cost to replace it, you should scrap it. If the repair cost is 50 percent or less, ask yourself some questions: What kind of shape is the appliance in? If it's already been fixed several times, it may not be worth another overhaul. Do newer models offer vastly improved features? For example, new refrigerators use less energy than old ones, so you may be able to recoup part of the cost of replacement that way. Consider whether the appliance is unique. If it fits into an odd space or it's an unusual color, it may be too expensive and difficult to replace. Finally, figure out how old the appliance is. Over the years, experts have figured out the average life of most household appliances.

Air conditioners: 8 to 15 years

Dishwashers: 5 to 12 years

Disposals: 5 to 12 years

Dryers: 8 to 12 years

Freezers: 15 to 20 years

Furnaces: 8 to 12 years

Heat pumps: 8 to 12 years

Refrigerators: 15 to 20 years

Stoves: 15 to 20 years

Washers: 8 to 12 years

Water heaters: 8 to 12 years

HOUSEHOLD

Don't just open up the phone book and get an estimate from the company with the biggest ad. Ask friends and family for referrals and check out the companies with the BBB and your county or state consumer protection office. Keep in mind that in some states appliance repair companies have to be licensed. If you don't have a solid referral, plan on getting more than one repair estimate on expensive appliances.

When you call for an appointment, be ready with the make and model number of the appliance. That way you can make sure the company services that brand, and the technician is prepared to bring the proper tools. Ask whether the company charges for estimates. Most companies waive that fee if you go ahead with the repair work. Find out the charge for the first half-hour of work and see if there's a minimum repair charge.

When the technician comes to your home, ask for a written estimate. That estimate should list all parts needed, plus labor charges. Some states require the technician to get your permission if the price is going to exceed the written estimate by more than 10 percent. Find out if the company offers a warranty and, if it does, get it in writing. Typically, repair companies guarantee their labor for thirty days, parts for ninety days.

Once you choose a repair company, alert the technician up front that you want your old parts back. This is a good way to make sure the technician really does replace those parts. Keep in mind that the technician cannot give you your old parts if they contain hazardous materials or if the manufacturer requires their return in exchange for warranty service.

Don't pay big bucks up front. Established companies should not ask you for any money at the beginning of the job. Certainly don't pay more than 10 percent or 20 percent. When the job is complete, pay by credit card, if possible. It's hard to fight the charges if you pay cash. If the company has misdiagnosed your machine, it should send a technician back at no charge. However, if the new repair requires different parts, you may get some money back or owe more.

If you take small appliances or electronics to a repair store, get a claim check before you leave your belongings behind. And pick your items up in a timely manner to avoid storage fees.

HOUSEHOLD

Beware of situations where appliance repair companies approach *you*. An air conditioning company called William B. and offered to tune up his AC unit for $34.95. Once the technicians got in the door, they claimed William's air conditioner needed much more than a tune-up. They persuaded him to pay $259 for all sorts of services he probably didn't need at all. Unfortunately, upselling like this is common.

Be the hunter, not the hunted! Don't do business with companies that come to you out of the blue. Beware of companies that call and claim to be subsidiaries or affiliates of the company you usually use. And don't panic if one of these companies tells you your appliance is a hazard. That's an age-old ploy. Stop using the appliance and get a second opinion.

DO YOUR HOMEWORK:

1. Figure out if the appliance is under warranty. If so, contact an authorized repair facility, and the fix should be free.
2. Check out appliance repair companies with the BBB and your state and county consumer protection agencies. Also check to see if they are properly licensed, if applicable.
3. Get an itemized written estimate and a written warranty.

4. Apply the 50 percent test to decide whether to repair or replace the appliance.
5. Don't do business with appliance repair companies that contact you unless you've checked them out first.

WHERE TO COMPLAIN:

If you have difficulty with an appliance repair company, contact your county and state consumer protection offices and the Better Business Bureau. If the company must be licensed, complain to the state agency that licenses that industry.

SEE ALSO:

HOME IMPROVEMENT: Contractors; HOUSEHOLD: **Home Warranties**

HOUSEHOLD

Cable

Here's a cable quiz for you. How much does the simplest cable package cost? You're probably thinking $25 to $35. That's what cable companies want you to think. What they call "basic" cable is actually their mid-range offering and usually includes dozens of channels. The cost of this "basic" service always seems to be on the rise.

There is an alternative that cable companies don't advertise. It's usually called "lifeline cable" or "broadcast basic." For $8 to $12 a month you get your local network affiliates-ABC, NBC, CBS, FOX, WB, and UPN. You also get the local PBS station and some extras like college channels or government access stations. Not all cable companies provide lifeline cable, but chances are one of the ones in your community does.

It's perfect if all you're looking for is better reception than you can get with an antenna. Or maybe you don't watch much television, but you want to be able to see emergency weather coverage.

DO YOUR HOMEWORK:

1. Contact all the cable companies in your area and see if they offer lifeline cable. You may have to pry the information out of them. They are in competition with satellite services, and don't like to make life easy for satellite customers.

WHERE TO COMPLAIN:

In some jurisdictions, public service commissions regulate cable companies. Otherwise, complain to your county consumer protection office.

Carpet Cleaning   HOUSEHOLD

I love writing about carpet cleaning scams because there are so many great clichés to use and abuse! There's no such thing as a "magic carpet." Don't let a crooked carpet cleaner "pull the rug out from under you." Don't let him "walk all over you" either. If a carpet cleaner tries to take advantage, "call him on the carpet." This is an industry that needs to be "cleaned up." Ah, yes. I could do a carpet-cleaning story every year, because cleaners continue to cheat and consumers continue to complain.

Coupon carpet cleaners that charge "by the room" are the scourge of the industry. You've seen them. Those coupons that promise, "Three rooms and a hall, just $29.95." It's a ploy. Bait and switch. Once the coupon carpet cleaner gets in your door, you learn that next to nothing is included in the price. You'll pay extra for pre-treatment solutions. Extra if you have a spot. Extra if the carpet cleaner has to walk up stairs. Some coupon carpet cleaners refuse to leave unless you agree to these "upcharges."

You may be wondering what happens if you stick to your guns and demand the three-room deal. The carpet cleaner either makes an excuse to leave: "I'm sorry ma'am, the dispatcher just called and we've got a carpet-cleaning emergency across town." Or the carpet cleaner does the work and does it badly. Vengeful coupon carpet cleaners have been known to soak customers' carpets with water, then leave without sucking it back up.

George R. found out about coupon carpet cleaners the hard way. He responded to a flier slipped under the door of his home in a retirement community. The coupon promised three rooms and a hall for $24.95. When the carpet cleaner arrived, he put on the hard sell. He saw George's dog and claimed he could smell urine in the carpet. The answer? Deodorizer: $55. He recommended a flea treatment, "just in case": $47. The cleaner wanted extra for cleaning the carpeting in George's closets: $32. And he demanded money to move the furniture: $50. Finally, the carpet cleaner pushed a protective spray: $108. George gave in and ended up paying $317 instead of $24.95.

Chances are, George didn't even get the extra services he paid for. Coupon carpet cleaners routinely charge for treatments they never perform. I once had a fun stroke of luck while investigating a coupon carpet cleaner. The cleaner accidentally left a jug of his protective spray at a customer's house, so I had it tested. It turned out to be 99.9 percent water! A former employee of another coupon carpet-cleaning company once tipped me that his company was using dishwashing liquid on peoples' carpets. Dishwashing liquid is sticky and attracts dirt. What a mess.

So what can you expect of a *good* carpet cleaner? Reputable carpet cleaners charge by the square foot, not by the room. Most will not give quotes over the phone, because they need to measure your house in person. Good cleaners include pretreatments and spot cleaning in their price, and they vacuum your carpets before they get started. The most experienced cleaners use truck-mounted equipment, which is many times more powerful than the self-contained equipment coupon carpet cleaners use. It's possible to do a good job with smaller equipment, but it takes more elbow grease. Careful cleaners will prop your furniture up on little blocks to give the carpets a chance to dry. That drying time should be brief.

HOUSEHOLD

DO YOUR HOMEWORK:

1. Seek out a carpet cleaner when you need one. Don't respond to those that come in search of you. Ask friends for referrals.
2. Check with the **Institute of Inspection, Cleaning and Restoration Certification, at www.iicrc.org,** to see if carpet cleaners your friends recommend are listed. IICRC trains carpet cleaners in proper techniques.
3. Then cross-check to see if the IICRC member has a complaint record with the BBB or your county or state consumer protection office.
4. Have the carpet cleaner come to your house and give you a detailed, written estimate.
5. Make sure the work comes with a money-back guarantee.

WHERE TO COMPLAIN:

If you have trouble with a carpet cleaner, contact your county and state consumer protection offices and the BBB.

HOUSEHOLD

Energy Efficiency

Energy is a boring thing to spend money on. Here are a few do-it-yourself tips and power company perks that will save you energy—and money.

You should know that power companies don't always read your meter to determine your bill. Some power companies alternate between manual readings and "estimated" readings. Others won't read your meter if it's blocked by shrubs or snow. Sometimes power companies *do* read your meter, but then estimate your bill anyway, if the reading seems abnormally high or low. Did you hear that? Abnormally *low!*

That's right. It happened to me. When I bought my condo, the first month's heating bill was *huge*. I was floored because I had waited a month to move in, and during that month the heat wasn't on and nobody used any appliances. Sure enough, the power company had estimated my bill based on the former owner's usage the previous year. I demanded a *real* reading, and the power company adjusted my bill.

There are lots of other instances, though, where the power company is your friend. A rich friend! For example, did you know many power companies have programs to reimburse you if you buy an energy-efficient air conditioner or heat pump? It's free money that you won't get unless you ask. If you repair your ductwork, your power company may split the bill with you. If you're building a new home, you may be able to get rebates for installing double-pane windows or insulator wrap. In other words, the power company will *pay* you for things that *also* save you money later!

HOUSEHOLD

Many utilities also offer home energy audits. For little or no money, a power company expert will walk through your home and identify ways to save energy and money. The expert may suggest you caulk around your windows or turn down your hot water heater or add extra insulation to your attic or basement. Other common mistakes: letting cold air seep in from your garage and placing lamps near your thermostat, which then gives false readings.

If your power company offers a "kilowatchers" program, that can be another source of savings. You agree to let the power company cycle your air conditioning unit off for short intervals during times of peak use. This saves the power company's grid and saves you money. The power company attaches a little radio receiver to your air conditioning unit to control it. You probably won't even notice the difference, but you will notice the $35 to $135 refund on your summer energy bill.

If you're not ready to let big brother take charge of your AC, try these do-it-yourself steps to save. Use compact fluorescent lightbulbs in place of regular bulbs. They cost $10 or $20 each, but they last ten times as long and use 75 percent less power. The weird color these bulbs throw off is masked by nice lampshades. I like to use compact fluorescent bulbs in ceiling fixtures that are hard to open. That way I only have to change them once every few years.

Buy a programmable thermostat with several settings. You can arrange for the heater to kick on an hour before you get up to make your house nice and toasty while you eat breakfast. Then you can let the house cool down while you're at work. Finally, set the system to warm up again just before you get home. Programmable thermostats even let you set a different schedule on weekends. For every degree you reduce the temperature, you save 3 percent on your energy bill over the course of the winter.

Here's another hint: Don't just clean the lint trap inside your dryer; clean the air duct that leads to the outside as well. This can dramatically reduce drying time and energy bills. Also, clogged air ducts are a fire and carbon monoxide hazard.

When you're considering buying a house or renting an apartment, call the power company. Someone there can tell you how much the monthly energy bills for that location were over the past several years. You'll know what to expect and whether you can afford it.

I apologize in advance, because this last tip is as repetitive as the dentist who nags you to floss your teeth. CHANGE YOUR FILTERS! AC and heating filters only cost a dollar, but dirty ones can drive your energy bills up by $20 a month.

HOUSEHOLD

DO YOUR HOMEWORK:

1. Check your power bills after vacations or other times of unusual use or nonuse to make sure they seem right. Demand a real reading if necessary.
2. Find out what kinds of rebates your power company offers. When it's time to replace appliances, choose energy-efficient models to get the rebate. If you're building a house, do it right from the start and cash in on power company freebies.
3. Get a home energy audit.
4. Consider joining a kilowatchers program.
5. Use compact fluorescent light bulbs, buy a programmable thermostat, and change your filters!

WHERE TO COMPLAIN:

The state public service commission usually regulates power companies. If yours doesn't, contact your county or state consumer protection office for a referral.

SEE ALSO:

HOUSEHOLD: Shocking

Home Warranties

Home warranties. They can give you peace of mind, but they can also make you want to give somebody a *piece* of your mind! Home warranties are essentially service contracts on used homes. Unfortunately, most states don't regulate them. They typically cost between $300 and $450. The seller often provides a home warranty to the buyer when a house changes hands, or you can also purchase one yourself. Sounds great, except that a home warranty can give you a false sense of security. You see, home warranty contracts exclude a lot of things. And the things they *do* cover have age limits.

When her air conditioner started blowing hot air, Jackie H. felt like the world's smartest consumer. After all, for years she had been spending $375 a year on a home warranty. She figured now it was about to pay off. Jackie called the company and arranged for one of its authorized service technicians to come out. The visit cost a flat fee of $75. Sure enough, the technician said her AC unit was hopeless and needed to be replaced. But then came the letdown. The warranty company refused to cover Jackie's air conditioner because it was twenty-one years old. The policy only covered appliances up to twenty years old.

I once had a home warranty myself. It came with the condo I bought. What lousy service! The seller was supposed to give me the home warranty paperwork at closing, but it hadn't arrived. Another couple of months passed. Still nothing. I called the company to complain and couldn't get through, got put on hold, got transferred, you name it. Six months into my one-year contract, I finally received a copy of my policy so I would know what was covered. That's a pretty clever way for a company to minimize claims! Of course, I demanded that the coverage begin on the date the company sent me the paperwork. What a hassle!

HOUSEHOLD

DO YOUR HOMEWORK:

1. Compare and contrast different home warranties. Figure out what's covered and what's not. Watch out for companies that won't cover things that "predate" the policy.
2. Check the warranty company's reputation with your county or state consumer protection office. If the warranty company is based in another state, check with the BBB in that state.
3. See how much you have to pay for a service visit and whether the company has plenty of partner technicians in your area. Better yet, go with a warranty company that lets you choose your own contractor.
4. Call the warranty company's claims line and see how long it takes you to get through. If you have an emergency, you don't want to suffer like I did.
5. When buying a house, never ever substitute a home warranty for a thorough home inspection.
6. Better yet, don't pay some outside company. Develop your own home warranty by putting aside money each year for a repair fund.

HOUSEHOLD

HOW TO COMPLAIN:

Even though home warranties are essentially insurance policies, most states don't regulate home warranty companies. Your best bet is to complain to the Better Business Bureau and your state and county consumer protection offices.

SEE ALSO:

BEFORE YOU BUY: Contracts; HOME BUYING AND RENTING: Home Inspectors; HOUSEHOLD: **Appliances**

Security

Americans spend about $19 billion a year on security products and services, but those products and services are not foolproof. They are only as good as their weakest link—and often that weak link is *you.* Here's what you need to know so you won't have a false sense of security.

First of all, if you buy an alarm system, you need to *use* it. Sometimes homeowners grow tired of taking the time to punch in the code when they enter and exit the house. Other times, a single sensor malfunctions, tripping the alarm, and instead of getting the sensor fixed, the homeowner gives up on the system. You also need to test your system once a month to make sure it's working. I tested a viewer's system for a report once, and sure enough, some of the motion detectors weren't working.

You also need to make sure you understand your alarm company contract. Most alarm companies explicitly state that there's no guarantee that you or your valuables will be safe. A couple of companies *do* offer guarantees now, but you pay extra for that promise. Denise M. was upset when she accidentally set off her alarm and nobody from the company called to check on her. It turns out there was nothing in her contract that said the alarm company would always call. The contracts I've read emphasize the equipment and say little about monitoring. For years I've gotten complaints that some alarm companies don't monitor their clients' alarms at all. If that's true, I've never been able to prove it.

Burglar bars used to be an urban security strategy. Now I see them in the suburbs, too. They work well. Problem is, the same bars that keep the bad guys *out,* can keep you *in.* Fire deaths, in general, are on the decline, but deaths due to *burglar bars* and fire are rising. There is a solution. For a little bit more money, you can buy a burglar bar with a safety release catch. It's designed so you can swing open the burglar bars from the *inside,* but intruders can't open the bars from the *outside.* The proper safety bars do not require a key, special tools, or extreme strength to open.

You can install standard burglar bars on most of your windows, as long as one window in each room has a safety release. In many states it's the law. Building codes require every bedroom to have a direct exit to the outside. If that exit is covered with burglar bars, they must have a safety release. Problem is, often the law applies only to multifamily buildings like apartments and condominiums. Fire officials inspect those to make sure they are up to code. But if you own a single-family home, you're on your own.

I once did a live demonstration where we had a man try to break out of some burglar bars. He rammed the bars with a baseball bat and a wooden bench, but they didn't give at all. Next, we had firefighters show us what they go through trying to break in through burglar bars. They carry gasoline-powered saws with special blades in their trucks for these occasions. Sometimes the saws won't start, and, even when they do, it takes an extra five minutes to cut through the bars. Fires double in size every minute. I have covered several fires in which entire families died trying to escape through burglar bars.

Here are a couple of other security tips I've learned in my years of covering crime and consumer issues. Mark your house with large, lighted address numbers and prune your plants so those numbers are never covered. Drive by your house at night and see if you can read the address. If you live in a warm climate, paint your address on the curb, too. You want police, firefighters, and ambulances to be able to find you in an emergency. Emergency workers tell me that finding people who've called for help is one of their greatest challenges.

HOUSEHOLD

Lock the door between your *garage* and your house. Admit it, you leave that door unlocked! Most people don't install alarms or burglar bars on their garages. Heck, plenty of people leave their garage doors wide open. That means the garage provides easy access. And once the bad guy is in your garage, he can enter your house.

DO YOUR HOMEWORK:

1. Check out alarm companies before you do business with them. Contact your county or state consumer protection office, the BBB, and trade organizations.
2. Compare different alarm companies before you buy. Ask for copies of their contracts and read them to see what is—and isn't—included.

3. Keep in mind that you'll typically pay one price for the alarm equipment and another fee for monthly monitoring.
4. Make sure the alarm company registers your alarm with the local police. You should receive paperwork showing this has been done. Police respond only to registered alarms. Be aware that if you have too many false alarms, police may fine you.
5. If you invest in an alarm system, use it. If it breaks down, get it fixed immediately before spare parts are no longer available.
6. Test your alarm system once a month. Walk by motion detectors. Open doors and windows. See if the monitoring service calls to check on you. (Just make sure the alarm company doesn't call the police and cause you to be fined.)
7. If you have burglar bars, make sure one set in each room has a safety release. If none does, invest in the proper kind or remove all the bars. If you're a landlord, improper burglar bars are a real liability.
8. Put big, legible address numbers on your house, the biggest ones you can find, and make sure they are well lit.
9. Lock the door between your garage and house and close your garage door if you're not going to be around.

HOUSEHOLD

WHERE TO COMPLAIN:

If you have a problem with an alarm company, contact your county and state consumer protection offices. You can also try complaining to local police, if the alarm is registered with them. If you are renting in a building with improper burglar bars, contact your local fire inspector and ask if that's illegal. If so, the fire department will ticket the landlord for you.

SEE ALSO:

BEFORE YOU BUY: Contracts; INSURANCE: Homeowner's Insurance, Renter's Insurance

Shocking

Deregulation in the power industry was supposed to be a big plus for consumers. You know, all that competition was going to lower prices and raise innovations. But first, something shocking had to happen. Not brownouts in California. Not the collapse of Enron. Nope. *Consumer* shocking. That's the catchy term the feds coined for when a company switches your service provider without your permission. This rogue behavior started in the long-distance phone industry, where it's called "slamming." I suspect it will happen in every business where deregulation suddenly creates competition.

One day, Phyllis M. got a bill from a power company she had never heard of. When she called the number on the bill, a representative told her she had agreed to switch to the company's service. Phyllis had done no such thing. It turns out her elderly mother, Margaret, had met with a salesman who came to the door. Margaret only signed an acknowledgment that she listened to the sales pitch, but the aggressive salesman then copied her signature onto a contract.

HOUSEHOLD

When we investigated, we found the rogue power company had also switched dozens of other people without their permission, including one hundred consumers who lived in the same apartment complex. Sometimes power companies "shock" consumers as part of an unwritten company policy. Other times, greedy sales representatives do it on their own to snare more commissions. Sometimes these new power companies charge astronomical prices and make it hard for you to have those charges reversed.

If you live in a state that has deregulated power companies, here's how it typically works. You can choose to stay with your traditional utility company or you can choose a new company, often called an "energy supplier." Energy suppliers don't have their own delivery systems; they pay to use the utility's system. You end up paying the supplier for energy and paying the utility for delivery. Why would anybody bother with such a complex arrangement?

Some energy suppliers are willing to work with smaller profit margins, so you get a better price. Others may offer helpful billing options or environmentally friendly fuels. Don't switch providers lightly. Unlike the phone industry, which lets customers switch back and forth as often as they want, many power companies require you to sign a contract for one, two, or three years.

Energy suppliers and old-style utilities are usually licensed and regulated by state public service commissions and public utility commissions. In some states, a department, called the "office of people's counsel," also plays a role. These bodies establish rules to try to smooth deregulation. For example, in one state, power companies must be licensed. In another, only the person whose name is on the bill is allowed to switch to a new service provider, and the power company must give that person ten days to cancel the contract. If a new power company approaches you, ask questions. You have the power to make your own decision!

HOUSEHOLD

QUESTIONS TO ASK:

1. What is the supplier's name and number? What is the salesperson's name?
2. Is this company licensed by the state public service commission? What is its license number?
3. How long has the company been in business? How many customers does it serve?
4. How much will the service cost? Does it vary by use, season, or time of day? How does it compare to the old company's price? Are there any automatic increases or decreases in price scheduled?
5. Will I have to pay membership or start-up fees? What about other penalties or late fees?
6. How long is the contract? Does it renew automatically?
7. Can I cancel? Is there a fee for canceling early? Can the company cancel on me?
8. Will I receive one bill or two?
9. What are the benefits of signing up with this supplier?

DO YOUR HOMEWORK:

1. Once the company answers all your questions, check its reputation with the public service commission, the office of people's counsel, the BBB, and your county and state consumer protection agencies.

WHERE TO COMPLAIN:

Fortunately, if you have problems, power companies are more regulated than most industries, so you'll get more help. Contact your state public service commission, public utility commission, or the office of people's counsel.

SEE ALSO:

HOUSEHOLD: **Energy Efficiency;** TELEPHONES: Slamming and Cramming

HOUSEHOLD

Termites

Eating you out of house and home. It's a phrase you can use quite literally if you're talking about termites. Every year termites do $2 billion in damage. The problem is so bad that homeowner's insurance doesn't even cover it. Some termite inspectors play on this homeowner's horror and bug you with bogus estimates. We once did a hidden camera investigation at a home we *knew* did *not* have termites. We went undercover and invited termite companies to inspect and give us estimates.

One inspector wanted to charge us a couple hundred dollars to spray the soil around the house. He said it would "burn up" the termites. A university entomologist said that was ridiculous, because termites live beneath the soil, so surface sprays are useless. The other company never even inspected inside our house, even though an interior inspection was required by state code. Nevertheless, the inspector proclaimed that we *definitely* had termites, and he wanted $500 for a subterranean treatment.

If you're buying a *brand-new* home, you could face termite troubles, too. Your contractor will hire a termite subcontractor to treat the area before building your home. Chemicals are injected into the soil to form a barrier so termites do not emerge from underground and crawl up inside the walls of your home. Problem is, the chemicals used for these new home treatments are very expensive. To compete, some unscrupulous subcontractors charge the contractor *less* than the chemicals actually cost. How can they afford it? They spray water on the soil instead of chemicals, leaving your home totally unprotected.

Scams like this are why you need to check out termite companies before you hire them. Contact your county and state consumer protection offices as well as the Better Business Bureau to see if other consumers have complained. Then go a step further, because consumers may not *realize* they were cheated. Contact the **National Pest Management Association** to see if the company is a member: Go to **www.pestworld.org.** NPMA may also be willing to tattle on unsavory companies in your area. Finally, get estimates from three or four firms before plunking down any money.

There are three methods of treating for termites. The most common technique is to inject chemicals into the soil. Pest-control experts also treat infested wood to prevent termites and try to kill any that are already there. Baits are the newest and most promising method. Pest-control experts install bait stations in the ground. Termites eat the bait and spread the poison throughout the colony. "Sentricon" is one brand name for this bait method.

Technically, you cannot buy insurance to cover you if you get termites. But pest-control companies *do* offer "warranties" that accomplish the same thing. They don't call it "insurance," because they don't want to be subject to insurance laws and regulations. Most companies treat your home, then sell you a warranty. If you are interested in an antitermite warranty, shop around. Some of these warranties just cover retreatment; others cover repairs. Think about it. If you get termites despite the company's treatment, do you really want the company just to treat your home again? No. You want the company to pay for repairs *and* retreatment.

There are some things you can do to prevent a termite infestation in the first place. Termites like moisture, so don't let water accumulate near your foundation. Make sure downspouts and hoses drain away from your house. Keep shrubs and vines away from the base of your house. Termites like shade and plants provide it. Don't pile mulch or wood chips against your foundation. The wood attracts termites, which will then move on to the wood in your home. Make sure contractors don't bury scrap wood in your yard, especially near the house, where it could lure termites. Establish a gap of at least eighteen inches between the soil and any wood on your house. Look for mud tubes on your foundation. Termites construct these to travel back and forth between the soil and your house.

HOUSEHOLD

DO YOUR HOMEWORK:

1. Check out termite contractors before you use them. Check with your county and state consumer protection offices, the BBB, and the National Pest Management Association.
2. If you're buying a home, keep in mind that houses built before 1988 may be more termite-proof. That's because the government banned a strong but environmentally unfriendly chemical, called "Chlordane," in 1988.
3. If you're having a home built, insist on choosing your own termite subcontractor. Pay extra if necessary and plan to be present for the treatment.
4. If you *already* have termites, find out which treatment method your pest-control company plans to use. Ask the pros and cons of the other methods or suggest a combination of all three.
5. If you are skeptical about the advice you're given, contact your local **agricultural extension service** for advice. The extension is usually run through the county or a local university.
6. Consider a termite warranty, but only buy the kind that pays for repairs as well as retreatment.
7. If you don't purchase a warranty (which usually includes annual inspections), pay for a pest-control expert to inspect your house once a year.

8. Follow do-it-yourself steps to protect your house from these wood-eating monsters.

WHERE TO COMPLAIN:

You can gripe about pest-control companies by contacting your county or state consumer protection office and the BBB. If your state requires pest controllers to be licensed, also complain to the licensing agency.

SEE ALSO:

HOME BUYING AND RENTING: **New Homes**; HOME IMPROVE-MENT: Contractors

HOUSEHOLD

CHAPTER 5

Home Improvement

Building Codes

Building codes are the nitty-gritty laws that counties and states put in place to make sure buildings are constructed safely and soundly: things like how big the beams have to be to hold up the roof and what kind of fireproofing is required. Building codes can seem obscure, even obnoxious, but failing to follow them can come back to bite you. It's bad for you as a resident of the house. It's even worse when you go to sell. If the buyer hires a really hotshot home inspector, he or she could find code violations that you're required to fix before the house changes hands.

At key phases during construction, county inspectors swing by to make sure the work is "up to code." Unfortunately, many contractors try to cut corners, and most building inspectors are overworked and underpaid. They're bound to miss things. That's why, for big home remodeling jobs, you may want to hire your own home inspector to make sure the contractor follows all applicable building codes. If you've used architects or engineers on your job, you can also pay them to do a final inspection for you.

DO YOUR HOMEWORK:

1. Ask your contractor about code requirements. Make him or her aware that you care about doing things by the book.
2. Consider hiring a home inspector who specializes in construction.
3. Consider having the architects, civil engineers, soil engineers, and structural engineers who drew plans for you come back and do a final inspection.
4. At the very least, try to attend the inspections conducted by the county.
5. Also be aware of any "codes, covenants, and restrictions" required by your homeowner's association. If you fail to follow them, you could be forced to do the work over again.

HOME IMPROVEMENT

WHERE TO COMPLAIN:

If your contractor fails to do the work up to code, try to get the county building department to step in and help you. If that fails, complain to the department that licenses contractors in your state (*if,* in fact, they're required to be licensed.) If all else fails, you may end up in court.

SEE ALSO:

HOME BUYING AND RENTING: Home Inspectors; HOME IMPROVEMENT: Contractors, **Permits**

Contractors

Crooked contractors are one of the leading causes of consumer complaints nationwide. Unlicensed contractors are the worst, but even licensed contractors can cause headaches and heartache. I've seen contractors build sinks so close to showers that there's not enough room to bend over and wash your face. I've heard about a carpenter who dropped a toolbox on his own foot, then sued the homeowner for medical expenses. And I've gotten call after call about contractors who take big bucks up front, then never return to do the work. Hiring a contractor to repair or renovate your home is one of the more expensive things you'll ever do. Make sure you do it right.

Develop a short list of contractors by asking friends and family for referrals. If your neighbors have a handsome new addition, stop by and ask about their contractor. Ask contractors for references and don't just *listen* to the references; *look* at their homes! Another idea: ask contractors for the names of three clients they're currently working for, then call those clients to see how it's going. Chances are, if their projects are behind schedule, yours will start late and drag along, too.

Thirty-six states require home improvement contractors to be licensed, and nearly all states license plumbers and electricians. Make sure the contractors you're considering are properly licensed. This is utterly crucial—and more complicated than it seems. For starters, don't take the contractor's word for it, even if he or she shows you a license card. Ask for the full name of the company, the owner's name, and the license number. Call your state and verify the license by company name, owner name, and license number. Find out whether your county has its own licensing requirements in addition to state requirements. If so, check with the county, too.

Do not accept a contractor's license from a state or county other than where you live. Local law will protect you only if the contractor is licensed to do business in *your* jurisdiction. Some cities, counties, and states do have reciprocity agreements with their neighboring governments, which means if the contractor is licensed in state A, state B also considers him or her qualified to be a contractor. But it's *not* automatic. Make sure your state has certified, in writing, that your contractor is allowed to work there.

You also need to know the difference between a contractor's license and a business license. A contractor's license is a specialty license obtained through testing or apprenticeships. By contrast, business licenses are nonspecialized. Business owners have to have

HOME IMPROVEMENT

one whether they're opening a flower shop, a shoe store, or an accountant's office. It's possible your contractor needs a contractor's license *and* a business license. Just know that the latter is *not* proof of competence.

There's also something called an occupancy license or certificate of occupancy. Many local governments require businesses to pay for one of these any time they move to a new location. It's simply a mechanism for local governments to collect more fees for the treasury and keep track of which companies are doing business in the area. For you, it's useless.

Next, it's time to do a background check. The same state or county office that keeps track of licenses should be able to tell you if the contractor has a complaint record. Check with the Better Business Bureau and your county and state consumer protection offices, too. You should inquire about complaints listed under the company's name *and* under the owner's name. This is important, because crummy contractors often change company names to erase their past.

HOME
IMPROVEMENT

If your state issues contractor's licenses to individuals rather than to companies, ask whether the individual who holds the license will be directly involved in your project. This is important because shady contractors have been known to "borrow" licenses from other people, which is illegal.

Find out how long the contractor has been in business. If it's an expensive project, you want to be doubly sure that you're dealing with a well-established company. Ask the contractor how many projects like yours he or she has done. You want to establish that the contractor has experience doing the kind of work you need.

Make sure the contractor has insurance: personal liability, worker's compensation, and property damage coverage. Ask to see certificates of insurance and make sure they're current. If you do business with an uninsured contractor and something goes wrong, you could end up paying for it.

If you're spending a ton of money and you want to be the ultimate savvy consumer, go to the courthouse and find out if the contractor has ever been sued. If so, is the lawsuit cause for concern?

While you're there, see if the contractor has ever filed for bankruptcy. This could be a sign of an unstable company.

Phew! At last it's time to get some estimates (or competitive bids in the case of larger jobs). Keep in mind, many contractors charge a fee for providing an estimate or proposal. Ask, so you'll know what to expect. Even if you have to pay, be sure to get at least two quotes. The more extensive your project, the more contractors you may want to interview. Some companies charge by the hour, known as a "time and materials" proposal. Others charge by the job, known as a "lump sum" proposal. I prefer to be quoted a price for the job, so there are no expensive surprises if the project takes longer than expected. Get estimates in writing and make sure they're detailed. I've seen contractors scrawl a price on the back of a business card. That's not acceptable.

Once you've chosen your contractor, that detailed estimate needs to be converted into an even *more* elaborate contract. The contract should include the work to be done, the precise materials to be used, labor costs, subcontractors' names, a construction schedule, a payment schedule, completion date, lien releases, and warranties. Make sure the contract includes cleanup. Contractors are notorious for leaving junk lying around in your yard. Also beware of clauses that allow the contractor to jack up the price without your permission. Instead, you should approve *all* "change orders" in writing. Don't accept any oral promises. Have them added to the written contract. When you're satisfied, you should sign the contract, as should the contractor. If the contract is signed at your home, then you have three days to cancel it, under the "Cooling-Off Rule."

HOME IMPROVEMENT

Possibly the most important part of your contract is the payment schedule. Personally I prefer not to pay *any* money up front. Unfortunately many contractors won't agree to that. At the very least, don't pay your first installment until the end of the first day the contractor's crew begins the project. You're trying to guard against situations in which you pay, but the contractor never shows up to do the work. Some states prohibit contractors from taking more than a third of the estimated price up front. I think that's way too much. One fair way to structure the payment schedule is to have it closely follow the construction schedule. Don't allow your payments to get ahead of the contractor's progress. If the contractor were to suddenly go bankrupt, he or she would have your money, and you wouldn't have the cash to complete the renovation.

Avoid paying cash for a remodeling project. Using a credit card is a better choice. If you're paying for your project with a construction loan, make sure the bank makes the check out to you, not the contractor. Be leery of contractors who try to persuade you to get your loan from a friend of theirs. If your home has been damaged and your insurance company is providing the money for repairs, get the check written out directly to you as well.

Before you make your final payment, live with the renovations a few days to make sure you're satisfied. Even though you have a warranty, it's a lot easier to get the contractor to make fixes when he or she is still trying to earn the fee. Look at the work in different types of light. Test every button, switch, handle, and appliance. When you're comfortable with the work and you're sure the contractor has paid all the subcontractors, then you can sign a certificate of completion and make your final payment.

HOME IMPROVEMENT

KNOW THE SIGNS:

1. Contractors who go door to door looking for business are often unsavory.
2. The same goes for contractors who claim they'll give you a good deal because they "just finished a project down the street."
3. If a contractor offers to give you a discount without saying what the actual price is, that's a bad sign.
4. Avoid contractors who want you to contact them only through post office boxes, pagers, or answering services. A reputable contractor should be happy to give you his or her permanent information.
5. Hard-sell contractors often claim they'll give you a deep discount if you agree to let your house be used as a "demonstrator model." This is just a sales ploy. You're getting the same price as everybody else.

6. Contractors have been known to use scare tactics to make a sale. "If you don't replace that furnace, you're gonna have a fire in here." Don't succumb. Quickly arrange for a second opinion.
7. Contractors who show up in unmarked vehicles may be suspect. Some states require contractors to list their license numbers on their vehicles, on their estimates, and in their advertising.

DO YOUR HOMEWORK:

1. Find contractors through referrals from friends and neighbors.
2. Check with your state and county to see if the contractor is properly licensed.
3. Remember, licenses in other states, business licenses, and occupancy licenses don't count.
4. Check the contractor's reputation with the licensing agency, your state and county consumer protection offices, and the BBB.
5. Get multiple written estimates.
6. Insist on a detailed contract. Make sure everything covered in this chapter is included.
7. Don't pay much—if any—up front. Let the payment schedule follow the construction schedule.
8. Don't make the final payment until you're satisfied.

HOME IMPROVEMENT

WHERE TO COMPLAIN:

The most effective way to complain about a contractor is to hit him or her where it hurts: go after the contractor's license. File a formal, written complaint with whatever agency licenses contractors in your state. It could be the home improvement commission, the board of contractors, or the department of licensing and regulation. Also file complaints with the BBB and your county and state consumer protection offices. If a lot of money is at stake, you may have to go to court.

SEE ALSO:

HOME IMPROVEMENT: **Government Guarantee**, Lien Releases,

Permits, **Store Contractors, Unlicensed Contractors;** BEFORE
YOU BUY: Contracts, Cooling-Off Rule

Government Guarantee

Free money. It's one more reason to make sure you hire a *licensed*
contractor when you remodel. (That's *if* your state licenses contractors. It still shocks me that some don't.) Many states stockpile funds
to compensate people who've been wronged by licensed contractors. States call their contractor kitties different things—the construction recovery fund, contractor guaranty fund, construction
industries fund—to name a few. *I* call it a *coup* for consumers! The
only bad thing about these funds is that not enough people know
about them.

Beatrice B. wanted to add an apartment to her son's house, so as
she got older she could be near family, but still be independent. She
and her children scraped together a $13,000 down payment and
hired a contractor. The contractor had some plans drawn up and
cleared some trees, but then months passed and he never returned.
Beatrice didn't want to sue the contractor, because she figured that
would cost more money than she had lost in the first place. That's
when she called my tip line. We told Beatrice about her state's contractor guaranty fund.

Here's how it works: Every time contractors renews their licenses they have to contribute to the fund. That pool of money covers
shoddy, incomplete, or abandoned jobs. In some states, if a contractor takes advantage of you, you can apply directly to the fund for
compensation. In other states, you have to file and win a lawsuit
first. Typically, the state investigates and tries to mediate with the
contractor first. If the contractor won't pay up, then you get a hearing. You can typically represent yourself at the hearing. You don't
need a lawyer. If you prove your case, the state gives you the cash.

Different states have different caps on the amount of money they
will give you. I know of one state that limits each homeowner to
$10,000 and another that awards up to $50,000. Some states require
you to demonstrate that you've tried everything to get the contractor to pay you back, like taking out liens against his or her personal

**HOME
IMPROVEMENT**

property. Other states specify that their funds are only meant for situations where the work was not done up to code. Time limits for making a claim also vary.

DO YOUR HOMEWORK:

1. If your state or county requires contractors to be licensed, make sure you hire a company licensed to perform work in your jurisdiction. A license from another state or county is not valid.
2. Have that contractor give you a detailed written proposal. Some states won't let you tap into the compensation fund without it.
3. Refuse to pay too much money up front. That way, if your state's compensation fund is capped at, say, $10,000, you'll be covered.
4. If you have problems with your contractor, research your options *immediately*, so you can file a claim within the time allowed.
5. Whether you have to go to court or to a state hearing, be organized. Bring at least two copies of all your paperwork, so you can hand one copy over and refer to the other. Document problem spots with photographs or videos.

HOME IMPROVEMENT

WHERE TO COMPLAIN:

To complain about a contractor and get information about your state's compensation fund, contact the state agency that licenses contractors. It may be called the Board of Contractors, the Home Improvement Commission, or the Department of Licensing and Regulation.

SEE ALSO:

HOME IMPROVEMENT: **Contractors,** Store Contractors, Unlicensed Contractors

Lien Releases

When you hire a general contractor, he or she hires all sorts of subcontractors. Normally, you pay the general contractor, who then pays the subs. So what happens when the contractor doesn't pay the subs? A big, ugly mess, that's what. If you haven't taken steps to protect yourself, those subcontractors can place a lien against your property. A lien is a court decision giving a creditor the right to seize or sell your property to satisfy a debt. You can't sell your house until you've satisfied all the liens against it. Subcontractors can even go to court to force you to sell your home to pay them.

Here are some of the professionals who might be entitled to file a lien against your home: plumbers, electricians, drywall specialists, painters, suppliers, architects, landscape designers, interior designers, engineers, and surveyors.

Now for some safeguards. Before you hire a contractor, ask who the subcontractors will be and ask for their numbers. Call them up and ask them whether the contractor has paid them promptly in the past. Remember, even if you pay the main contractor in full, if he or she doesn't pay the subs, they can come after *you*.

As the project progresses, and you start paying bills, obtain "lien releases" or "lien waivers" from anybody who works on your home. These are written documents stating that the subcontractors have been paid and will not place a lien against your home. You can either make it part of your contract with the main contractor that he or she must obtain lien releases from all subs for you, or you can get them directly from the subs yourself. Some county building departments provide blank lien release forms.

DO NOT make your final payment until you have lien releases. If you're paying in installments as the work progresses, get the relevant lien releases as you go. Always hold back at least the final 10 percent of the payment as a carrot to get the contractor to complete lien releases for you. Before you make your final payment, obtain an affidavit from the contractor naming all subs who worked on the project and stating that they have been paid.

I have also heard of two, more novel approaches. See if the main contractor will provide you with a performance bond, a signed promise that all work will be done to your satisfaction and all subcontractors will be paid. Alternatively, some insurance companies offer policies that protect you in case subcontractors come after you for money.

HOME IMPROVEMENT

DO YOUR HOMEWORK:

1. Learn the contractor's lien or mechanic's lien laws in your state and act accordingly.
2. Insist on knowing the names, addresses, and phone numbers of every subcontractor who will work on your house.
3. Contact those subs and ask if the contractor has paid them promptly in the past.
4. Make sure your home improvement contract includes a promise to obtain lien releases from subcontractors.
5. As an alternative, get the paperwork from the subs yourself.
6. Never make a payment without receiving a release of lien.
7. Explore performance bonds and construction lien insurance policies.

WHERE TO COMPLAIN:

If you live in a state that licenses contractors, contact the licensing department for advice regarding lien releases. The local building department may be able to help as well.

HOME IMPROVEMENT

SEE ALSO:

HOME IMPROVEMENT: **Contractors**, Permits, Store Contractors, Unlicensed Contractors.

Permits

Government regulations are meant to protect you when you remodel, but they can come back to bite you, instead. Huh? How?

Counties typically require you to "pull permits" for any substantial construction work. If you're just building a new linen closet in your house or laying new tile in your bathroom, you probably don't have to have a permit. But if the work will affect the structural integrity of your home, you definitely need a permit. Same goes for significant electrical and plumbing changes. If the project will change the footprint or height of the house, you'll also need a permit. Check with your city or county building department for specific requirements. You could get in trouble with the law if a permit is required and you don't have one.

Reliable contractors routinely obtain construction permits for you. That way, if city or county inspectors find fault with the work, the contractor is responsible for making corrections. If you pull the permit *yourself,* you are essentially assuming liability for the job, and you could be forced to pay for fixes. Proper permits benefit you, because county building inspectors come around to make sure the work is being done correctly and in compliance with building codes. If the contractor pressures you to get the permit yourself, that may be a sign that you're dealing with an unlicensed company.

DO YOUR HOMEWORK:

1. Find out if your project requires a permit.
2. Ask the contractor to pull it for you.
3. Look for the paper permit at the construction site; it should be posted.

SEE ALSO:

HOME IMPROVEMENT: **Building Codes,** Contractors, Store Contractors, Unlicensed Contractors

Store Contractors

Americans spend $84 billion a year remodeling their homes. Obviously, if you're going to pay big bucks for home improvement, you should know who you're dealing with. But what if you can't *tell* who you're dealing with? That's exactly what happens sometimes when consumers hire big box stores to do their renovations. Typically these stores sign customers up on stationery bearing the store's name and logo, but they don't do the work themselves. They pass it along to outside contractors. The problem is, when something goes wrong, the big box store sometimes refuses to take responsibility.

Mary Anna L. hired a big box store to remodel her bathroom and kitchen. The store arranged for a regional contractor to do the work. The regional contractor did an appalling job. The sink was so close to the shower that Mary Anna couldn't bend over it to brush her teeth. The kitchen wasn't even completed, because the contractor never got the required permits. And none of the work was done up to code. Naturally, Mary Anna called the big box store to complain. The store manager said it wasn't his responsibility and referred Mary Anna to the contractor. She didn't even know the contractor's individual company name! When she figured it out, the contractor wouldn't return her calls.

I haven't mentioned the name of the store because I've had similar complaints about several. These stores try to be all things to all people. They should stick to selling stuff you can use to build stuff instead of selling building services. But they won't. So it's up to you. If you want to hire a contractor through a big box store, you still have to check out the individual contractor the way you always would. Keep in mind, the store probably takes a cut of the contractor's profit, and whenever there's a middleman, you pay more.

HOME IMPROVEMENT

DO YOUR HOMEWORK:

1. If you want to hire a store contractor, ask the store to give you at least three choices. Then check out those contractors just as you would if you were hiring them independently.
2. If you still get a raw deal, contact bigwigs at the big box store's corporate headquarters and complain like crazy. Tell them you're going to call every investigative reporter in town—it worked for Mary Anna!

WHERE TO COMPLAIN:

Complain about shoddy contractors by contacting the state agency that licenses them, if applicable. Complain about the contractor *and* the store by contacting your county and state consumer protection offices and the BBB.

SEE ALSO:

HOME IMPROVEMENT: Contractors

Unlicensed Contractors

Did you know you could be arrested for using an unlicensed contractor? It's true. In states that require licensing, *hiring* an unlicensed contractor is illegal. Did you know an unlicensed contractor who gets hurt on your property could sue you—and win? Unlicensed contractors are unlikely to carry proper insurance, so this has happened. These are the extremes, but even the *average* experience with an unlicensed contractor can be devastating. Most consumers who call me for help complain that the unlicensed contractor did shoddy work. Others report the contractor made off with their money and did no work at all!

HOME IMPROVEMENT

Elease W. saved for two years to build a ground-floor bathroom in her home, because she has arthritis and it's hard for her to climb stairs. She paid a contractor $10,000 to do the work. Two years later it still wasn't done right. For months, Elease and her daughters felt like prisoners in their home, because the contractor had left gaping holes in the walls, so they didn't dare leave. The water pipes were built outside the structure, where they froze in the winter. The foundation was unstable and the siding immediately started peeling off. Of course, the family didn't check out the contractor until after everything went wrong. It turned out he was unlicensed and had a complaint record a mile long.

Paul H. needed a new roof. He got a couple of different estimates, but felt he couldn't afford them. Then he spotted an ad in one of those free neighborhood newspapers. The ad promised the lowest roofing rates in town. Paul hired the man to reroof his home for $5,000. The man demanded full payment in advance. He climbed around on Paul's roof for a few minutes, then said he was going to get supplies. He never returned. When I investigated, I learned the phone number in the ad actually belonged to an answering service. The address the man gave Paul didn't even exist! And the state didn't have a record of a licensed contractor by that name.

Licenses are generally required for any work that affects the plumbing, structural, or electrical integrity of the building. I've done a couple of different undercover investigations where we invited unlicensed contractors to give us estimates for roofing work. First of all, it was easy to find unlicensed contractors. We spotted their ads in local newspapers and found their business cards at home improvement stores. Unlicensed contractors tend to use the cheapest possible means to market themselves.

When we confronted them we heard every excuse. One man said he couldn't afford a contractor's license, even though the state where he worked only charges $300. Another man said he was working "under" somebody else's license. That's illegal. Only bona fide employees are allowed to work under the umbrella of a licensed contractor. A third showed us a contractor's license for another state. That doesn't count. The contractor must be licensed in the state where the work is to be done. Several guys presented us with occupancy licenses, which are just business permits that anybody can buy. They don't make a contractor legal.

HOME IMPROVEMENT

If an unlicensed contractor nails you, you have next to no recourse. There's no license that the state can yank to threaten the contractor's livelihood. If you complain, the contractor will just change the name he or she does business under. You can't tap into the contractor's insurance policy because he or she doesn't have one. Even suing an unlicensed contractor—and winning—is often futile, because unlicensed contractors don't have deep pockets.

KNOW THE SIGNS:

1. Unlicensed contractors often go door to door claiming they "just finished a job down the street."
2. They may rush you and say if you act now, you'll get a special price.

3. Unlicensed contractors either neglect to pull construction permits or they ask you to do it for them. If you do, you are assuming liability for the project, including their mistakes.

4. Some states require contractors to list their license numbers on their vehicles, their estimates, and their advertising. If a contractor has not done that, it may be a bad sign.

5. Find out how many letters, numerals, and digits licenses in your county or state are supposed to have. If you see a license number in an ad that doesn't fit the format, it may be a fake.

6. Be wary if a contractor provides only a post office box or pager number. That may mean he or she doesn't have roots in the community and plans to move on as soon as people start to complain.

7. Unlicensed contractors often ask for a lot of money up front. Try not to pay any money in advance. If you must, keep the amount minimal, less than 10 percent of the total.

HOME IMPROVEMENT

DO YOUR HOMEWORK:

1. Find out what the licensing requirements are for contractors in your state. Also check with your county. If you live in an area where contractors do not have to be licensed, you're going to have to be extra vigilant about who you hire.

2. Try to find your contractor through word of mouth. A satisfied friend or neighbor is a much better source than a free newspaper.

3. Ask to see the contractor's actual paper license. Unlicensed contractors often put fake license numbers in their advertisements.

4. Get the contractor's full name, company name, and license number and double-check all three with the county and state departments that license contractors.

5. Also ask those departments if the contractor has a history of complaints.

6. Don't be fooled by "occupancy permits" or business licenses. These pieces of paper are worthless to you. Any business owner can get one. When I say "licensed contractor" I'm talking about a person who has proven his or her skill in the field and been awarded a specialty license just for contractors. Hint: Ask the

contractor if he or she had to take a test to get a license. A licensed contractor should have.

7. If the contractor is licensed in another state, but not the one where the work is to be done, that offers you no protection. Some states do have reciprocal agreements, where a contractor with a license in one state can be "fast tracked" to get a license in another. However, until the contractor goes through that process, don't do business with him or her. Demand written proof.

8. Also make sure the contractor is licensed to perform the type of work you need done. A licensed electrician cannot do plumbing work, for example.

9. If you hire a general contractor, make sure the specialists he or she hires—for example, plumbers and electricians—are licensed, too.

10. Once you're confident the person is not an unlicensed scumbag, follow the procedures in the section on Contractors in this chapter.

WHERE TO COMPLAIN:

If you learn your contractor is unlicensed, contact the county and state departments that license legitimate contractors. Also call your county and state consumer protection offices and the BBB. They can advise you and possibly pursue criminal charges against the unlicensed contractor.

SEE ALSO:

HOME IMPROVEMENT: **Contractors, Government Guarantee, Store Contractors**

HOME
IMPROVEMENT

CHAPTER 6

Credit

Advance Fee Loans

"No money? No job? No problem!"This is the seductive sales pitch of an advance fee loan scam. Con artists say they can guarantee you a loan or credit card *if* you pay a hefty fee up front.The fees range from $50 to $500.This scam targets people who are down on their luck: the unemployed, the poor, and people with bad credit.The ads appear in the newspaper, on telephone poles, and on the Internet. Telemarketers also hawk advance fee loans. Don't fall for their pitch!You'll give up your money and you'll get . . . nothing.The bad guys have no intention of giving you a loan or a credit card. Plus, it's illegal to guarantee somebody a loan in exchange for a fee.

A telemarketer promised Jennifer P. a low-interest credit card with no annual fee.All she had to do was send a $199 processing fee and the offer was guaranteed. The one-day special even included her choice of a laptop computer or satellite dish. Sound too good to be true? The telemarketer was friendly and persistent, and Jennifer fell for it. She waited weeks and never received her credit card. She tried to contact the company, but it had disappeared. The company was called U.S. Credit Services, but when Jennifer did some research she learned it was based in Canada. She called Canadian authorities, and they told her she had been scammed.

KNOW THE SIGNS:

1. Be suspicious of companies that claim they'll guarantee you a loan despite bad credit, bankruptcy, or unemployment. That's ridiculous. Legitimate lenders base their entire decision on whether you'll be able to repay your loan.

2. If the salesman says you are *guaranteed* to get a loan, walk away. No bank can guarantee you a loan up front.

3. If the company asks for a lot of money up front, that's wrong, especially if it's a generic "processing fee." A real lender may ask for money to cover a credit check, but credit checks don't cost very much. I've never heard of a credit card company asking for a credit check.

4. If the company claims it will refund your money if you don't get a loan, don't believe it. That's a common claim and part of the scam.

5. Advance fee loan scammers sometimes ask you to call a 900 number to choose the loan you want. Then they try to keep you on the line as long as possible to rack up 900 number phone charges.

6. If the company wants you to forward your payment by some method other than U.S. mail, be very wary. The company is probably trying to avoid mail fraud laws.

7. Many advance fee loan scams originate in other countries; Canada is the most common. I've also heard from consumers who sent their advance fees to companies in the Caribbean.

8. If the company *does* send you a card, it will be a card good for only its own merchandise—not a credit card. The company may claim that by buying its merchandise and then paying your bills you can reestablish good credit. The truth is, the merchandise is overpriced, and your payment record for this kind of card isn't a factor in your credit rating.

CREDIT

DO YOUR HOMEWORK:

1. Never agree to a loan over the phone. Insist on seeing written documentation. If the company refuses, run the other way!
2. Never give out your Social Security number, bank account number, or credit card number over the phone, unless *you* initiated the call.
3. Lenders may have to be licensed and bonded in your state. Find out if that's a state requirement and whether the company in question has met that requirement.
4. Know the difference between an advance fee loan and a secured credit card. Secured credit cards are legitimate tools for people who are trying to reestablish good credit. You deposit, say, $500 with the credit card company, and the company issues you a card with a $500 limit. You get the flexibility of paying by credit card instead of cash or check. If you make payments faithfully, the credit card company eventually increases your limit and refunds your deposit.

WHERE TO COMPLAIN:

If you are the victim of an advance fee loan scam, it's a criminal matter. Contact your state attorney general. If the company is based in another state or country, you may have to go to the FBI. Complain to the Better Business Bureau as well, so other consumers will be forewarned.

CREDIT

SEE ALSO:

CREDIT: Credit Counseling, Credit Repair

Collection Agents

Their calls send chills down your spine. They make ordinary people feel like common criminals. They are collection agents, debt collectors. If you're in debt, it's probably your own fault and it's *definite-*

ly your responsibility. But you don't have to take abuse. Debtor's prisons don't exist anymore, but debtor's *rights* do.

At age nineteen, Drew H. owed his creditors more than $10,000. He had about fourteen credit cards, and he used the new ones to pay the minimum balance on the old ones. He used caller ID to screen out calls from collectors. It was too much for Drew, so he took a drastic step: He joined the army. There, the collection agents couldn't get to him. This gentle, artsy soul spent two years fixing helicopters just to avoid his mountain of debt and those constant phone calls.

Collection agents make commissions that range from 15 percent to 50 percent of what you owe. I asked a couple of them to share their brand of psychological warfare. Collectors know an awful lot about you, but *they* don't even use their real names. They use fake names in case they ever encounter a case of debtor's rage. To get you on the phone, they alternate between using your first name and your last name. Here's another trick: Collectors will pretend they're putting you on hold to plead your case to a manager. They act like they're on your side, but instead, they doodle or go get some more coffee.

Despite creative tactics like this, federal law requires collection agents to treat you fairly. They're not allowed to call you before eight in the morning or after nine at night. One call a day is the accepted industry standard. If they know your employer discourages personal calls, they are not supposed to call you at work. After a collection company calls you, it has five days to mail you a notice stating how much you owe, to which company, and what to do if you dispute the debt.

Collectors are not allowed to embarrass you publicly or discuss your debt with anyone else. They can call other people only to find out where you are. Collection agents are not allowed to pretend they're with the cops or the courts. They can't imply that you've committed a crime or threaten to arrest you. And they can get into serious trouble if they use foul language or threaten violence. Collection agents are not allowed to collect more than you owe. If you write a postdated check, they can't cash it early.

If you want a collector to stop calling, ask the person for his or her name and address. By law, the collector must provide it. Then

CREDIT

send a certified letter demanding that the collector cease and desist. After that, the collection agency can notify you only of specific actions it plans to take against you, like lawsuits. If you believe you don't owe the money, you should write the collection agency a letter within thirty days. The collector is not allowed to contact you again until he or she verifies your debt and forwards you the documentation.

Often, collection agents are willing to negotiate. After all, if *you* don't pay, *they* don't get paid. Say you owe $300, but you only have $200. If you offer to forward it right away, the collector may agree to call it even. If your credit record is in terrible shape anyway, cutting a deal like this won't make it much worse. If in doubt, contact a counseling service like Consumer Credit Counseling.

DO YOUR HOMEWORK:

1. If a collection agent calls you, remain calm and get the agent's name, the collection company's name, the name of the merchant the company is collecting for, and the amount.
2. If you don't want a collection agent to call you anymore, ask for the company's address. Send a certified letter asking the company to stop contacting you.
3. If you are deeply in debt, consider negotiating with the collectors who call. They may be willing to accept a smaller amount than you actually owe, or they may waive late fees and fines.

CREDIT

WHERE TO COMPLAIN:

If you believe a collection agent is harassing you or violating the law, you have the right to sue in a state or federal court within one year of the violation. If you simply want to file a complaint, contact your state attorney general and the Federal Trade Commission.

SEE ALSO:

CREDIT: Credit Card Debt, **Credit Counseling, Credit Repair,** Credit Reports, Credit Scoring, Credit *Re*scoring

Credit Card Debt

Between 1990 and 2001 the average credit card balance rose from $3,000 to $7,500. Credit card debt is a cancer that's spreading in American households. I used to have this disease myself. The malignancy started when I received my first credit card in college. Like many students, I was issued a credit card even though I had no job and no way of paying. I quickly racked up about $2,500 in debt. My parents bailed me out. I racked up *another* $5,000 in debt. The second time I dug *myself* out, dollar by dollar. What an achievement! I can't tell you how good it feels to be free of credit card debt. Here are some strategies to help you liberate *yourself*, too.

What I'm about to say may make you break out in a cold sweat. CUT UP YOUR CREDIT CARDS. Are you feeling the withdrawal symptoms yet? Credit cards give us a sense of possibility that we just don't have with cash. They allowed me to live beyond my means for years. But I paid for it. Just as an alcoholic can't drink a drop without relapsing, a credit card junkie shouldn't have any credit cards. Zero. Zilch.

You may argue that in this high-tech age, it's impossible to conduct business without a credit card. True, you can't pay cash when you shop online, and hardly anybody uses personal checks anymore. But your argument falls flat in the face of debit cards. A debit card allows you all the convenience of a credit card, with all the limits of your own bank balance. It's an excellent substitute.

If you believe you must have a credit card on hand in case of an emergency, I've got an incredibly creative suggestion for you. Cut up all but one credit card. Then take the lone survivor and drop it in a Tupperware container full of water. Pop the container in the freezer and put your credit card spending on ice! This way you'll have to think about it for several hours if you want to use that card. You're unlikely to thaw this consumer culture ice sculpture to make an impulse buy. But if you have a true emergency, it will be there for you.

My financial planner boyfriend (now husband!) put me on a spending freeze back in my debtor days. I wasn't allowed to spend money on nonessential items. For me, that meant no new clothes, no home decorating, and no dinners out. Not using your cards anymore really is the first step in paying them off. Most people who are in a credit card crunch charge their cards to the limit, pay the minimum each month, then spend right up to the limit again until they get their next bill.

After you stop spending, you need to *start* paying. Here's how I did it. I didn't make much money in my credit card debt days. I lived from paycheck to paycheck. When my credit card bill came, sometimes I didn't have much money to send in, so I sent what I could. At other times of the month, I occasionally *had* extra money. In the old days, of course, I would have spent it! Instead, I began sending money to my credit card company even when I didn't have a bill due. I preaddressed and stamped several envelopes so I had them ready. Anytime I had extra cash in my checking account, I popped it in an envelope and kissed it good-bye.

Your savings account is another source. Sound sacrilegious? I get into this argument with people all the time. I know lots of smart people who have a savings account *and* credit card debt. It's ludicrous! I know, I know, you feel it's important to save for emergencies. Trust me, credit card debt *is* an emergency. But here's my less flippant explanation. If your savings account yields 3 percent interest and your credit card charges 19 percent interest, you can instantly "make" a 16 percent "profit" by using your savings account to pay off your credit card debt. That would be an impressive gain in the stock market! Then, instead of pulling out your credit card to make impulse buys, you can fall back on it in emergencies—a much sounder use for it.

CREDIT

If you're deep in debt, try calling your creditors and asking if you can negotiate a more manageable payment plan. Some credit card companies may be willing to lower the interest rate for you. Others will let you make smaller monthly payments. This is exactly what a credit counseling organization would do for you, but it is possible to do it yourself.

You could also look for a debt consolidation loan, but don't count on it. Reputable banks don't make debt consolidation loans to people with no collateral. *Crooked* lenders may offer you a consolidation loan, but the interest rate will probably be higher than what you're already paying on your credit cards. They'll try to trick you by offering you a lower monthly payment than what you currently pay, but the loan will last so long that you end up paying far more money than you should have.

If you own a house, you may be able to take out a home equity loan to pay off your credit cards. This option sounds great because you can then deduct the interest you pay on your tax return. But beware! Home equity loans come with closing costs, which just add to your debt. And if you miss payments, you could lose your *house*. If you miss a payment on a credit card, you just lose your good credit rating.

DO YOUR HOMEWORK:

1. Cut up all your credit cards or keep one and put it on ice!
2. Use a debit card instead of a credit card.
3. Impose a spending freeze.
4. Send payments more than once a month—whenever you have spare money.
5. Use your savings account to pay off your credit card debt, then use your credit card in emergencies.
6. Negotiate a better payment plan with your credit card company.
7. Beware of debt consolidation loans. Most make your problem worse.
8. Consider a home equity loan, *if* you have plenty of extra equity in your house and you know you can make the payments on time.
9. Teach your children about the perils of credit card debt and how to use a credit card responsibly.

WHERE TO COMPLAIN:

You can whine and complain all you want, but if you've got killer credit card debt, it's your own darn fault!

SEE ALSO:

BEFORE YOU BUY: How to Pay; CREDIT: Advance Fee Loans, Collection Agents, **Credit Card Strategies, Credit Counseling, Credit Repair**

CREDIT

Credit Card Strategies

I have my fifteen-digit credit card number memorized. Scary! That's how much I use it. Fortunately, I no longer *abuse* it. In fact, these days my credit cards work for me, instead of me working for them! There are a couple of different strategies for managing your credit cards, depending on your situation.

If you carry a balance, you need to find the card with the lowest possible interest rate. First, try negotiating with your current credit card company. You may be able to get a lower rate just by asking, because the company wants to keep you as a customer. In a recent survey, 56 percent of consumers were able to wrangle a lower interest rate with one five-minute phone call. The average drop was six percentage points! You can negotiate lower service fees, too. By getting lower interest rates on your current cards, you buy yourself time to shop around and see if you can find an even better deal elsewhere.

Next, get a list of low-interest-rate credit cards and see if any of the banks can beat the rate you've just negotiated with your current card company. The **Federal Reserve** regularly publishes a list of credit card offers. It's available by going to **www.federalreserve .gov.** Click on "consumer" and look for the credit card links. Web sites **www.cardweb.com** and **www.bankrate.com** also offer lists of low-interest credit cards. One caution: years ago I obtained one of these lists and, fearful that I'd have trouble qualifying, I applied for *several* different cards. I got denial letters back from every single one. The reason? "Excessive credit applications." Bankers get suspicious when you apply for too much credit at once.

You may be able to lower your interest rates even more by doing the introductory rate dance. This is a dicey proposition, but it can be done. Basically, you transfer your balance from one card to another to take advantage of low introductory rates. That's right, you know all those credit card offers that come in the mail every day? If you have credit card debt, read them. The key is finding cards that offer a low rate, a long introductory period, and few fees. Some credit card companies charge you so much to transfer balances that it

CREDIT

wipes out the benefit of the low interest rate. Read the fine print. Make a note on your calendar of when the introductory rate expires and switch to another card before it does. If you fail to transfer before the higher rate kicks in, the bank will charge you that rate on your entire existing debt.

Now, once you pay off your balance and start paying in full each month, you want a totally different kind of credit card. Low interest rates are no longer a concern. Shop around for a card that offers you a benefit you will actually use. My husband used to have a card that earned him points toward a General Motors car. Problem was, he didn't *want* a GM car. When we got married, I persuaded him to switch to two credit cards that offer fabulous frequent-flier mile benefits. We've traveled to Europe, Hawaii, and Australia, thanks to our credit card points. Cards that offer benefits usually charge higher interest rates and an annual fee, so make sure you aren't going to need to carry a balance and calculate whether the benefits are worth that fee.

Here are some other tricks and terms to look out for as you shop *for* a credit card and shop *with* a credit card!

Some banks will send you offers that blare in bold print, **"No Annual Fee!"** But if you read the fine print, you may find that only applies for the first year. Often, you *will* be charged an annual fee in subsequent years. Be careful.

CREDIT

Banks realize consumers are wise to "low introductory rates" that don't last for long, so they're modifying their marketing. I've actually seen credit card offers that state, "This is NOT an INTRODUCTORY rate." Again, when you read the fine print it turns out that's *exactly* what it is.

Some credit card companies advertise phenomenal introductory rates, but then charge enormous transfer fees that wipe out the benefit of the low rate. Read, read, read.

In addition to the annual fee and interest rate, you need to consider the credit card's grace period. This is the amount of time the company gives you to pay off your monthly bill before interest starts accruing on new purchases. The average used to be twenty-five days, but some banks have now reduced that to just twenty days. Look for a card with a generous grace period, especially if you pay your bills in full each month.

If you open a checking account and credit card at the same bank, you may have unknowingly signed a linked banking form allowing the bank to tap your checking account if you don't pay your credit card bill on time. This can cause you to lose track of your bank balance and bounce checks. Either revoke the bank's right to link the two accounts, or get your credit card through another company.

When you check into a hotel or rent a car, the merchant may *block* a portion of your credit card. Say the hotel is $100 a night, and you plan to stay for a week. When you check in, the hotel will probably block $700 to make sure that much credit is available when you check out. If you are near your card limit, this can cause you to go over if you make other purchases during the week. If you pay with a check or a different card when you check out, the block will stay on your original card for an average of fifteen days. The solution? Either pay with the same credit card you used at check-in or ask the clerk to remove the block.

Have you ever noticed the extra numbers printed on your credit card in tiny type that is *not* raised? It's usually a three- or four-digit number, and it can be on the front or the back. It's a security code. Bob R. got a call from a telemarketer who promised him a free gift. The telemarketer said he just needed to know the little numbers on Bob's credit card to validate the offer. Turns out, if strangers have your account number, expiration date, and security code, they can use your card. The three- or four-digit code is there so merchants can verify that the person making a phone or Internet purchase is actually holding the credit card.

Your buying patterns can also get you into some sticky situations. Gus V. used his credit card to get gas. Then he went home and went online to try to order a new computer. His credit card company rejected the transaction. Gus was furious until he learned that it's a security precaution. Crooks often test stolen credit cards at the gas pump, where they don't have to face a clerk or sign their name. If the card works, they move on to big purchases—like computers. Shopping overseas can also trigger a security alert on your card. If

CREDIT

you're going to be traveling or making unusual purchases, ask your credit card company what you need to do so your transactions will not be denied.

DO YOUR HOMEWORK:

1. If you carry credit card debt, negotiate with your current card company to get a lower interest rate and lower fees.
2. Obtain a list of low interest credit cards and see if there's one that fits your needs. Apply for them one at a time and leave some breathing room between applications.
3. If you're deeply in debt—and you're disciplined—do the introductory rate dance. Just be sure to read the fine print and look out for transfer fees.
4. If you don't carry a balance, get a credit card that offers you some benefit. Make sure the benefit is worth the price of the annual fee. Also check to see that the card has a generous grace period.
5. If you pay your bills in full every month, it's best to keep only one or two credit cards. That's the optimum number for a high credit score, plus it's easier to keep track of fewer bills.
6. Understand the tricks and terms credit card companies use and make them work in your favor.

CREDIT

WHERE TO COMPLAIN:

If you want to gripe about a credit card company, try the Federal Reserve. The Fed reviews consumer complaints and refers them to other agencies if necessary. You could also contact your state department of banking.

SEE ALSO:

CREDIT: **Credit Card Debt,** Credit Counseling, Credit Repair

Credit Counseling

If you're trying to lose weight, and dieting on your own hasn't done it, you might sign up with a diet counselor. That counselor will give you pep talks, help you develop a menu, even weigh you to measure your progress. If you're trying to shed *debt*, and doing it on your own hasn't worked, you can go to a *credit* counselor. That counselor will give you pep talks, help you develop a budget, and weigh in on your progress! Credit counseling is a lifesaver, as long as the counselor you choose is reputable.

Here's how it works. You meet with a credit counseling service, usually a nonprofit. You and a counselor develop a budget by looking at your income, your expenses, and your debt. Once you know how much money you can afford to put toward your debts each month, the counselor calls your creditors and negotiates a workable payment plan. This is something you can certainly do yourself, but credit counseling services have ongoing relationships with various banks and may have better luck. The counselor will try to get your creditors to waive late fees, lower interest rates, or accept smaller monthly payments—or maybe all of the above. Once the payment plan is set, you send a single check to the counseling service, which then forwards the money to your various creditors. You may have to agree not to take on any more debt while you participate in the program. Most credit counseling services also want you to attend educational classes to help you stay out of money trouble in the future.

Now here are the negatives. Some credit counseling services receive funding from credit card companies, so they may have a conflict of interest. Critics say these services aren't likely to tell you if bankruptcy is your best bet, because they don't want to lose their wealthy backers. Credit card companies hate bankruptcies, because that means the customer gets off scot-free. Card companies prefer customers who enroll in credit counseling programs because at least they're paying, even if they're doing so slowly. Perhaps the best thing to do is to get advice from a bankruptcy lawyer *and* a credit counseling service and see which seems best for you.

CREDIT

You should also know that enrolling in a credit counseling service does not keep creditors from putting negative entries on your credit report. The counseling service won't report anything to the credit bureaus, but your creditors will. If a creditor agrees to accept a smaller payment from you, it may report the loss. At the very least, your creditors will probably report that you are part of a credit counseling program. Lenders that see that on your credit report later may consider it a negative that you couldn't manage your money on your own. On the other hand, you'll have better luck getting loans later if your credit report shows a steady stream of payments than if you go it alone and default entirely.

You should know that illegal credit *repair* firms often mimic genuine credit counseling services to try to lure customers. Credit repair companies don't emphasize paying down your debt. Instead, they claim they can help you erase negative entries from your credit report—even if those entries are accurate. It's a scam and it's illegal; it's also the subject of the next section.

DO YOUR HOMEWORK:

CREDIT

1. Interview several credit counseling services before making a commitment. Think about it. You're sending these people most of your money each month. You want to make sure they're legit. In recent years, consumers have complained about sleazy credit counseling firms that didn't forward their payments on time or failed to disclose their fees. Be careful! Two reputable national firms are **Consumer Credit Counseling Service, (800) 388-2227**, and **National Credit Counseling Service, (800) 955-0412.** You can also get help from your local **Cooperative Extension Service,** a service of counties and universities. Check out the Web site, **www.money2000.org.**

2. Before you sign anything or start sending money, do a background check. Call the Better Business Bureau and your county and state consumer protection offices to see if any complaints have been lodged against the counseling service.

QUESTIONS TO ASK:

1. Do you offer educational materials? Are they free? Can I get them online?
2. Will I work with one counselor or several? What kind of qualifications do your counselors have?
3. What are your fees, and what are they based on? Do I have to pay a fee before you can help me?
4. Where do you get your funding?
5. Is a debt repayment plan my only option? What about bankruptcy? What about counseling?
6. Will I have a formal written agreement or contract with you?
7. Who regulates or oversees your agency? Are you audited?
8. What is your privacy policy? Will my address and phone number remain confidential?
9. Can you get my creditors to lower or eliminate interest, finance charges, and late fees?
10. How do you determine the amount of my monthly payment? What if I can't afford it?
11. How will I know my creditors have received my payments?
12. Is client money put in a separate account apart from your operating funds?

CREDIT

WHERE TO COMPLAIN:

The Federal Trade Commission accepts complaints about credit counseling services, but doesn't resolve those complaints. For individual help, try your county or state consumer protection office or the BBB. Some states have banking and credit divisions that may be able to help you, especially if the credit counseling service is funded by the banking industry.

SEE ALSO:

CREDIT: Collection Agents, Credit Card Debt, Credit Card Strategies, **Credit Repair,** Credit Reports

Credit Repair

It's ironic. People who are too strapped to pay their bills somehow scrape together enough money to pay a credit repair company. Credit repair companies claim they can erase negative entries on your credit report—even if those entries are accurate. Sorry, NOBODY CAN DO THAT FOR YOU. Now, if there are *mistakes* in your credit file, you can correct those yourself. But companies that claim they can purge *accurate* information from your file are operating illegally—and if you hire one, you could be breaking the law, too.

Tiffany D. heard an advertisement for credit repair on the radio. Her credit was a mess, so she was intrigued. When she called, the company told her it could almost instantly "clean up" her credit record. So Tiffany made a $450 down payment to get the company's help. A couple of months later, she still couldn't get a loan to save her life. She got suspicious, put a hold on her bank account so the company wouldn't take out any more payments—and called me.

I sent a producer into the company undercover. He signed up to get his credit repaired. A few days later, the company sent him three sealed envelopes that he was supposed to forward to the major credit bureaus. Of course, we opened them first! The company had written dispute letters claiming our producer had never made a late payment—even though he had. The company wrote all sorts of other lies, then forged our producer's name at the bottom!

Credit repair companies use a couple of different strategies. The first is known as "bombardment." They flood the credit bureaus with paperwork disputing every single item in your credit report. They try to take advantage of a law that says credit bureaus must drop an entry if it can't be verified within thirty days. Trouble is, that same law allows creditors to put an item *back* in your credit file, once it *is* verified. So even if a credit repair company succeeds in creating chaos at the credit bureau, it won't last for long.

Another strategy is called "file segregation." Some credit repair companies counsel their clients to apply for an employee identification number, which has the same number of digits as a Social

CREDIT

Security number. Credit repair firms claim you can create a new financial identity by using this number instead of your old Social Security number. If you try it, you'll be breaking not one, not two, but *three* federal laws. It's illegal to apply for an employee ID number under false pretenses, to misrepresent your Social Security number, and to make false statements on a credit application.

Of course, many credit repair companies don't bother with all these fancy strategies. Their method is much simpler. They just take your money—and disappear.

The Federal Trade Commission says it has *never* seen a legitimate credit repair company. (Credit *counseling* companies are another matter—and another section.) But just in case, the FTC has crafted a series of rules such companies must obey. Credit repair companies are not allowed to take money up front before they do any work. They're not supposed to make false claims about their services. They must tell you that you have three days to cancel, and then honor that waiting period. And they have to give you a written contract that includes the price, the precise services they are offering you, how long it will take to get results, any guarantees, and the company's official name and business address.

KNOW THE SIGNS:

CREDIT

1. Credit repair companies claim they can quickly fix your credit situation, no matter how atrocious it really is These grandiose claims are a real red flag.
2. If a company asks you to pay for credit repair services up front, that's a bad omen, indeed, because it's illegal.
3. Credit repair companies often discourage you from contacting the credit bureaus directly.
4. If somebody suggests that you apply for an employer identification number and use that instead of your Social Security number when you apply for credit, that's a telltale sign of fraud.
5. Credit repair scammers may advise you to dispute *all* the information in your credit report, even entries you know are accurate.

DO YOUR HOMEWORK:

1. If, after reading this chapter, you still somehow believe a credit repair company could be legit, then, for god's sake, check out the company with the Better Business Bureau and your county and state consumer protection offices.
2. Read the Credit Reports section and learn how to dispute errors in your credit history yourself—for free!
3. Read the Credit Counseling section and discover people who really can help you dig yourself out of debt and establish good credit again.

WHERE TO COMPLAIN:

Since credit repair companies operate illegally, contact your state attorney general if you have been victimized. Also file a complaint with the BBB to help other consumers.

SEE ALSO:

CREDIT: Advance Fee Loans, Credit Card Debt, **Credit Counseling, Credit Reports**

CREDIT

Credit Reports

Half of all credit reports contain negative information that is not true. Your task is to make sure yours isn't in that half! The first time I ordered my credit reports, they were loaded with errors. For example, the same credit card was listed three different times—so it looked like I had three times as much debt as I really did. One report claimed I had worked at Sears—not that there's anything *wrong* with that—but it's not true! I filled out dispute forms and got the credit bureaus to correct my record. Then, when I ordered my reports again a year later, some of the same errors resurfaced. Aaargh!

Banks, credit card companies, and landlords have long used credit reports to get a sense of a person's reliability. Now, employers and insurance companies are using credit reports more and more, too, so it's important that you know what's in that report. Credit bureaus are required to provide copies to consumers who ask for them. You get to see what businesses are saying about you as well as which businesses have *asked* about you. I recommend reviewing your credit reports every year—especially before any big purchase.

You're entitled to a free credit report any time you're turned down for credit. The institution that told you "no," is required to list the reason for your rejection, plus the name of the credit bureau it used. You then have sixty days to request your free report. You can also qualify for a freebie if you're on welfare, if you're unemployed and about to launch a job hunt, or if you believe your credit report is inaccurate due to fraud. If you plan to pay for your credit report, it will only cost you about $10.

If you find mistakes on your credit report, you should dispute them. Simply fill out the dispute form provided by the credit bureau. If you want the bureau to know that you've never worked at Sears, just say so. If you're trying to prove a bigger point—like you never made a late payment on your credit card—you should try to provide documentation. If you don't *have* documentation, but you know you're right, try disputing it anyway. The credit bureau has thirty days to research your claim and get back to you.

If your credit record changes as a result of your dispute, you can ask the credit bureau to send a fresh copy to any business that has received an inaccurate report about you in the past six months.

CREDIT

If the credit bureau says you haven't made your case, and refuses to change your report, you can write a dispute letter and have it placed in your file. You can also write a letter if you *agree* with entries in your report but want to explain the circumstances. For example, maybe you got behind on your bills because of a serious illness. Future businesses that pull your report will be able to see your letter and take it into account.

If there are unflattering entries in your credit report, and they're *true*, time is the only remedy. After seven years, the credit bureaus are required to stop reporting late payments or other adverse information. Lawsuits and judgments last seven years or until the statute of limitations runs out. If you've declared bankruptcy, that will remain on your record for ten tough years.

DO YOUR HOMEWORK:

1. Order your credit reports from the three major credit bureaus once a year and a couple of months before making a big purchase. Go to **www.experian.com, www.equifax.com,** and **www.transunion.com** to get started.
2. Dispute inaccurate entries swiftly and thoroughly.
3. If necessary, write a succinct letter to be placed in your file to explain your side of the situation.
4. If you don't want to receive endless credit card offers, tell the credit bureaus you want to opt out. You can do this by calling **(888) 567-8688.**

WHERE TO COMPLAIN:

If a credit bureau mistreats you, complain to the Federal Trade Commission.

SEE ALSO:

CREDIT: Credit Counseling, Credit Repair, Credit Scoring, **Credit Rescoring,** Identity Theft

CREDIT

Credit Scoring

You've got a phone number, a Social Security number—even an IQ number. In the twenty-first century, people know us by our numbers. So do you know your credit score? That's the number that predicts whether you'll pay back your loans and do it on time. Scoring formulas are closely guarded, but a typical scale ranges from three hundred to eight hundred. Every bank does it differently, so your score could vary depending on where you apply for credit. Your score also changes with every single payment you make—or *fail* to make.

So how is your credit score calculated? Statisticians studied peoples' payment patterns for years. They looked at things like late payments, types of credit, home ownership, occupation, length of credit history, and the ratio of debt to credit. They learned which factors are good predictors that you're likely to pay your bills. Then they assigned numerical values to those predictors and created statistical models. Banks calculate credit scores by gathering information from your credit report and your credit application and comparing it to those statistical models.

Banks are *not* allowed to make race, gender, marital status, national origin, or religion a factor in their credit scoring models. They *are* allowed to use age as a predictor, *if* they can prove their model is well designed and doesn't discriminate against the elderly. Credit scores are less biased than bankers. After all, scoring applies the same mathematical, methodical standards to everybody. The one thing that's missing is human empathy. If your late payments are the result of an illness in the family, the scoring model won't account for that. In those cases, many banks allow you to plead your case to a real live human.

Credit scoring is fast and impartial, but it's not perfect. Here are a couple of examples. A person can be filthy rich and have a terrible credit score. Credit scoring models give preference to people who *have* credit, *use* it, and pay it off responsibly. If somebody is so wealthy that he pays cash for most things, he won't have much of a credit history, which will hurt his credit score. That person could be turned down for . . . a Sears card! For that matter, if you're *not* rich, but you just don't believe in using credit cards, you could score low and have trouble qualifying for a bigger loan when you want it.

CREDIT

Here's a flaw that affects *me*. To earn frequent-flier miles, my husband and I charge everything we possibly can on our American Express card. American Express cards have no official limit because they are *charge* cards rather than *credit* cards. Credit reports usually list the credit limit for every account a consumer has. Since American Express cards *have* no limit, credit bureaus list the amount of your most recent *bill* instead. Unfortunately, that makes it look like you are always right *at* your limit. Remember, credit-scoring models compare your debt to your available credit and subtract points if you are maxed out. So, even though my husband and I pay off our Amex bill in full each month, our credit score suffers. From what I understand, the eggheads who design credit-scoring models *are* working to get rid of flaws like this.

Credit card companies were the first to use credit scoring. Auto loans came next. Banks started basing their mortgages and small-business loans on credit scores in the 1990s. Today, even insurance companies use credit scores. They've discovered a correlation between people who pay their bills late and people who make excessive insurance claims. Credit scores are bound to come into play in other industries, too.

If you're going to win in this game, it's important for you to know the score. For many years, banks and credit scoring companies resisted telling you your own score. Not any more. Now they're eager to *sell* it to you. The three major credit bureaus, Equifax, Experian, and Transunion, all provide credit scores, along with their credit reports, for prices starting at $35. I would order from Equifax first, because Equifax's credit scores are calculated in partnership with Fair Isaac, the company that invented credit scores. Fair Isaac, or "FICO," scores are still the most commonly used.

If you don't like what you see, can you improve your score? Yes. Fortunately, scoring models emphasize the present more than the past. So with every bill you pay on time and every debt you wipe out, your score will rise. It's also important not to take on any *new* debt. Even credit *applications* can count against you. Bankers grow suspicious if you suddenly apply for a bunch of new credit cards. (Hmmm, does this guy have a gambling problem? Is he trying to finance an independent film? Will he pay us back?)

If you're one of those who opens new store cards to get the 10 percent discount, don't! That counts against you, too. Having a ton of open credit card accounts hurts your score, even if you cut the cards up and never use them. They are considered to be *potential* liabilities. The optimum number of credit cards to achieve the highest possible credit score is one or two. That's right. *Uno* or *dos. Un* or *deux.* Doesn't seem like very many, does it?

If you don't have any credit card debt, then you should cancel all but two of your cards. Write to the companies and ask them to close your accounts so they appear on your credit report as "closed by consumer." Order a credit report and make sure your requests were honored. There's one exception. If you carry a lot of debt, then you should *keep* those extra, unused accounts. Why? Because they

CREDIT

improve your credit-to-debt ratio. Remember, you get demerits if you're maxed out.

Studies show your score can vary by as much as fifty to a hundred points, depending on which credit bureau calculates it. Mortgage lenders often base their loan on your lowest score, because that way they can charge a higher interest rate and make more money. That's why it's important to order your credit report regularly from all three bureaus and make sure each has all your financial information—and has it correct. When you apply for a mortgage, ask the lender which credit bureau it uses and what your score with that bureau was. If it seems low, ask the lender to take an average of all three scores or use the one in the middle.

DO YOUR HOMEWORK:

1. Order your credit score from one of the credit bureaus: Go to **www.equifax.com, www.experian.com,** or **www. transunion.com.**
2. Along with your score, you'll get an explanation of why it isn't higher. If the reasoning doesn't make sense to you, order your credit *report* and check it for errors. Keep in mind, credit scores are derived from credit reports.
3. If your score is low and it is your fault, start taking steps to improve it. Pay your bills on time. Pay down your debt. Don't apply for any new credit. And close accounts you don't use, *if* you don't have a lot of debt.
4. Remember, different financial institutions use different scoring models. If you get turned down at one bank, try another. Each one has different standards and different levels of risk tolerance.
5. If your credit score is just below the threshold for getting a loan or getting a good interest rate, don't despair. Read the Credit *Re*scoring section and learn how a professional can help you quickly raise your score.

CREDIT

WHERE TO COMPLAIN:

If you are turned down for credit or a loan, the bank that rejects you is required to tell you where it got its information about you. Your score is based on your credit report. Complain to the credit bureau in question.

SEE ALSO:

CREDIT: Credit Repair, Credit Reports, **Credit Rescoring**

Credit Rescoring

Somebody *else's* mistake may be costing you thousands of dollars. Then again, your *own* mistake may be costing you thousands of dollars. Either way, credit *re*scoring, also known as "rapid rescoring," can help. If there's an error on your credit report, or if you haven't structured your debt very wisely, your credit score may not be as high as it could be. Rapid rescoring is a service offered by local credit bureaus (which are affiliated with the big national credit bureaus). Unfortunately, the service isn't available directly to consumers. You'll have to go through your mortgage broker or lender.

Here's how it works: If there's a mistake on your credit report, you have to provide proof. The rapid rescoring expert researches your story and gathers written documentation. Next, the expert forwards your materials to the three national credit bureaus and asks for a correction. You can do this yourself, but it takes weeks. Companies that offer rapid rescoring have dedicated phone and fax lines they use to communicate with the big credit bureaus. In twenty-four to seventy-two hours, your credit report is corrected, and your credit score rises as a result.

Valerie B. wanted to refinance her townhouse to provide stability for her daughter and to pay for graduate school for herself. She had never checked her credit score, but she was confident she would score high because she had always been careful to pay her bills on time. But when the mortgage broker pulled Valerie's score, it was just 598 on a scale of three hundred to eight hundred. She needed to score at least 650 to get the low interest rate she wanted.

So Valerie's broker recommended rapid rescoring. When the local credit bureau pulled up Valerie's credit report, it showed she had

CREDIT

never finished paying off her car loan. The bank had written off the loss, which is a huge black mark on any consumer's credit. As it turns out, a big national bank had purchased Valerie's local bank around the same time she was making her final car payment. The new bank lost her paperwork, never recorded her final payment, and ruined her credit.

Once the local credit bureau corrected the mistake, Valerie's score soared from 598 to 790—near the top of the scale. At the lower score she was only able to qualify for a mortgage rate of about 8 percent. After rapid rescoring, she landed a loan at just 6 percent. You do the math! Over the life of the loan, Valerie was set to save $72,000, thanks to rapid rescoring.

In addition to correcting *errors,* a rescoring expert can help you *restructure* your debt to improve your score. For example, say you have three credit cards, and one of them is near the limit, but you hardly use the other two. By transferring some of that debt to the other two cards, you may be able to improve your score. Why? Credit scoring models are biased against consumers who are near their credit limits. Sounds dumb, but you can sometimes have the *same* amount of debt and achieve a higher score just by spreading it around. Rapid rescoring experts say you should check your credit limit on each card and keep your balance at less than 50 percent of that limit—30 percent is even better.

CREDIT

Here's another trick. Say you're young and your credit score is low because you're just getting started. Ask somebody with established credit (like a parent) to put you on his or her credit card account as an "authorized user." Their credit card company will issue you your own card, but you don't even have to use it. Even though it's not really your account, and you don't even get the bill, the account will become part of your credit record. This long-standing account will factor into your credit score. On the flip side, if you are an "authorized user" on somebody else's account and that person manages the account poorly, a rapid rescoring expert may suggest you cut your ties to that account to improve your score.

I hope rescoring experts will soon make their services available directly to consumers and for purchases other than real estate.

Credit scores are calculated using hundreds of different variables, and some of those variables actually cancel each other out. You can take commonsense steps on your own, but if you're about to make a big purchase and you need points fast, consult a professional. Thanks to rapid rescoring, you could *score!*

DO YOUR HOMEWORK:

1. When you're ready to buy a house, don't paint yourself into a corner. Research your credit situation in advance so you'll have time to make adjustments and corrections.
2. If a mortgage company turns you down or doesn't offer you a low interest rate, ask if you're a candidate for rapid rescoring. It's a fairly new procedure, so you may have to educate your mortgage broker about it.
3. Do everything you can to gather written evidence that proves negative entries in your credit report are false. That's the ammunition the rapid rescoring expert needs.
4. Make sure the rescoring expert looks not just at errors on your credit report, but also at ways to restructure your debt to achieve a higher score.

CREDIT

SEE ALSO:

CREDIT: **Credit Reports, Credit Scoring,** HOME BUYING AND RENTING: Mortgages

Identity Theft

You may have an evil financial twin. Every year, a million or more Americans discover they are victims of identity theft. It is the nation's fastest-growing financial crime, doubling or tripling every year. The average victim spends 175 hours clearing his or her name—that's more than four weeks! And that effort is usually spread out over a couple of years. Unfortunately, preventing identity theft isn't easy. And fighting back after the fact is even worse.

Your name, Social Security number, and date of birth. That's all it takes to step into your shoes and start spending. How do crooks get this information? Identity theft is evolving. Old-style identity thieves are avid dumpster divers. They search peoples' trash for bank statements and credit card offers. They also target unlocked mailboxes in rural and suburban neighborhoods. Sometimes one crime leads to another. If thieves snatch your purse or break into your car, they may get just the information they need to steal your identity next.

These days, though, authorities say about half of all identity theft is committed by insiders. Mortgage brokerage employees with access to sensitive financial information, car salesmen who take your loan application, even people who work at the big three credit bureaus. This is much more sinister. You can shred your mail and lock up your trash, but it's impossible to do business without sharing some financial details about yourself.

Francisco and Gloria V. don't know how their financial information was swiped, but they now know how devastating it can be. The crook called their bank and ordered a new box of checks. Then he went on an $80,000 spending spree, with their home equity line as collateral. The theft shook Francisco and Gloria's finances and it shook their relationship. Gloria actually wondered whether Francisco himself took the money, until Francisco pointed out that the signatures on the checks were not in his handwriting and weren't even spelled right!

CREDIT

Originally, people whose identities were stolen were not even acknowledged as victims, because they are not responsible for the fraudulent debts. True, they lost countless hours and their good credit rating, but *banks* were the ones losing *money.* Authorities refused even to update the individual victims on the progress of their investigations. Today, that's changed, but there's still a hole in law enforcement's response. Local police often consider identity theft outside their jurisdiction and refer people to the Secret Service. But the Secret Service, which is responsible for investigating financial crimes, only takes cases involving a lot of money. If you're a small-time victim, you may get caught in the no-man's-land in the middle.

Private industry has come out with innovative new products to address identity theft, but if you're a victim, it may seem like too little too late. The major credit bureaus now offer credit-monitoring services. For $70 or more a year, they will alert you if an account is opened in your name. By the time you hear about it, the account is already open, but at least you can respond quickly. Another offering is identity theft insurance. A typical policy costs $25 per year and gives you $15,000 dollars worth of coverage. The insurance pays for lost wages, certified mail, notary public fees, long-distance phone calls, and some legal fees.

KNOW THE SIGNS:

1. If a monthly bill doesn't show up on time, an identity thief may have stolen it. Call the company and inquire.
2. If you see mysterious charges on your credit card bills or a company mentions a charge you didn't make, investigate further.
3. If you have always had impeccable credit and suddenly you are turned down, find out why. Maybe somebody else is tapping into your good credit.
4. If you order checks and they don't arrive in a timely fashion, call your bank and track them down. The fact that banks send checks in those unmistakable little boxes is one of my pet peeves!

CREDIT

DO YOUR HOMEWORK:

1. Shred sensitive documents before you throw them away, including bank statements, brokerage statements, credit card bills, and credit card offers.
2. If you have a freestanding mailbox, get a different one. You want a mailbox that only you and your mail carrier can access.
3. Don't pay bills by leaving them in your mailbox with the flag up. That's an invitation to identity thieves.
4. Don't carry your Social Security card in your wallet, where it's readily available to pickpockets. You probably have the number memorized, and you almost never need to present the card. Keep it in a secure place, instead.
5. Don't print your Social Security number on checks.

6. If your DMV uses Social Security numbers as driver's license numbers, ask for an alternate. Same goes for student IDs.

7. Ask your health plan to use a substitute number instead of your Social Security number.

8. Don't give out sensitive financial information over the phone unless you initiated the call.

9. Ask your bank and your credit card companies to add a password to your accounts, so that no business can be transacted without that secret word. Make sure it's an unusual password that's hard to predict. Don't use your mother's maiden name!

10. Order your credit report once a year and dispute any errors you find on it.

11. If you find unfamiliar accounts on your credit report, immediately alert the credit bureau's fraud department. Also call and write to the creditor. Send your letter by certified mail.

12. Consider subscribing to a credit-monitoring service. I recommend using one provided by one of the three major credit bureaus. Don't go with a no-name company that could just be trying to get your personal information.

13. Weigh whether you want identity theft insurance. Chubb and Travelers were the first companies to offer it. You simply add it to your homeowner's or renter's policy.

FIGHTING BACK:

1. If you learn your identity has been stolen, you are eligible for a free credit report. Order yours from all three major credit bureaus: Go to **Experian.com, Equifax.com,** and **Transunion.com.**

2. Ask the credit bureaus to "flag" your record, with a fraud alert that includes a warning that creditors should call you for permission before opening new accounts in your name.

3. Immediately file a police report. If your local police department doesn't want to be bothered, raise a ruckus if necessary. You're going to need this official document. Be sure to keep a copy for yourself. Try to get the local police to actually investigate the crime.

CREDIT

4. Cancel all your credit cards and get brand-new ones. Be sure to ask for a password for the accounts.
5. Report the thefts to your bank. Stop payment on all outstanding checks. Close your bank accounts and open new ones. Get passwords. Get a new ATM card and choose a different PIN (personal identification number).
6. For every fraudulent account that appears on your credit report, write a letter to the creditor and send it by certified mail. Include an affidavit (a letter written by you and witnessed by a notary) stating that the account is fraudulent. Include a copy of the police report. Ask the creditor to close the account, correct your credit record, and send you a confirmation letter.
7. If the identity thief stole your mail, file a complaint with the U.S. postal inspector's office, which investigates mail fraud.
8. Contact the **Social Security Administration** to verify that your retirement benefits are being credited properly and that your name is listed correctly. The number to call is **(800) 772-1213.**
9. For additional tips and support, contact the **Federal Trade Commission.** Congress appointed the FTC to be the clearinghouse for identity theft complaints. Go to **www.ftc.gov.**

CREDIT

WHERE TO COMPLAIN:

In addition to the FTC and the postal inspector, you can make a report to the Secret Service. If your driver's license was stolen, alert your Department of Motor Vehicles.

SEE ALSO:

CREDIT: **Credit Reports**

CHAPTER 7

Finances

ATMs

I haven't been inside a bank to do business in years. Heck, some banks now offer a free checking account if you *promise* not to come inside. How do you spell convenience? A-T-M. But watch out, because these days it's also how you spell scam.

Once again, some clever con artists have used their brains for all the wrong reasons. The bad guys have two tactics. They install fake freestanding automatic teller machines in malls and other public places, or they attach a false front to a real ATM. Either way, when you insert your card, the con artists capture the card number and the PIN (personal identification number). Then they're able to clone your card and drain your account.

When this scam first surfaced, the card-reading devices were crude, clunky-looking things that only read ATM *card* numbers. Now they're sleeker and more realistic and they grab your secret code too. After the computerized device reads your card, it sends you a message that the ATM machine is out of order. You move on, and the bad guys move in to retrieve their computer.

Sigh . . . this is one more reason to be on your guard and ever-vigilant. Try to use one "home base" ATM whenever you can. That way, if something looks different about it, you'll notice. Your next best bet is always to use ATMs operated by your own bank, since they should all look roughly the same. Pay particular attention to the slot where you slip your card. Try to avoid freestanding ATMs, especially if they have no familiar markings.

DO YOUR HOMEWORK:

1. Next time you use your "home base" ATM, take a few minutes to memorize the look of it.
2. If you have to withdraw cash away from home, look around and practice healthy skepticism. That's also a good way to keep from getting mugged at a cash machine.
3. If you try to use an ATM and it displays a message that your transaction cannot be processed right now, make a mental note of the location of the ATM and the wording of the message. Call your bank and see if that ATM has been out of order and, if so, what the notification message was supposed to say.
4. Stay on top of your bank balance and bank statements. Personally, I *hate* cross-checking my receipts against my statement, but it *is* a worthwhile habit.

FINANCES

WHERE TO COMPLAIN:

The U.S. Secret Service is the agency investigating this ATM scam; file a report with the office closest to you. For good measure, also contact your local police department's financial crimes unit.

SEE ALSO:

FINANCES: **Checking Account,** SCAMS: Bank Examiner, Nigerian Letter

Charity

Giving to charity should make you feel good and help a good cause. But beware. There are fake charities out there. And even *real* charities may make poor use of your donation dollars. Experts estimate that 10 percent of donations are misused. Americans are generous, so that 10 percent is a number in the billions of dollars. That's why you shouldn't write a check until you've checked out the charity.

Here's the thing. There's no law requiring that any particular percentage of your contribution must go toward the cause. Poorly run charities may spend your money on executive salaries and additional fund raising instead of on charitable programs. In addition, for-profit solicitors that raise money for charities may *keep* most of the cash and give only a tiny percentage to the organization you intended to help. It's perfectly legal and utterly frustrating.

That's why you need to do your homework—especially if you're prepared to make a generous gift. Charity watchdogs say that at least 60 percent of the money a charity spends should go toward its stated mission. More is even better. You can ask the charity itself what portion of your money will actually do some good, but you may not get a straight answer. For example, some charities have been known to count telemarketing and direct mail fund-raising campaigns as "educational" efforts.

Instead, check out the charity by contacting your state government and a private watchdog group. Many states require charities to register and provide basic information about their finances to operate legally in the state. Usually the state attorney general or the secretary of state carries out this function. Some private groups scrutinize charities, too. The **BBB Wise Giving Alliance,** probably the best known, now bestows a seal of approval on charities that meet certain strict standards.

As you do your research, beware of charities that play the "name game." Counterfeit charities often assume names and logos that are very close to those of reputable, established charities. Often they just change one word—like "society" instead of "foundation." If a

FINANCES

charity name seems a little "off" to you, check it out. If you receive a telemarketing solicitation, hang up and get the number of the well-known charity from information. Call and see if that charity is currently soliciting by phone.

Lori R. was livid when she received a call from a group with a name very similar to that of the American Diabetes Association. The caller asked for money. Lori gave him a piece of her mind instead. You see, Lori's on the board of the American Diabetes Association. For years, she's had to inject herself with insulin to avoid losing her sight, her kidneys—even her limbs. She says the pinpricks no longer hurt, but it does pain her to know that fake charities are stealing money from her cause. One footnote: sure enough, the group that contacted Lori was under investigation by the government for fraudulent solicitation.

Charities that lend their names to for-profit enterprises are another twist you need to be aware of. The charities figure that it's money they wouldn't have gotten otherwise. But donors need to realize that often only a minuscule amount of money makes it to the charity. Again, that's perfectly legal. For example, I once investigated gumball machines with charity logos on them. I found one machine labeled with the name of a charity that had gone under years before. Of course, the for-profit vendor was still collecting the coins. I got a copy of another charity's vending contract. The charity rented out its name for $1.25 a month per machine, but the vendor made about $110 per machine every month! Of course, a quarter isn't a big investment, and you do get a gumball for your money, but charities also lend their names to big-ticket businesses like used-car dealers that run donation programs.

Not only do you need to make sure your donation is legitimate, you may also want to be sure your *tax deduction* is legitimate. Fake charities often brag that they're tax-exempt. That just means they don't have to pay taxes. Just because a business is tax-exempt, doesn't mean your contribution is tax-*deductible*. Other ploys: unscrupulous operators may go on and on about having a "tax ID number." Meaningless. All companies have to have tax ID numbers. Fake charities may also print, "Keep this receipt for your records," on their paperwork to give the impression you're going to get a tax break. Don't fall for it. The IRS could prosecute *you* for claiming a fraudulent deduction.

For that matter, even if the IRS really has granted nonprofit 501(c)(3) status to a group, that's no indication of quality. The IRS doesn't have the time or staff to carefully scrutinize those organizations that apply for charity status. I once got a tip about a 501(c)(3) company. The IRS had overlooked the fact that the founder was a convicted felon who kept most of the group's money for himself and didn't even register with the state as required by law.

KNOW THE SIGNS:

1. Be alert to names that sound slightly "off." The same goes for logos.
2. If a group refuses to send you written information, that's a bad sign.
3. If the person soliciting your contribution can't answer basic questions about the organization, be wary.
4. If you receive a thank-you note or an invoice for a contribution you never pledged to make, that's a classic tactic. Don't fall for it.
5. Solicitors who pressure you to give on the spot are not to be trusted. The need will still be there after you've done your homework.
6. Charities that offer to send a courier or private shipper to pick up your contribution may be trying to avoid mail fraud laws.

QUESTIONS TO ASK:

FINANCES

1. What's the full name, address, and phone number of the charity?
2. Do you work directly for the charity, or are you a paid fundraiser? If you're a paid fund-raiser, what percentage does your company keep?
3. What will my contribution be used for?
4. Can you send me literature about the charity and a financial statement so I can decide whether to give?
5. Is my contribution tax-deductible?
6. Are you a 501(c)(3) organization?

DO YOUR HOMEWORK:

1. Before you give, make sure the charity is registered with your state, if required. Some tiny charities and church groups do not have to register.
2. Also check with one of the private watchdog groups that monitors charities. These groups can tell you what percentage of the organization's revenue goes toward the cause. The **BBB Wise Giving Alliance's** Web site is **www.give.org**; you can find the **American Institute of Philanthropy** at www.charitywatch.org.
3. The state or a watchdog group should be able to tell you if the group is a bona fide 501(c)(3). You can also check with the **IRS** by going to **www.irs.gov** and looking for publication number 78. Or call the IRS customer service number, **(877) 829-5500.**
4. Make your payment by check or credit card, so there's an independent record of your gift. Never give cash.

SEE ALSO:

CARS: **Donations**; SCAMS: **Police and Fire Funds**

Checking Accounts

FINANCES

It's printed right on your checks—all the information somebody needs to rob you blind. The numerals in the lower left-hand corner are your account number and your "routing and transit number." With these digits in hand, a thief can issue a blank check, called a "demand draft," for any amount of money. Or the thief can withdraw the funds electronically without doing any paperwork at all. He or she doesn't even need your signature. By the time you discover the scam, the thief has wired the money to another state or country and disappeared.

This is a popular ploy with fraudulent telemarketers, especially those pushing sweepstakes, magazines, and "guaranteed" credit cards and loans. Smooth-talking salespeople have all sorts of excuses for asking for your account information. Alternatively, if you send a check through the mail to buy something, the person on the other end could also get your account information *that* way.

Shirley S. got a call from a man selling cellular telephone service. He made it sound like he was with a major phone company. In addition to a cell phone, he promised her all sorts of extras like insurance, frequent-flier miles, and long-distance service. Shirley agreed to let the caller debit $19.95 from her account and gave him those all-important numbers. The salesman told Shirley she could cancel within seven days of receiving a package from the company. Of course, the package never came, but the money in her account started to go. When Shirley reported the matter to her bank, the fraud department found a Canadian company draining her account.

KNOW THE SIGNS:

Crooks often claim they need your account information:

1. To make the transaction faster and easier for you.
2. To break what you owe them into monthly payments as a courtesy to you.
3. To check your credit.
4. To verify your ability to make payments.
5. To verify your account or payment information.
6. To credit your prize money to your account.
7. To verify your identity.
8. For confirmation.

DO YOUR HOMEWORK:

FINANCES

1. Never give your bank account number out over the phone or the Internet—*especially* to someone who called *you.* Use a credit card instead.
2. Review your bank statement each month and compare it with your checkbook.
3. If you do want to pay a regular monthly bill by direct debit, make sure you've given written authorization to your bank.
4. Think twice before signing documents that ask for a checking account number.

WHERE TO COMPLAIN:

If a thief taps into your checking account, let your bank know the moment you discover the crime. With speed and luck, your bank will be able to demand reimbursement from the crook's bank.

SEE ALSO:

FINANCES: **ATMs**; SCAMS: Bank Examiner

Home Equity Loans/ Lines of Credit

Home equity loans and lines of credit are beneficial—but risky. You have "equity" in your house if it's worth more than you still owe on it. Once you get to the point where you have lots of equity and don't owe so much anymore, banks are more than happy to send you back into debt. The key is to make sure you can afford to make the monthly payments out of your current income.

First, the good news. If you've got sizable equity in your home, banks now offer you a way to tap that wealth without selling the house. Home equity loans and lines of credit can help you do things like go back to school or add on to your house. Sober purposes like this are the best use of the money.

Home equity loans and lines can also help you get out from under credit card debt faster than you'd be able to otherwise. They offer lower interest rates and the possibility of writing off the interest on your taxes. (Whether the interest is deductible depends on the amount of the loan and the amount of equity in your home.) However, this only works if you are making good progress in paying off credit card debt and just want to speed it up.

If you're having *trouble* making your credit card payments and you consolidate them with a home equity loan, what makes you think you won't have trouble paying off *that* loan too? If you default on your credit cards, you just lose your good credit rating. If you default on a home equity loan, you could lose your *house* (plus all the equity you've built up in it.) Serious stuff.

Now, let me detail some more dangers. Some lenders offer loans equal to 100 percent or more of the equity in your home. They're not doing you any favors. If you decide you want to sell your house and home prices have dropped, you will have to pay off the mortgage and home equity debt out of your own pocket. Never accept a loan that eats up so much of your equity.

"Equity stripping" is another concern. Some predatory lenders calculate their loans based on how much equity you have in the house rather than on whether your income will allow you to repay the loan. They may even fabricate your loan application to make it *look* like you make more money than you actually do. When you inevitably fall behind in your payments, the lender takes possession of your little piece of property.

Balloon payments are the other pitfall. If your loan or credit line is structured so that you owe a large final payment, you may not be able to make it. If that happens, you'll be forced to take out another loan—possibly at a time when interest rates are unfavorable. Worse yet, you could lose the house.

Home equity loans and lines of credit are basically second mortgages, only dressed up with less burdensome-sounding names. You should know that both come with closing costs, another thing that cuts into their usefulness. Keep in mind, when lenders state the APR, or annual percentage rate, of a home equity loan, they're required to include closing costs and fees in that rate. When they state the APR of a home equity *line of credit,* closing costs and fees are not included. They're extra. You're comparing apples and oranges. Here are the other ways in which loans and lines of credit differ.

FINANCES

A home equity *loan* is basically just a second mortgage. It's for a set amount of money, and the bank cuts you a check for that amount up front. Home equity loans come with fixed interest rates. Your monthly payment stays the same for the life of the loan. You can usually choose whether you want the loan to last, say, five, ten, or twenty years. Home equity loans work best if you have a fixed expense you want to pay for, like remodeling or building a pool.

A home equity *line of credit* is more like a credit card. You have a credit limit, and you can tap into the line as you need it. Your bank will give you checks, an ATM card, or a credit card to access the credit line. Home equity lines have variable interest rates, so your monthly payment will change over the course of the loan. You should know that some home equity lines start with a low introductory rate, then jump to a much higher interest rate. Some banks also charge transaction fees each time you tap into the account. Home equity lines of credit are better suited for fluctuating expenses like college tuition and books.

A couple of cautions: because you access your home equity line using financial tools you're used to, like checks and credit cards, it can be tempting to charge a great vacation or a fabulous wardrobe. But remember, this is not a normal source of money. Your house and your financial future are on the line. On the flip side, if you end up *not* using your home equity line very much, that can be a bad deal, too, because of all those closing costs you paid.

DO YOUR HOMEWORK:

1. Consider how much money you really need and never borrow more than that.
2. Do some soul searching before you use the equity in your home to pay off past purchases you made with credit cards.
3. Figure out which would work better for you, a home equity loan or line of credit.
4. Shop around for the best interest rate and fees. Be sure to try the bank where you have your checking account and the lender who holds your mortgage. They may offer incentives to existing customers.
5. If you are unhappy with the loan once you've signed it, you have the right to cancel within three days, as long as you do so in writing. The lender must refund all fees.
6. Don't carry home equity line checks with you. You don't want to risk somebody stealing them and tapping the equity in your home, your biggest investment.

FINANCES

SEE ALSO:

CREDIT: Credit Card Debt; FINANCES: Predatory Lending, Refinancing; HOME BUYING AND RENTING: **Closing Costs,** Mortgages

Investment Fraud

They promise they can turn water into oil, sand into gold. They are investment swindlers, and you could be hearing from them soon. Investment fraud falls into two broad categories: fraud committed by *real* investment brokers and fraud committed by *fake* investment brokers. Both are devastating to the victims.

Brokers who are licensed and work for legitimate investment firms can still cheat you. It's a tricky situation, because often the same person you look to for investment *advice,* is also trying to *sell* you something. I mean, how can you be sure the advice is unbiased? Your nest egg is riding on that broker's integrity—or lack of it. I would never do business with a broker who cold-called me out of the blue. (Remember, be the hunter!) Instead, find an investment advisor through friends who've had a good experience. Make sure that person is licensed and has a clean record before you hand over your precious savings.

One way bad brokers get you is by churning. Since many brokers are paid a commission each time they make a trade for you, they have a powerful incentive to trade as often as possible. The broker will switch you rapidly from one investment to another instead of investing for the long term. One way to avoid this is by asking for a "fee-based" account. With that kind of arrangement, the broker makes a small percentage of your account's value each year. He or she is motivated to make your account grow rather than to make multiple trades.

An individual broker could also mislead you because of pressure from his or her own firm. By now, the stories are infamous: Wall Street firms that recommended lousy stocks just to get investment banking business with those same companies. Sometimes the moti-

FINANCES

vation is simpler than that. Some investment firms offer their brokers a bonus every time they sell a particular mutual fund. The broker may push you into that investment, even though it's not the best one for your needs.

Caroline R. discovered an unscrupulous broker had embellished her elderly mother's investment application to get her into a high-risk real estate investment. He invented assets like a vacation home and thousands of shares of stock so she would qualify. Caroline's mom lost $15,000. The broker lost his license.

Unlicensed brokers who sell *fake* investments are even *more* devastating. They typically find their victims via the phone. They've also been known to advertise in newspapers and magazines or pay their initial investors to give them referrals. These days, investment swindlers also operate on the Internet, sometimes creating entire firms that aren't real. One of the most obnoxious tactics for finding new victims is known as an affinity scam. Investment swindlers play to your religion or your ethnicity and get referrals by building on that trust.

Just as the brokers and brokerages are unlicensed, the investments they sell are typically *unregistered*. Even though registered securities are unpredictable, at least securities exchanges have standards for what companies they'll accept and strict rules to ensure fair dealing. Unregistered securities have no such rules.

Ponzi schemes are one type of unregistered investment. They're named after Charles Ponzi, who defrauded countless people in the 1920s. Ponzi operators promise investors a high rate of return and often say it's guaranteed. The very first investors *do* get paid, which helps create hype. But where does the money come from? From the funds contributed by *later* investors. There is no actual business that makes money. It's all a transfer game. When the Ponzi operator can't find any more new recruits, the top-heavy structure collapses.

I once investigated a company that persuaded hundreds of investors to plunk down money for schemes like Internet shopping malls. Of course, it turned out the investment opportunities didn't even exist. The boiler room operation closed down, and the con men made off with the money.

They left so fast they didn't have time to destroy their training manuals and audiotapes. As investigators combed the offices for evidence of fraud, they let me inspect what was left behind. In one document, entitled "The Psychology of the Sale," the company advised, "by making your clients feel important and wanted, you will build their ego. This is the key." In a sales script, called "The Greed Close," the company told its telemarketers to promise: "You could make over $3 million in just twelve months."

I listened to an audiotape of an actual call in which a salesman tried to get an elderly woman to invest her money in an Internet shopping mall. Here's their exchange. Woman: "I'm not too up to date on any Internet or computer-type things. At my age, I didn't think it was necessary." Salesman: "You don't even need to know how to turn on a computer to be an investor with us in this project. What you simply need to have is some vision, some foresight, and some courage to take advantage of the tremendous opportunity that you have before you."

KNOW THE SIGNS:

1. If a caller says you have to buy now or miss out on the opportunity of a lifetime, that's a warning sign. Usually unscrupulous operators have some excuse why you need to act now. Never allow yourself to be pressured into making a quick decision.
2. Another worn out catchphrase is, "Get in on a ground-floor opportunity." If a *stranger* is offering you this great opportunity, you have to wonder why *me?*
3. If the broker promises huge returns, that's illegal. Brokers can't *guarantee* you'll make *any* money on an investment—especially big money.
4. If the broker says you're guaranteed not to *lose* money, run! Downplaying risk is a huge red flag. Fake brokers may even try to insult you and say something like, "Obviously you don't have the courage to take advantage of this fantastic opportunity."
5. If the broker wants to be a joint owner of your account, that's a telltale sign of fraud.

FINANCES

6. If you're asked to send money to an address other than that of the brokerage firm or the company listed in the prospectus, ask questions. Demand answers.

QUESTIONS TO ASK:

These questions should weed out bad brokers and scare off fake ones.

1. How did you get my name? (Don't accept oily answers like, "You're part of a list of highly qualified investors.") Demand a specific source.
2. What does the company you want me to invest in do or make? Who are the principals and officers? You'd be amazed how many people invest in a company without understanding what it does.
3. Is this a registered security? Which exchange is it traded on? What's the ticker symbol? These specifics will help you verify whether the investment is for real.
4. What government agency regulates the company? An investment swindler won't like the sound of this! If he or she does tell you the name of the agency, say you want to check the company's record with that agency, then follow through.
5. What type of regular accounting statements do you provide? A con artist won't have a good, detailed answer for you, since he or she doesn't send any statements at all.
6. Would you mind explaining this investment to my attorney, banker, or investment advisor? Heh, heh, heh. This is my favorite question!
7. How much are the fees and commissions? A real investment broker will answer this for you. A con artist will, too, but he'll make something up.
8. Can I liquidate the investment any time I want? If you learn you can't sell the investment, or you have to pay a fine for doing so, consider whether that's in your best interests.
9. If a dispute arises, how will it be resolved? A legitimate firm will have a detailed answer for you. A crook will be impatient with this line of questioning.
10. What stocks, bonds, or mutual funds would you recommend for me? If the broker has an instant answer and hasn't even gotten

FINANCES

to know you or your needs yet, that's not good. Investments should be tailor-made for each individual based on the individual's goals and tolerance for risk.

DO YOUR HOMEWORK:

1. If you're not investment-savvy, ask another brokerage firm, an accountant, or an attorney for input. State securities officers may also offer guidance. Asking friends is not enough, since in some cases friends are the ones who draw other people into affinity scams.
2. Do a background check on the brokerage company and/or the investment by calling your local Better Business Bureau and your county and state consumer protection offices.
3. Find out if the broker is licensed. You can do this by calling whatever department regulates securities dealers in your state. Often it's the office of the state comptroller or the division of banking and finance.
4. If the broker is licensed or was once licensed, the same office can give you a Central Registration Depository or "CRD" report on him or her. It will include the broker's work history, whether he or she has ever been disciplined or involved in lawsuits, settlements, and criminal cases.
5. If you don't like the idea of getting investment advice from the same person who wants to sell you investments, you could look for a **Certified Financial Planner** (CFP) who charges an hourly rate for advice.
6. Make sure you obtain, read, understand, and keep copies of all your investment paperwork. Don't sign anything you don't understand.
7. Review your statements to make sure no unauthorized trades appear. If you find a discrepancy, ask for a written correction.

FINANCES

WHERE TO COMPLAIN:

To complain about an *unlicensed* broker, contact your county and state consumer protection offices and the state agency that licenses brokers. The licensing agency will probably be the one to conduct an investigation. To file a complaint about a *licensed* broker, contact the state agency that licenses brokers and the National Association of Securities Dealers.

SEE ALSO:

FINANCES: Savings Bonds; INSURANCE: Life Insurance.

Predatory Lending

If buying a home is the American dream, then predatory lending is the American nightmare. Predatory lending typically occurs in refinancing deals. Unscrupulous lenders cause people to lose their homes and neighborhoods to lose their luster. Aggressive mortgage brokers target the poor, the elderly, minorities, and women, but it can happen to anyone.

Charles K. is a combat veteran who lives on a fixed income. He was a month or two behind on his mortgage, so he wanted to refinance in hopes of arranging a lower monthly payment. The mortgage broker promised Charles he could lower his payment from $980 a month to $880. The broker advised Charles to stop making payments to his old mortgage company, because his new loan would be ready soon. But then the broker waited more than a month to schedule Charles' closing. At that closing, Charles learned his new monthly payment was $1,250—hundreds more than the old payment he had been struggling to make. By now, Charles' old mortgage company was threatening to foreclose on his home, so he felt trapped and he signed for the new loan.

When I investigated Charles's case, I learned his monthly payment was jacked up illegally. By law, the broker was supposed to inform him the price was going up. The *reason* the monthly payment was so high is that the brokerage firm charged $13,000 to process the loan. Pure profit for the broker. This abusive fee was then rolled into Charles's loan, so he ended up owing $146,000 on a house that was only worth $126,000. Charles couldn't afford his new monthly payments. Eventually, he declared bankruptcy, and the bank sold his home on the courthouse steps.

FINANCES

That's just one example. There are dozens of variations on predatory lending. Predatory lenders often work through home improvement companies. These contractors approach people about sprucing up their homes. If the homeowners say they can't afford to, the contractor then steers them toward a predatory lender for a construction loan. Of course, the loan fees are high and the quality of the carpentry is low.

Some predatory lenders purposely structure their loans so the monthly payments are too high for the borrower. When the borrower defaults, the lender offers yet another loan with additional closing costs and fees. This is called "flipping." Consumer advocates have documented cases in which homeowners were flipped into more than ten different loans in just four years. One homeowner paid $29,000 in closing costs to get a loan for $26,000. Outrageous!

KNOW THE SIGNS:

1. Predatory lenders often promise one set of terms when they talk to you, then jack up the price at closing. It's a sign that you're in for a rough ride.

2. If a mortgage broker asks you to sign a blank application form, that's a red flag. The broker may intend to falsify your credit history so you'll qualify for a loan you can't afford.

3. Adding cosigners is another ploy. Unscrupulous brokers may ask you to come up with a cosigner, knowing full well that person doesn't really intend to contribute to the payments. It's another way of getting you an expensive loan that the broker will make a lot of money on.

4. If a lender refuses to give you a copy of the good faith estimate, that's a signal that the estimate will change. The lender doesn't want you to have written proof of the terms you were first offered.

5. Predatory lenders often structure loans with balloon payments at the end. The monthly payment seems manageable, but in a few years' time you could owe tens of thousands of dollars all at once. Of course, the broker is hoping you won't be able to afford the balloon payment and you'll refinance *again*, generating more fees for the firm.

FINANCES

6. If you see "credit life insurance" as a line item in your loan, beware! This kind of insurance is supposed to pay off your loans if you die. It's a rip-off. A basic life insurance policy is all you need. Predatory lenders charge exorbitant premiums for credit life as well as credit disability and involuntary unemployment insurance.

7. The same goes for homeowner's insurance. Predatory lenders have been known to add expensive homeowner's insurance to a loan even though the homeowner already has insurance through an outside company.

8. Some predatory lenders continue to abuse you *after* you've gotten your loan by tacking expenses onto your monthly payments. They may charge late fees even when your payments are on time. If you try to refinance with another lender, they may refuse to provide you with an accurate payoff statement.

DO YOUR HOMEWORK:

1. Be the hunter, not the hunted. Don't borrow money from a company that slips a flier under your door or blares at you in a TV commercial. Find your own mortgage company. Check with the company that currently holds your mortgage if you want to refinance. Go to the bank where you have your checking account. Ask friends and neighbors if they've had a good experience.

2. Once you narrow down your list, check out the mortgage brokers or lenders by contacting the BBB and your county and state consumer protection agencies.

3. When a mortgage broker or lender gives you an estimate, get it in writing and make sure you have your own copy.

4. If you want a loan to make home repairs, hire your lender and contractor separately.

5. Never sign any paperwork that contains blanks.

6. Never obey a mortgage broker who suggests you stop paying on your old mortgage loan. This could affect your credit record and trap you into accepting a predatory loan.

7. Demand a copy of your closing paperwork a couple of days before the closing. Review it to see if the terms are different from what you were offered initially.

FINANCES

8. When you refinance with a different lender, you have the right to back out of the loan for three days after your closing. If you detect problems at your closing, immediately ask a real estate attorney for an opinion, so you can take advantage of that window.

WHERE TO COMPLAIN:

If yours is an FHA loan, complain to HUD, the Department of Housing and Urban Development. If you've got a veteran's loan, complain to the Department of Veterans Affairs. Contact your state banking department and your county and state consumer protection offices, too. If they can't help you, they'll give you a referral. Your city or county office of fair housing may also be able to help. Complain to the BBB so other consumers will have a paper trail to follow.

SEE ALSO:

HOME BUYING AND RENTING: **Closing Costs,** Mortgages; FINANCES: **Refinancing**

Refinancing

Refinancing can be a gold mine where you find money—or a mine shaft down which you *pour* your money. It all depends on three factors on a sliding scale: how much you can reduce your interest rate, how much you'll pay in closing costs, and how long you plan to live in the home.

FINANCES

The old rule of thumb is that you should refinance if you can get a rate at least two percentage points less than your old rate. That's still a reasonable rule, but it's not enough. The lower mortgage rates get, the less meaningful the 2 percent rule is. Let's rewrite the rule: If you can get a rate two percentage points less than your current rate, you should *consider* refinancing. If you plan to live in the house a *long* time, you should look into it, even if rates are just one percentage point lower.

The real key is the break-even point. That's the number of months you need to keep the home after refinancing in order to recover your closing costs. For example, if you pay $3,000 in closing costs and you manage to lower your mortgage payments by $150 a month, you would reach the break-even point in twenty months. As long as you plan to live in the home at least that long, refinancing could be worthwhile. It's a sliding scale. The smaller your savings, the longer you need to stay put.

There are a couple of strategies to minimize the price of closing costs when you refinance. One is to ask your current lender to refinance you. To keep your business, your lender may be willing to waive certain closing costs. For example, ask for a "drive-by" appraisal instead of a full appraisal. Try to get your lender to skip the credit check—after all, the company is intimately familiar with your payment record. If you bought the house fairly recently, you can ask the title agent for the "reissue rate" on your title insurance, often a savings of 50 percent.

Your other choice is to shop for "zero-cost" refinancing. It's not actually free, but it does allow you to avoid up-front costs. Negotiate an interest rate. Then ask the broker or lender to absorb your closing costs by raising that interest rate by an eighth or a quarter of a percent. True, you don't get the lowest possible refinancing rate, but if you only plan to keep the home for a few years, maybe that doesn't matter. The benefit is that you immediately cut your interest rate and monthly payment with no out-of-pocket costs.

Other factors complicate refinancing decisions as well. For example, did you ever consider that by reducing your interest rate, you reduce the amount you can write off on your income taxes? In close cases, this could tilt the teeter-totter in favor of sticking with your old loan. The length of the loan is another variable. For example, if you're approaching retirement and your old loan is almost paid off, refinancing could extend the length of your loan and cost you more.

When you refinance, be on the lookout for predatory lenders. If you currently have a "prime" loan, the kind given to people with good credit, but you've now fallen behind on your payments, don't believe anybody who tells you that you can refinance for less.

FINANCES

Missing mortgage payments plunges your credit score down to "sub-prime" loan levels, and these loans always carry higher interest rates. If you're promised a lower interest rate, chances are it's a bait and switch deal and the rate will rise dramatically at closing.

DO YOUR HOMEWORK:

1. Read the newspaper, go online, and ask mortgage brokers and lenders what their going rates are.
2. Be sure to check with your original mortgage company, too. Some lenders offer their current customers incentives to keep their business.
3. Go online and use a mortgage calculator or ask a mortgage professional to help you determine what rate would result in savings for you.
4. Do a break-even analysis to see how long you need to stay in the home to make refinancing worthwhile. The formula is: closing costs ÷ monthly savings = months you must keep the home.
5. Get written estimates of the rate you could qualify for, the monthly payment, and closing costs.
6. Insist on keeping a copy of this document to ward off predatory lenders.
7. Before you sign a refinancing contract, check out the reputation of the mortgage broker or lender.
8. Do what you can to keep your closing costs down and increase your savings.

WHERE TO COMPLAIN:

If a mortgage broker or lender steers you wrong, complain to your county and state consumer protection offices and the BBB. For mortgage lenders, you can also try your state department of banking or whatever agency regulates lenders in your state.

FINANCES

SEE ALSO:

CREDIT: Credit Scoring, Credit *Re*scoring; HOME BUYING AND RENTING: **Closing Costs, Mortgages;** FINANCES: **Predatory Lending**

Savings Bonds

Here's a consumer quiz for you. True or false: "You should hang on to U.S. savings bonds as long as possible." The answer is: FALSE. Today's U.S. savings bonds mature in thirty years. After that, they stop increasing in value. (There was a time when the government also issued *forty*-year bonds.) Unfortunately, millions of Americans either don't realize this or have forgotten they even *have* savings bonds.

Twenty-five million U.S. savings bonds have never been cashed in. If you were to line them up end to end, they would stretch all the way from Washington, D.C., to San Francisco, California. The total value of all those orphan bonds is about $9 billion! Most of us could use a little "found money." At the very least, you'll want to reinvest that money to get it working for you again. The U.S. Treasury Department has launched a campaign to help people claim their bonds.

Barbara S. heard about the campaign. She had been holding onto a savings bond for thirty-two years. A family member paid the discounted rate of $375 for it back in the 1970s, and gave it to Barbara as a gift. It had a face value of $500. Barbara had no idea how much it would be worth today. When she cashed it in, she got a pleasant surprise: $2,800!

DO YOUR HOMEWORK:

FINANCES

1. Check around your house to see if you can find any evidence of uncashed savings bonds. If you find the paper certificates, check them to see if they've matured yet.
2. To double-check whether there is an outstanding savings bond in your name, go to the Treasury Department's Web site, **www.publicdebt.treas.gov/sav/sbtdhunt.htm.**
3. If you feel fairly certain you own an outstanding savings bond, but it's not listed on the Web site, you can write to the **Treasury Department** and ask the agency to search old microfiche records by hand.

WHERE TO COMPLAIN:

The only thing you've got to complain about is if you don't have a long-lost bond that you get to cash in!

SEE ALSO:

FINANCES: Unclaimed Money

Taxes

I admit it. In a sick sort of way, I enjoy getting my tax stuff together. I don't actually *do* my taxes. No, no, no, no, no. That's a special form of torture that I leave to the professionals. I'm talking about gathering together all the receipts and bills and pay stubs I need to claim every possible deduction I'm entitled to. It's my version of clipping coupons . . . or bargain shopping. A wise accountant once explained it to me this way: Say you're in the 27 percent tax bracket. If you itemize, then for every hundred dollars of deductions you can claim, you save $27 on your taxes!

OK, so I nickel and dime the IRS. There *are* ways to save *bigger* chunks of money, too. If you're an investor, consider selling some stocks at a loss—especially at the end of the year. Even though you're taking a loss for tax purposes, you may not lose money at all. You see, after thirty-one days you're allowed to buy those stocks back. If you believe in a company, but it's going through a stagnant period, perhaps the price won't fluctuate much while you're out of it. You just buy the stock back and you're right where you started, except that you saved some money by offsetting your capital gains. Another variation is to sell a mutual fund at a loss. If you move your money to a similar fund in the same family, you won't even have to pay a commission. A thorough broker or investment advisor should offer you these options, but many don't, so ask.

FINANCES

If you think being taxed is a drag, being *audited* is devastating. It's unpleasant, even for people who have nothing to hide. You usually have to hire accountants and lawyers to help you prove your innocence. That's expensive. And even if you're cleared, the IRS doesn't reimburse you for the time and money you were forced to spend defending yourself. The IRS is the largest law enforcement agency in the United States—bigger than the police departments of New York City, Los Angeles, Chicago, Detroit, and Philadelphia combined. That's what you're up against.

Now, if you're one who doesn't mind tax time because you love getting a refund, a word of caution. Many accountants and tax preparation firms now offer what they call "rapid refund loans" or "refund anticipation loans." (They often put the word "loan" in smaller print.) These companies hype the fact that you can get your refund money in twenty-four to forty-eight hours. What they downplay is the fact that it'll cost you a lot of money.

You see, when you participate in one of these programs, the money you're getting is *not* coming from the Internal Revenue Service. IT'S A *LOAN* FROM THE TAX PREP COMPANY. With fees and interest, this loan can cost you up to 30 percent of your refund. Expressed as an annual percentage rate or APR, it's as much as 116 percent! Say you're expecting a $1,500 refund. That's $450 that you're giving away for no real reason. And that's just the cost of the loan; it *doesn't* include the price of preparing your return!

Here's how it works: You pay a company to prepare your taxes. The company lends you the amount of your expected refund. When your *real* refund comes through, you repay the loan, plus fees and interest. If the IRS reduces the amount of your refund for some reason, you still have to repay the high-interest loan. I don't think it's worthwhile at all. Consider this: If you file electronically and ask for direct deposit, the IRS itself can get you your refund in ten days to two weeks. So, by holding out for just a few days more, you save up to 30 percent.

In addition, over the years I've seen a lot of problems with these refund loan programs. Michelle C. needed her money fast, so she went to a tax preparation company and signed up for a refund loan. She expected the money in no more than three days, but it ended up taking three weeks. Why? Michelle didn't qualify for the fastest refund loan because of her tax status. And she didn't notice the fine print that said she would automatically be rolled into another, slower program. She paid all those fees when she could have gotten the money faster from Uncle Sam himself.

DO YOUR HOMEWORK:

1. Make a series of manila folders for different types of tax deductions and slip receipts into them all year long to reduce the pre-April 15th panic. For example, I have folders for business entertainment, business expenses, business travel, charitable contributions, mortgage interest, and job search expenses.
2. Ask your broker or investment advisor about selling stocks at a loss to offset your capital gains.
3. Give to charity before December 31 and take a deduction. If you're low on cash, donate used clothing and household items. You can also donate stocks to charity.
4. You can get another easy extra deduction by making your January mortgage payment in December. Of course, that means you won't have that expense for next year's taxes, but maybe you need it more this time around.
5. When you fill out your return, neatness and accuracy count. Triple-check your math and don't forget to sign your return. The IRS catches six million math errors every year. You don't want to increase your audit odds by making the IRS take a second look.
6. If you file for an extension, remember, you *still* have to pay your *estimated* tax on April 15. Many people don't realize that. You can look up the average tax for your income level online or in the back of a 1040 booklet. Make sure you pay at least 90 percent of what you owe to avoid fees and penalties.
7. If you need your refund fast, file online or have your accountant do it for you. Ask the IRS to deposit the refund directly into your bank account, and you could have your money in as little as ten days.

WHERE TO COMPLAIN:

Contact your county and state consumer protection offices and your state attorney general to complain about abusive refund loans.

FINANCES

If you want to complain about taxes in general, call your congressional representative!

Unclaimed Money

Have you ever put on a winter coat for the first cold snap of the season and found a $10 bill in the pocket? Nice, huh? Well, government unclaimed money accounts are like a winter coat with really deep pockets. The trick is to figure out *which* government agency keeps the winter coat. The other trick is to slap away the hands of all the opportunists who are trying to reach into those pockets and get *your* unclaimed money.

Unclaimed money consists of apartment and utility deposits, back pay, overpayments, tax refunds, health care reimbursements, and so on. If you fail to collect money that's owed to you, honest companies eventually turn that money over to the government—usually at the state level. Often the state comptroller or the division of banking and finance holds it, but every state is different.

Many states publish lengthy lists of people who are owed money in local newspapers. Trouble is, if you no longer live in that area, you won't see it. And if you still live in the area, you've probably already collected it. If you really want to find unclaimed money held in your name, you'll need to do a little detective work. Call the state information number or go to the state Web site for each state you've lived in. Find out which agency is in charge of unclaimed money, then contact that agency and ask if you're on the list of the lucky.

If you're trying to find pension money held for you from a long-ago job, that's a little trickier. First, think through whether you were vested in the pension plan at that old job. Usually it takes five years of employment. If you left the job after 1975, that helps, because federal law began protecting pensions more after that. You may have quite a chore ahead of you trying to track down that old company— especially if it has merged, been bought, or has gone out of business. For help, try the **Pension Benefit Guaranty Corporation**, at **www.pbgc.gov/search/default.htm.** For step-by-step guidance for finding a lost pension go to **www.pueblo.gsa.gov,** click on the money section, and read the article about finding pensions.

If you go out in search of unclaimed money, you may very well find it. If money-grubbers come in search of *you,* you may *lose* it. It's a classic scheme. Clever businessmen try to sell you something you can get from the government for free. They often use official-sounding names and logos to make it *seem* like they're with the government. Some promoters contact you and say there *may* be money held in your name. They have no idea; they're just trying to get you to pay them to do a search. Other promoters actually obtain government lists of people who are owed money and contact those people in hopes of earning a finder's fee.

If a private company contacts you about unclaimed money, try to get the caller to spill the beans on where the money is being held, then collect the money yourself. If the company won't say, at least you have a hint that there may be money out there in your name. If you do decide to pay a company to search for you, don't hand over any money up front. Also, use caution in providing personal information. It could be an identity theft scheme. Pay only when the unclaimed money is found and safely deposited in your account.

DO YOUR HOMEWORK:

1. Find out which state departments hold unclaimed money in places where you've lived, then contact those agencies and ask if you're on their list.
2. If you were vested in a pension at an old job and you haven't received it, launch a search. Spouses of the deceased are typically eligible for partial benefits, too.
3. If you get a notice saying there's unclaimed money waiting for you, verify whether the notice is from a public or private agency. If it's a private company, consider looking for the money yourself.

FINANCES

WHERE TO COMPLAIN:

If an unclaimed money promoter cheats you, and the solicitation originally came through the mail, contact your local U.S. Postal

Inspector's office, which investigates mail fraud. If the company contacted you in some other way, complain to your county and state consumer protection offices and the BBB.

SEE ALSO:

FINANCES: Savings Bonds

CHAPTER 8

Insurance

Cancellation and Nonrenewal

"Nonrenewal" sounds like a ridiculous corporate euphemism for cancellation, but, actually, in the world of insurance they're different. The amazing thing is that even if you make your payments on time and never make a claim, your insurance company could choose not to insure you anymore. This happens with both auto and homeowner's policies.

If your insurance policy has been active for more than sixty days, the company can't cancel it without cause. Legitimate causes include if you misrepresented yourself when you applied, failed to pay your insurance bill, or your driver's license has been revoked. In such cases, the company can cancel you at any time, and the implication is that it's your fault.

By contrast, with *nonrenewal*, the decision may have nothing to do with you. Perhaps the insurance company is getting out of the car insurance business or pulling out of your state. If you've gotten several speeding tickets recently, the insurance company may decide not to renew you because you're a greater risk than you were when you first bought the policy. Increasingly, insurance companies are choosing not to renew people who make even one homeowner's insurance claim.

Nonrenewal happens only when your insurance policy expires. The company must give you a reason and advance notice that you're being dropped. (The precise number of days varies according to the law in your state.) If you feel the reason for nonrenewal is unfair, you can appeal the decision to your state insurance commissioner.

If your insurance company didn't *renew* you, you won't necessarily pay more or have trouble getting insurance elsewhere. If your company *canceled* you, that's another story. Get ready to pay a higher price or participate in a state insurance plan for people who can't get insurance anywhere else.

DO YOUR HOMEWORK:

1. Don't use your homeowner's insurance to pay for small losses. Cover those yourself so your company won't refuse to renew you.
2. Even calling to *inquire* about making a claim can count against you, so don't give your name if you just want to call and ask about a possible claim.
3. If your insurance company doesn't renew your policy, find out why. Verify whether you've been canceled or "nonrenewed."
4. If the reason has nothing to do with you, be sure you have that in writing, so you can show the letter to other insurance companies when you shop for a new policy.

INSURANCE

WHERE TO COMPLAIN:

If you feel the company's reasons for not renewing you are unfair, file a written complaint with your state insurance commissioner, the office that regulates insurance companies to make sure they treat customers fairly.

SEE ALSO:

INSURANCE: **Car Insurance, Homeowner's Insurance**

Car Insurance

The first car insurance policy was purchased in 1898. Back then, there were only about a hundred cars in the United States. Today there are 160 million! If you've got one of them, then you also have to get insurance. Ugh. Dull thing to spend money on—but so important. Here are some tips to help you spend as little as possible.

Experts say you can find big differences in car insurance prices if you shop around. So many of us just fall in with the company our parents used, but that's not a good idea. If you've been with the same insurance company, paying the same premium for a long time, do yourself a favor and make a few calls. Market conditions may have evolved, and you could be paying too much. It's particularly important to reprice insurance policies if your circumstances change. For example, if you start taking public transportation instead of driving many miles to work, you will almost certainly save on your car insurance.

There are some classic ways to save. Number one: Raise your deductible. Switching from a $200 deductible to $500 can save you 30 percent. Number two: Insure your car and your home with the same company. Number three: Skip the collision and comprehensive coverage if you have an older car that's not worth repairing. (Only liability insurance is required.)

You can actually save on your insurance before you even buy a car! What? That's right. You should find out how much it will cost to insure a particular model before you go out and get one. Some cars are expensive to repair. Others attract irresponsible drivers. For example, say you're young and single and you've had a couple of tickets. If you buy a muscle car with a convertible top, you could pay up to $14,000 a year to insure it!

Here's another pricey proposition: If you're planning to lease, you may be required to get a hefty insurance policy to protect the car

INSURANCE

company. Here are the numbers: One major insurance company charges $1,447 to insure a leased American sedan for six months. If you were to *buy* that same car and insure it more modestly, it would only cost $987 for six months.

A state insurance commissioner recently warned me about another practice that can cost consumers. Every state has an insurance policy of last resort for people whose driving records are so bad they can't get coverage elsewhere. It's called "pool" insurance or an "assigned risk" plan—and it's expensive. Even though it's organized by the state, you buy the policy from a private agent. Some agents specialize in pool insurance and don't offer anything else. They've been known to push drivers with good records into the pool plan just to get the business and make a commission.

Beware of another sleazy tactic, called "sliding." That's when an insurance agent slides extra coverage into your policy that you didn't request. Roadside assistance, rental car coverage—things like that. The agent may claim the coverage is free or just try to sneak it in. Truly bold agents have been known to tell customers the extra coverage is required by law. Check with your state insurance commissioner to see what kinds of coverage really *are* required.

Once you've shopped around, be sure to review your insurance policy periodically for mysterious price hikes. Earl and Betty W. suddenly found they were paying more than ever before. They spotted some fine print in their policy that said the company was charging them a new rate because of their new zip code. Insurance companies base their rates on the number of crimes and accidents in your zip code. But Earl and Betty hadn't moved! The post office had changed their zip code, and the insurance company used that as an excuse to raise their rate. I investigated, asked the state insurance commissioner for help, and got the charges reversed.

INSURANCE

DO YOUR HOMEWORK:

1. Shop around when you first get insurance and every few years after that. Experts say you should get at least three estimates.
2. Take strategic steps like raising your deductible and doing all of your insurance business with one company to save money.

3. Check the insurance rate before you buy or lease a new car.
4. Don't allow an insurance agent to push you into pool insurance.
5. Scan your policy for unauthorized coverage you didn't want.
6. Be alert to mysterious price hikes like the "zip code zap."

WHERE TO COMPLAIN:

If you have a problem with an insurance agent or insurance company, contact your state insurance commissioner.

SEE ALSO:

CARS: Accidents, Auto Body; INSURANCE: **Cancellation and Nonrenewal**

Credit Life Insurance

I once put together a series of television stories entitled, "Money Blunders," and let's just say credit life insurance was one of them. It's insurance that pays off your consumer debts if you die. Credit life isn't normally sold all by itself. Salespeople typically sneak it in when you finance a big purchase like a car. Credit life generates hefty commissions for the salespeople. It is the most overpriced insurance product on the market.

For the amount of money you'd spend on credit life, you can buy far more regular life insurance. In addition, credit life coverage is severely limited. It doesn't cover pre-existing medical conditions. If you will turn seventy during the policy period, it often becomes null and void. And your family isn't even named as the beneficiary—the lender is!

When Don P. bought his first brand-new car, it was also a brand new financial experience. The salesman told Don the bank wouldn't give him the loan unless he bought credit life insurance: $3,600 worth! Don was so eager to get the car that he signed the paperwork. But he was troubled. He did some research and learned that it's illegal for salesmen to force you to buy credit life. When Don

INSURANCE

confronted the dealership, his car payments dropped from $326 a month to just $250.

DO YOUR HOMEWORK:

1. Scan any financing agreement carefully in search of signs of credit life. If you find any, ask that it be removed.
2. If the salesman insists that you must buy credit life to get the loan, check with your state insurance commissioner. (Some states allow lenders to require credit *property* insurance on loans in which you use property or possessions as collateral.)
3. If you learn you're already paying for credit life, you can cancel it any time you want. You should receive a prorated refund.
4. If you're single with no dependents, you probably don't need any kind of life insurance. If you *do* have a family you'd like to protect, see if your regular homeowner's or life insurance policy is large enough to cover the new consumer debt. Or open a separate term life insurance policy for the exact amount of the debt. One other idea: pay for a rider on your existing whole life policy to pay the outstanding debt if something should happen to you.

WHERE TO COMPLAIN:

If a salesperson tries to sneak credit life into your contract or tells you it's required, complain to your state insurance commissioner.

SEE ALSO:

CARS: Financing; INSURANCE: **Life Insurance**

INSURANCE

Health Insurance

Have you ever wondered how health insurance came to be an employment benefit? I mean, what's the connection? Turns out it's an accident of history. During World War II, workers were scarce and companies were cash-poor because of the Great Depression. Since they couldn't afford high wages, companies began offering "fringe benefits" to attract workers. Group health insurance was one of those benefits. Since it came about as such a fluke, it could disappear just as easily. If you lose your company health benefits, you'll want to be ready.

If you lose your benefits because you lose your job, that's simple. Thanks to the Consolidated Omnibus Budget Reconciliation Act, or "COBRA," you are entitled to buy into your previous employer's group health insurance plan for up to eighteen months after you leave your job. You'll have to pay the full premium instead of just a copay, but it's still cheaper than buying individual health insurance. The COBRA plan benefits you if you (1) leave a company and become unemployed or self-employed; (2) are less than twenty-three years old and your parent leaves a company; (3) are the divorced spouse of an employee who worked at the company for at least three years; or (4) are the survivor of an employee who worked at the company for at least three years.

If you *do* need to buy your own health insurance, there *are* ways to save. For example, after your COBRA eligibility expires, try asking that same insurance company to convert you from group to individual coverage. It'll be more expensive than what you're used to paying, but probably less than if you were to buy coverage from a company that doesn't know you. Another idea: try to get a group rate somewhere else. Trade associations, professional organizations, and alumni clubs sometimes offer group health plans. Some labor unions offer health care coverage if you work freelance in a union job just a few weeks a year. If you are over age fifty, you can join AARP and get access to an extensive health care plan. Here's an odd one: Some credit card companies offer health care coverage deals.

If you choose a managed care plan in which you must see certain doctors for your health care needs, beware of "balance billing." There are a couple of different variations of this practice. Many managed care plans negotiate discounted prices with their member doctors. Some doctors then turn around and try to bill the patient to make up the difference. Balance billing also happens when a managed care provider goes bankrupt and doesn't pay at all. In that case, the doctor may try to bill you for the entire amount. Balance billing is illegal in many states. Some even require managed care

INSURANCE

plans and their participating doctors to sign "hold harmless" agreements with each other, so patients are protected if the plan goes belly up. As long as you see a *plan* doctor for *covered* services, a copayment should be your only responsibility.

Winnie A. has a lot of medical problems. She's also a savvy consumer. Winnie's taken the time to educate herself about her HMO (health maintenance organization), so when a couple of different doctors started sending her balance bills, she was livid. Winnie returned the bills with a letter stating that they were illegal. The doctors sent more. Winnie contacted state authorities, but they showed little interest because the amounts were so low. Eleven dollars here, $29 there. Finally, Winnie contacted me, and I contacted her doctors and the state. Winnie's doctors *stopped* balance billing, and state officials *started* enforcing the law.

QUESTIONS TO ASK:

1. Ask yourself: Should I buy insurance that covers most medical care, including routine visits? Or should I just get insurance that covers more catastrophic problems? (Make this decision based on your health and your income.)
2. What's the deductible? After I pay it, what percent of my medical bills am I responsible for?
3. How much will it cost me to use an out-of-network doctor?
4. Is my current doctor covered by the plan? How easy is it to switch primary care doctors?
5. Do I have to get permission to see a medical specialist?
6. Are preexisting conditions covered? How are chronic conditions treated?
7. Does the plan cover alternative treatments like acupuncture and chiropractic care? What about preventive care like mammograms and immunizations? How about birth control?
8. Does the plan cover prenatal care and childbirth?

DO YOUR HOMEWORK:

1. See how different health plans are rated. Check with the **National Committee for Quality Assurance, www.ncqa.org,**

INSURANCE

or try the Joint **Commission on Accreditation of Healthcare Organizations, www.jcaho.org**.

2. Contact your state insurance commissioner or medical licensing board to find out how many patients have filed complaints about the plan. These agencies can also tell you how many patients drop out of the plan each year.

3. Ask your doctors which health care plans they've had positive experiences with.

4. Learn to recognize balance billing. Keep in mind, however, that doctors who do not participate in your plan are allowed to bill you for the amount your plan doesn't pay. Doctors may also bill you for procedures your plan doesn't *cover*, so check first before undergoing an unusual procedure.

5. If you're self-employed, don't forget to write off your health insurance premiums on your taxes.

WHERE TO COMPLAIN:

To complain about a health insurance company, contact your state insurance commissioner. To complain about a doctor, contact your state medical licensing board.

SEE ALSO:

INSURANCE: Life Insurance

Homeowner's Insurance

Your house is your most valuable asset, so you want to protect it. But that doesn't mean you have to pay a premium for your premiums! There are ways to save on homeowner's insurance. First, shop around. Insurance is a competitive industry and different companies offer different prices. (Just don't go with a company so cheap that you'll get lousy service if you ever make a claim.) Another idea: raise your deductible. By increasing your deductible from $250 to $1,000, you could save up to 24 percent.

    Insuring your home and car with the same company is another

INSURANCE

money-saver. Also, inquire about purchasing an insurance policy just for the value of your house, not the land it sits on. After all, theft, wind, fire, etc., don't affect the land much. You can cut your insurance costs by 5 percent to 15 percent by installing safety systems like dead bolts, burglar alarms, and sprinklers. Seniors get a 10 percent discount at some companies, nonsmokers get 5 percent off, and loyal customers who stick with a company for three to six years can save 5 percent to 10 percent.

Once you've purchased a policy, you should review it once a year to see if it's still appropriate for your circumstances. For example, if you remodel your house, it's probably worth more, so you'll want to bump up your insurance coverage. On the other hand, say a family member moves out of the house. You can probably reduce your insurance because you're not insuring that person's belongings any more. Don't wait until there's a big storm looming to review your coverage. Once a storm is named, or once it's within five hundred miles of the coast, your insurance company won't let you make any changes.

Many people assume valuables like jewelry are covered by their homeowner's insurance. Not true! Most homeowner's policies include just a thousand dollars worth of coverage for all your valuables—things like jewelry, furs, silver, art, and, sometimes, electronics. You need to purchase extra insurance to cover those items. This extra coverage is called a personal property endorsement, floater, or rider and it's attached to your homeowner's policy. It usually costs a dollar or two for every hundred dollars worth of valuables. Your insurance company will ask you to get the items appraised, then it will base the personal property endorsement on that appraised value. (A receipt showing the purchase price of the items is *not* enough.) The nice thing about personal property policies is that typically there's no deductible and they cover your valuables no matter what—even if you lose them. You should adjust this coverage each time you buy or sell valuables.

INSURANCE

Leslie and Jim A. are slowly trying to replace the treasures stolen from their home a couple of years ago. Losing their wedding rings caused them a lot of heartache. And their silverware cost just $1,600 in 1962, but now it's worth more like $16,000! Plus, Leslie and Jim didn't itemize their valuables on a personal property rider.

This couple now knows the value of the right insurance policy and the importance of getting an updated appraisal every few years.

Another thing that's *not* covered by your homeowner's policy is *flooding*. The general rule of thumb is that water damage that comes from inside your home is covered by your homeowner's policy (like a burst pipe). Water damage that comes from outside your home is not. If you live in a flood-prone area, you should definitely get flood insurance. In fact, your mortgage company may require it. You can purchase flood coverage through your insurance agent, but it's actually provided by the federal government. Flood coverage takes thirty days to kick in, so don't procrastinate until your TV weatherman announces a flood warning.

Speaking of warnings, here's one for you. If you file too many claims, your insurance company won't renew your homeowner's policy. Times are tight for insurance companies, and they're balancing their budgets by getting tougher with their customers. Some states prohibit insurance companies from dropping you for weather-related claims. But if you file claims for things like stolen bicycles, or if you file two or three claims within just a few years, you could find yourself without insurance. What's worse, insurance companies report information about you to a central agency, so you may have trouble finding another company to insure your house. Even if you call your insurance company just to ask about making a claim and then decide *not* to, that telephone inquiry is reported to the central agency and could count against you. The best advice? Save your insurance for catastrophes; that's what it's for. Don't file small claims. And if you call your company to inquire about making a claim, don't give your name. Tell the insurance company you're just doing research.

DO YOUR HOMEWORK:

INSURANCE

1. Shop around for the best rate offered by a reputable company and ask for every possible discount.
2. Call your state insurance commissioner and find out how many consumers have complained about the company you're considering before you sign up.

3. Make sure your insurance policy offers replacement value rather than depreciated value coverage.

4. Ask your insurance agent what valuables are not covered by the regular homeowner's policy and get personal property coverage for those.

5. Find out what happens if only part of a valuable is lost—like when a diamond falls out of its setting.

6. See whether you live in an area that's prone to flooding or earthquakes. If you do, you'll need to purchase special insurance for those. Also consider whether your policy covers landslides, mud slides, or sinkholes.

7. Take an inventory of your belongings. Write down makes, models, and serial numbers or photocopy the covers of your product manuals. Save receipts when you buy new things. You can also document these belongings with photographs or a videotape. Store these records away from home.

8. If disaster strikes, don't clean up the damage until your insurance adjuster has seen the extent of it. On the other hand, your policy may require you to do what you can to protect your home and belongings from *further* damage. For example, if a tree falls on your roof during a storm, don't have the tree removed until the adjuster has seen it but *do* spread tarps over your furniture to protect it from rain coming through the hole.

9. If your house is damaged in a disaster, beware of unlicensed contractors who prey on disaster victims. Don't make any quick decisions. Check out anybody and everybody before you hire someone to work on your house.

WHERE TO COMPLAIN:

Direct complaints about insurance companies to your state insurance commissioner.

SEE ALSO:

HOME IMPROVEMENT: Unlicensed Contractors; INSURANCE: **Cancellation and Nonrenewal, Public Adjusters**

Life Insurance

In murder mysteries, it seems like there's always one character who has a motive for murder because he or she stands to collect on the victim's life insurance policy. In real life, most people don't get rich from life insurance. Life insurance benefits are just meant to support family members when a breadwinner dies. In fact, if you don't have any dependents, you don't need life insurance at all. (You may *want* to start a policy for the future, because the premiums are cheaper when you're younger and healthier, but don't let anybody tell you you *need* it.)

If you *do* have family members who depend on you, and you *do* need life insurance, there are some sales schemes you should look out for. The first is known as "vanishing premiums." In this scenario, a salesman tells you that down the road your insurance will be guaranteed for life and you won't have to pay premiums out of pocket anymore. He tells you that after a specified amount of time—usually seven, ten, or fourteen years—you'll have so much cash value built up in the policy that payments can come out of that instead. The trouble is, some sleazy salespeople deliberately overestimate how fast the cash value of your policy can grow. So when your time is up, you find you still owe big premiums, and if you don't pay them you'll lose the policy.

Churning is another sales scheme. This one happens when you already own a policy. A salesman may approach you and suggest that you use the cash value in your current policy to buy a "better" policy. Truth is, the new policy isn't any better; it's just more expensive. The salesman makes another fat commission, but you have to start building up your cash value all over again. To make matters worse, you may not need or qualify for the new policy.

INSURANCE

KNOW THE SIGNS:

1. If a salesman claims your premiums will "vanish" after a set number of years, proceed with caution. It may be a vanishing premiums scam.

2. If a salesman suggests that you "upgrade" your existing life insurance policy, it could be a case of churning. Ask an independent professional with no interest in your current policy whether you need more insurance.
3. If the policy you're offered costs 30 percent to 50 percent less than its competitors', it may be too good to be true. Shop around to learn the average price range.
4. If the cash value in your insurance policy decreases or disappears, demand answers.
5. If the agent asks you to make a check out to him or her rather than to the insurance company whose product you're buying, that's suspicious. Agents have been known to pocket premium checks instead of forwarding them to the insurance company.
6. If an insurance agent tries to get you to sign blank forms or forms that are not completely filled out, that's a classic sign of fraud.
7. Be alert to penalties like severe surrender charges if you cash in your policy and buy a new one.

DO YOUR HOMEWORK:

1. When you buy life insurance, make sure the salesperson is licensed to sell insurance in your state. Contact your state insurance commissioner to confirm.
2. Also ask the insurance commissioner's office how many consumers have filed complaints against the company in recent years, especially if it's a company you've never heard of.
3. Contact a financial rating service like A.M. Best or Moody's to determine whether the insurance company is financially healthy and will be around to pay your dependents down the road. The life insurance company's reputation is key.
4. If you haven't received a copy of your policy within thirty days of applying for it, contact the company not the agent to follow up.
5. Get and keep a copy of every form you sign. Read and understand all of your insurance paperwork.
6. Compare the *guaranteed* rate of cash value accumulation with the *projected* rate, which is just an estimate. If the salesperson overemphasized the projected rate, you may be in trouble.

INSURANCE

7. Keep in mind, in most states you have ten days to review your policy once you receive it. If you're not satisfied, you can cancel during that time.

WHERE TO COMPLAIN:

Direct complaints about insurance companies to your state insurance commissioner.

SEE ALSO:

FINANCES: Investment Fraud

Public Adjusters

Most people see fires, floods, and tornadoes as disasters. But certain businesspeople make their living picking up the pieces. They are little-known professionals, called "public adjusters." Good ones can be a huge help. Bad ones can leave you homeless and penniless. When disaster strikes, your insurance company will send out an adjuster to calculate the cost of your losses. Of course, those adjusters work for the insurance company, so they may be biased. If you want, you can hire a *public* adjuster to represent *you*. That public adjuster will try to wrangle a better deal from the insurance company. Public adjusters charge a 10 to 15 percent commission on your total insurance settlement.

As Olivia G. lay in the hospital recovering from smoke inhalation, a man came to her bedside and awakened her. He said he'd heard about the fire at her house and his company could keep people from looting the place—for a fee. Olivia's glasses were lost in the fire, so she couldn't even see the contract the man had her sign. She thought he was just going to board up her windows. But it turned out the man was a public adjuster, and the contract gave him the power to be the middleman between her and her insurance company. This unscrupulous public adjuster persuaded Olivia's insurance company to send her $51,000 settlement check to *him*.

As part of his "service" to Olivia, the adjuster arranged for a contractor to fix up her damaged house. Olivia's front hallway used to

INSURANCE

have hardwood floors. The contractor installed linoleum instead—even though it's industry standard to return a home to its previous condition. Workers rebuilt Olivia's floor with the bathroom door closed and built it so thick the door wouldn't open. The roof was patched so poorly that it leaked immediately. The contractor left raw particleboard exposed in Olivia's kitchen and didn't install a garbage disposal, even though she had always had one.

The work was so shoddy that, two years after the fire, Olivia still couldn't move back in. Her replacement housing allowance ran out and she was forced to live with relatives. All this, even though she had faithfully continued to make mortgage payments on the house.

When I investigated, I discovered that the public adjuster *owned* the contracting firm that did the work. Olivia says he never disclosed that. By keeping repair costs down, the public adjuster was able to pocket the extra profit in addition to his 15 percent commission. I dug some more and learned the public adjuster was a convicted felon with a long list of complaints on file with insurance regulators in other states. Unfortunately, where Olivia lives, public adjusters are not regulated, so this man was able to do his dirty work for years.

Six states ban public adjusters outright, and many others regulate them. Some states bar public adjusters from soliciting at night. Others prohibit them from signing homeowners up within forty-eight hours of a fire.

Honest public adjusters say they can get up to 40 percent more money for you, because they know what to demand from insurance companies. They also have expertise in removing smoke from furniture and fabrics and preserving your possessions. According to the code of ethics of the National Association of Public Insurance Adjusters, public adjusters are not to engage in improper solicitation (like approaching people in the hospital), and they must disclose their business relationships (for example, if they own the contracting company).

INSURANCE

DO YOUR HOMEWORK:

1. If you are the victim of a fire, flood, or some other disaster, ask people at the scene for identification, so you will know whether

they are public adjusters or adjusters with your own insurance company. Unscrupulous public adjusters sometimes imply that they work for your insurance company.

2. Don't sign anything in the first couple of days after a disaster. Give yourself a chance to calm down.

3. You might want to try going through your insurance company first. If you're not happy with the settlement offer, then have a couple of independent contractors give you repair estimates to help you make your case.

4. If you're still not happy, ask your state insurance commissioner for help mediating the dispute.

5. If you do decide to hire a public adjuster, make sure the company has a spotless reputation. Check with your state insurance commissioner, the Better Business Bureau, and your county and state consumer protection offices.

6. Insist that settlement checks be made out to *you,* so you're in control of the money.

WHERE TO COMPLAIN:

If your state regulates public adjusters, then complaining to the state insurance commission will threaten the adjuster's license and should do some good. If not, complain anyway, and maybe your state government will get the message that it *ought* to regulate public adjusters. You can also try to get help from your county and state consumer protection offices.

SEE ALSO:

HOME IMPROVEMENT: Contractors, Unlicensed Contractors; INSURANCE: Homeowner's Insurance

INSURANCE

Renter's Insurance

Many renters don't realize that if something happens to their building, their landlord's insurance doesn't cover their belongings. That's why you need renter's insurance, but only 20 percent to 30 percent of renters have it. Say there's a fire. Your landlord's property insurance will pay to repair the apartment and replace appliances owned by the landlord. But if you don't have renter's insurance, you'll have to come up with the money to replace your furniture, clothing, computer, stereo, CDs, and so on. Even the lowliest college student usually has about $20,000 worth of possessions that have been accumulated over a lifetime.

A typical renter's policy costs between $75 and $225 per year—it's a good deal. It protects you in case of fire, theft, windstorm, hail, vandalism, etc. Many renter's policies even include replacement housing if you have to live somewhere else while your place is being repaired. As with homeowner's insurance, flood and earthquake coverage are not included. And you'll have to pay extra to insure valuables like jewelry and expensive electronics.

DO YOUR HOMEWORK:

1. Shop around for a renter's insurance policy. Prices do vary from one company to another.
2. Purchasing car insurance and renter's insurance from the same company could get you a discount.
3. Be generous when you calculate the value of your belongings. Renter's insurance is so inexpensive, it's better to have too much than not enough.
4. Discuss with the insurance agent whether you need extra coverage for jewelry, electronics, or other valuables.
5. Figure out if you need flood or earthquake insurance.

WHERE TO COMPLAIN:

INSURANCE

Complaints about insurance companies should be directed to your state insurance commissioner.

SEE ALSO:

INSURANCE: Homeowner's Insurance

CHAPTER 9

Employment

Business Opportunities

Vending machines. Display racks. Radio licenses. Medical billing businesses. Internet kiosks. These are some of the most common fraudulent business opportunities offered by con artists. What makes them scams? High start up costs, grossly overestimated earnings potential, small or poor-quality territories, and products nobody wants. Fraudulent business opportunities are advertised in newspapers and magazines, on the Internet, and through infomercials.

The people pushing these "opportunities" promise you can earn big money even if you have no experience. They claim the opportunity is only going to be available for a short time, so you need to make a quick decision. They say it's a "sure thing" that will set you up for life. They gush that you can work from home and set your own hours. They promise to coach and support you every step of the way. And they tell you the very same program made *them* rich.

If you're still skeptical, they give you a few references to call. The company pays these fake references or "shills" to say glowing things about the opportunity. If that's not enough to draw you in, the promoter promises you can get your money back if you're not satisfied. But good luck getting a refund. The Federal Trade Commission (FTC) ends up suing business opportunity promoters every couple of years.

DO YOUR HOMEWORK:

1. Do a background check on the company by contacting the BBB, your county and state consumer protection offices, your state attorney general, and the FTC. Ask if the company has any unresolved consumer complaints.
2. If the company makes earnings claims, get them in writing. If the company refuses to give you written documentation, don't buy into the business.
3. If the business opportunity involves selling name-brand products, call the company that manufactures those products and confirm its relationship with the company offering the business opportunity.
4. Ask the company for a list of every person who has purchased the business opportunity. Don't accept a narrow list of references, as they may be fakes, called "shills." Choose from the list of participants at random and visit them at their places of business to verify that they really are involved in the business.
5. Many business opportunities are considered franchises, so they're required to follow the FTC's franchise rule. Ask if the opportunity is a franchise. If so, request a copy of the company's franchise disclosure document. It includes: (a) a profile of the company's executives, (b) the total number of franchises in your area and their locations, (c) the number of franchises terminated or canceled the previous year, (d) company revenue and profit information, (e) lawsuits by former franchisees, and (f) details of any claims about potential earnings.

EMPLOYMENT

WHERE TO COMPLAIN:

If you have a problem with a fraudulent business opportunity, contact your county and state consumer protection offices and your state attorney general. Send a copy of your complaint to the BBB, too. The Federal Trade Commission can't mediate your individual case, but FTC lawyers want to hear about fraudulent opportunities.

SEE ALSO:

EMPLOYMENT: **Work-at-Home Schemes**

Classified Ads

My dad has worked for the same company his entire career. He started just before I was born. In today's world, he is a statistical oddball. (Sorry, Daddy!) A more typical American will hold seven to ten jobs in his or her lifetime. Searching for the next position can be treacherous. You know how people say searching for a job is a full-time job? If that's the case, then get ready to work double shifts. That's what it takes to read between the lines of all the misleading "Help Wanted" ads in the newspaper.

When Earl G. was looking for a job, he spotted an ad in the paper that said, "Warehouse Work." He liked the idea of some good, honest physical labor. So he spent two days—and his last ten bucks—traveling to apply for the job. When he got there, he found out it wasn't a warehouse job at all. In fact, there wasn't a warehouse in sight! The company wanted him to sell toys and trinkets on the street—and recruit other people to sell, too.

I sent a photographer in undercover to apply for that same "warehouse" job. Sure enough, when he got to the company, nobody ever mentioned warehouse work. The company made our photographer and a horde of other applicants sign waivers agreeing to an unpaid "observation day." Then company leaders had them unload boxes of merchandise from a truck and try to sell it on the streets. Some "observation" day! Remember, our photographer and the others were not being paid. That's a violation of state labor laws.

During that same investigation, I spotted another intriguing ad in the paper. The heading read, "Advertising! Sports marketing!" I had a producer apply. Of course, she had no trouble landing an interview,

EMPLOYMENT

even though advertising and sports marketing are highly coveted careers. When our producer got to her "interview," it turned out to be a group initiation—just like with the "warehouse" job. A spokesperson told the group about the company's "exciting, authoritative, commanding" marketing approach. The next day, our producer got to see that approach for herself. And what was it? Selling pizza and health club coupons door to door. Right. "Advertising and Sports Marketing."

KNOW THE SIGNS:

1. Truly glamorous jobs aren't usually advertised. Cheesy sales firms and multilevel marketing companies often try to lure applicants by using buzzwords like "advertising," "public relations," "sports," and "television."
2. Misleading job ads like this tend to run unchanged for weeks and weeks. The companies advertise constantly because applicants drop out as they learn the true nature of the work.
3. If you answer an ad, and the company grants an interview without asking for any details about you, that's a bad sign.
4. If you get to the interview, and it's a group initiation instead of a one-on-one meeting, that's another red flag.
5. If you are asked to pay money to get a job or buy a stake in a company, you could be dealing with a multilevel marketing firm or even an illegal pyramid scheme.

DO YOUR HOMEWORK:

1. If you see a want ad that seems too good to be true, scan the classifieds for other similar ads. Often these "offers" come in groups.
2. As you conduct your job search, be aware of ads that run for weeks on end.
3. If the company doesn't ask you about yourself when you call, say, "Don't you want to know anything about me?" If the person on the other end of the line grows impatient, perhaps you have your answer.

EMPLOYMENT

4. If you get to the firm, and it's a group interview, be on guard and consider just walking away.

5. Try to network through friends, family, and professional organizations. Most truly worthwhile jobs are filled before they're ever advertised—if they're advertised at all.

WHERE TO COMPLAIN:

If the company runs an ad that bends the truth, there's little regulators can do. But if you are asked to work without pay, file a complaint with your state labor department. If you believe the company may be an illegal pyramid scheme, contact your state attorney general.

SEE ALSO:

EMPLOYMENT: **Government Jobs,** Multilevel Marketing, **Trade Schools;** SCAMS: Pyramid Schemes

Executive Counseling Services

According to a recent poll, half of all workers say they hate their jobs. But looking for a *new* job is a dreaded task, too. For that reason, you may be tempted to *hire* somebody to help *you* get hired. After all, they say it takes money to make money—right? Wrong! That old adage is fine for investments, but job hunters should not spend money *up front* on headhunters. If you pay in advance, what motivation does the executive counselor have to work hard for you? He or she has already made all the money to be made off of you. To earn his or her next paycheck, the counselor's got to go find the *next* job seeker who's willing to pay in advance.

Headhunters, executive counseling services, job search services, career agents. No matter what you call them, if they want money up

EMPLOYMENT

front, it's a bad deal. When I investigated this industry, I called every single executive counseling service listed in the employment section of the newspaper, and they all wanted thousands of dollars in advance. It's not that I'm against seeking professional help to advance your career. I have an agent myself for my television work. But I don't pay him a dime until he gets me a job. Then he gets a percentage of the salary he negotiates for me, so he's motivated to get me the best deal possible. That's how it works for actors and athletes who employ agents too.

Stephen A. was looking for a new job, in a new city, in a new field. He was overwhelmed, so when he spotted an ad in the paper for an executive counseling service, it seemed like the answer. Stephen paid the firm $4,000 to help him find his dream job in biology. The firm gave him interviewing tips—but didn't get him any actual interviews. Problem is, Stephen's contract had no time limit within which the firm was supposed to find him a job. The way it was written, the search service could have spent years—and Stephen could have starved. Eventually, Stephen found his own job.

Hugo P. wanted help transitioning from the military to a career in the civilian world. He paid an executive counseling service $2,500 up front and agreed to pay another $4,500 later. The company was able to string Hugo along for six months, without doing anything for him. When he landed a job on his own, he angrily demanded his money back. Get this! Hugo's contract stated that he owed the headhunter the balance of his payment when he got a job—no matter who got it for him! The company actually had the nerve to try to collect. Abusive contracts are one of the hallmarks of the bad boys in this industry.

There are several kinds of companies that match up employers and employees, so here's the lowdown. "Executive counseling services" are the questionable companies I've been ranting about. You pay up front for job search advice and, possibly, job leads. Placement agencies find temporary and permanent jobs, mostly for people with administrative or accounting skills. Their fees are typically paid by the employer, but sometimes they are split between employer and employee. Companies hire retained search firms to find executives for them. The company often pays the firm on an ongoing basis, rather than for each new hire. Finally, job-listing services offer

EMPLOYMENT

lists of openings. These companies often sell you information you could easily get on your own for free.

KNOW THE SIGNS:

1. Executive counseling services that advertise in the paper should be approached with caution. After all, how exclusive can they be if anybody can contact them?
2. If the search firm "guarantees" it can get you a job, get serious. How can any third party make that promise?
3. In case I've failed to bludgeon you with my point, IF THE COMPANY ASKS YOU FOR MONEY UP FRONT, THAT'S BAD. RUN! If the company promises a refund if you're not satisfied, chances are you'll never get your money back.
4. Some firms charge money up front, but suggest that your new employer will reimburse you for the fee once you get a job. Don't believe it.
5. Beware of contracts with no time limit for finding you a job.
6. Beware of contracts written so that the company's obligation to you is fulfilled once the company gets you just *one* interview. This is common.
7. Don't fall for a contract that requires you to pay the headhunter a fee when you get a job—even if you secure that job on your own.
8. Executive search firms often change names once they've sufficiently pissed off enough people. Key into clues, for example, a company that advertises under one name and answers the phone under another.

DO YOUR HOMEWORK:

1. Ask firms in your industry whether they employ headhunters and, if so, which ones.
2. Check out any search firm with the BBB and your county and state consumer protection offices before signing up. Find out who owns the company and do a search under that name as well, in case the company name has changed.
3. Some states require employment agencies to be licensed. Find out if that's the case in your state and follow up.

EMPLOYMENT

4. Read and understand your contract with the search service before signing it. Have a lawyer look at it if necessary.
5. If the firm makes oral promises that are not included in the written contract, be on your guard and ask that the oral promises be put in writing.
6. Ask the firm for the names of employers it has placed people with in the past. Call those employers and confirm.

WHERE TO COMPLAIN:

If an executive counseling service does you wrong, complain to your county and state consumer protection offices and the BBB. You may also be able to get help from your state attorney general.

SEE ALSO:

EMPLOYMENT: Modeling

Government Jobs

Schemers are always trying to get people to pay for information the government provides for free. In this case, the people who fall victim are those who can least afford it: the unemployed. Heartless bad guys place classified ads offering to sell lists of government jobs. Sometimes, they take your money up front even when there aren't any jobs available. Other times, the lists they sell are fake. But mostly, they provide the same information that's available for free online. Sometimes these scam artists charge another fee to help you *apply* for those jobs. They use official-sounding names like "U.S. Career Agency" or "Federal Job Clearinghouse" to make it sound like they're part of the government, but they're not.

First of all, federal agencies never charge application fees. Nor do they guarantee people jobs. And they don't sell study guides for their tests. If you have to take an exam to qualify for a government job, the agency usually provides free sample questions when you sign up for the test. Some federal agencies, like the U. S. Postal

EMPLOYMENT

Service, rarely have openings and give priority to military veterans. If a private company tells you the postal service is hiring, check with your local postmaster first. If somebody claims to be able to teach you to score well on the postal entrance exam, that's very deceptive. The exam tests your general aptitude, which is not something you can learn from a study guide or a class.

Fifi T. was considering going to a school that advertised training for government jobs. The tuition to prepare for the postal exam was $360. When Fifi questioned whether he was guaranteed to get a job after spending that money on tuition, the school counselor started swearing at him. That sounded suspicious to me, so I sent a producer to the school with a hidden camera.

The school's lobby was decorated with U.S. flags, and eagles adorned the school's business cards—all in an attempt to make it seem like a government agency. The counselor told our producer the school would train him to pass the postal exam and then *place* him in a full-time position paying $22 dollars an hour. Of course, I did some checking and learned the postal service had never heard of this school. Furthermore, the postal exam is offered only when jobs are available—sometimes as seldom as every seven years. The only postal jobs available at the time were for mechanics and paid just $11.70 an hour. And guess what? Those jobs didn't even require the exam the school was training people to take!

KNOW THE SIGNS:

1. Beware of private companies that try to seem like government agencies by using official-sounding names, American flags, eagles, or seals in their advertisements or literature.
2. If somebody guarantees you a high test score, guarantees you a job, or says no experience is necessary, that's another tip-off it's a rip-off.
3. Con artists often promise to give you information about "hidden" or "unadvertised" government jobs.
4. Classified ads that refer you to a toll-free number are suspicious because the operator may try to sell you job listings or practice tests.
5. Toll-free numbers that refer you to 900 numbers are even worse.

EMPLOYMENT

DO YOUR HOMEWORK:

1. If you're interested in getting a government job, go to **www.usajobs.opm.gov** for information.
2. If you like the idea of postal work, go to your local post office and inquire or check out **www.usps.gov**.

WHERE TO COMPLAIN:

If you find a private company misleading people about government jobs, complain to the Federal Trade Commission at **www.ftc.gov**. If postal jobs are at issue, contact your local postal inspector.

SEE ALSO:

EMPLOYMENT: **Trade Schools**

Modeling

Wouldn't it be nice if, through the luck of genetics, you could make millions as a model? It would be like winning the lottery without even entering! Well, I've got news for you. Pursuing a modeling career really is like gambling. Experts estimate only a quarter of the agencies in the business are legitimate. You can improve your odds, however, by learning to recognize the scams.

Angela D. was browsing at a bookstore when a man approached her. He told her she had a great look and asked if she'd ever considered becoming a model. Of course, Angela was flattered, so the man made her an appointment to visit what she thought was a modeling agency. When she got there, the staff gushed that she had tremendous potential and could make big bucks. Angela told the staff that she didn't have a U.S. work permit, but they seemed unconcerned. Little did she know, that's because the company's business was teaching modeling *classes,* not getting people modeling *jobs.* The company persuaded Angela to write a check for more than a thousand dollars.

EMPLOYMENT

When I investigated, I discovered the company had more than five thousand complaints on file with the Better Business Bureau. I tracked down a former scout for the company, who decided to tell all. The company had coached her to approach anybody and everybody on the street and tell them they had modeling potential. The more people the better. The company paid her a commission each time one of her recruits signed up and paid for classes. None of her recruits ever got a modeling job. In fact, the company folded before most of them could even take a modeling class.

My investigation contained both of the classic modeling scams. The first is the mall talent scout. We've all heard the right-place-at-the-right-time stories of supermodels who got discovered. This scam plays on those same hopes and dreams. The "talent scout" approaches people in public places and plays to their egos. Actually, the scout is usually a victim, too. Even if the scout sends in dozens of prospects, he or she only gets paid if those prospects plunk down money for classes. The modeling school often skips town without paying its scouts or providing classes to its recruits.

The second scam is even worse—even more widespread: Up-front fees. Legitimate modeling agencies don't charge you any money until they get you a job. Once you've worked, then they take a percentage of your earnings. Unscrupulous modeling agencies make their money by charging in advance for photographs, screen tests, classes, and so on. The problem has grown so bad that some states have passed laws making it illegal for modeling agencies to double as modeling schools or to charge any fees up front. Even if it's not illegal in your state, you should never, ever pay a modeling agency money in advance.

Finding a legitimate modeling agency is tricky. If you know anybody who's ever actually made money as a model or actor, ask who their agent is. Reputable photographers should be able to name agencies that actually get people work. You could also try contacting an advertising agency to see where it gets its models. Another idea: some print ads include the name of the photographer and agency. If all else fails, call each agency listed in the phone book and ask if it charges any fees up front. If it does, and you want to end up on the *runway*, then *run* the other way!

EMPLOYMENT

KNOW THE SIGNS:

1. If the modeling "agency" advertises in the paper or in the phone book, that's a strike against it. Top agencies rarely advertise. They don't have to.
2. If the agency claims to be a major player in the industry, and you live in a small city, that's unlikely. The big American modeling agencies are concentrated in New York, Los Angeles, and Miami. Most of the others are smaller players.
3. If the agency charges you for photos, that's unprofessional and possibly illegal. It's just another up-front fee.
4. If the agency insists that you use a particular photographer, that's not good either. The photographer may get kickbacks from the agency.
5. Agencies that charge up-front fees and require you to pay those fees with cash or a money order are not to be trusted.

DO YOUR HOMEWORK:

1. Before signing up with a modeling agency or school, check out its reputation with the Better Business Bureau and your county and state consumer protection offices.
2. Find out if your state requires modeling agencies to be licensed or bonded. If it does, make sure the agency is.
3. Ask the agency for names and numbers of models it has placed recently. Contact those people to verify.
4. Ask for names of clients the agency has worked for recently and call those clients, too.
5. Before signing a contract, get a blank copy to take home and study. Show it to a lawyer if necessary.
6. If the agency makes any verbal promises, have them added to the written contract.
7. Make sure the agency gives you a signed copy of your contract and keep it in a safe place.

WHERE TO COMPLAIN:

EMPLOYMENT

Complaints about modeling agencies and modeling schools can be directed to your county and state consumer protection offices and your state attorney general. Also lodge a complaint with the BBB for the sake of those who come after you.

SEE ALSO:

EMPLOYMENT: Executive Counseling Services

Multilevel Marketing

People often confuse illegal pyramid schemes and legitimate multilevel marketing (MLM) companies. You definitely want to avoid pyramids. But the truth is, even if a multilevel marketing company is *legal,* it may not be *profitable.* For one thing, most MLMs allow an unlimited number of people to become distributors in a single market. That's in contrast to traditional businesses, which often give each salesperson an exclusive territory. Furthermore, even though multilevel marketing companies pass the government's legal litmus test by actually offering products for sale, sometimes they are still structured in a pyramid shape that rewards longtime distributors more than new recruits. In a traditional business, a veteran and a newcomer make the same amount of money if both of them sell the same item.

Because of these inherent disadvantages, dropout rates in multilevel marketing are astronomical. One major MLM says 50 percent of its sales force bails out every year, and only 9 percent of its people last ten years. According to the Web site, **www.MLMSurvivor.com,** less than 1 percent of multilevel-marketing participants make a profit—and even fewer make a living at it. If all of that is not discouraging enough, consider whether you want to turn your friends and family into sales prospects. Years ago, some acquaintances invited my parents over to dinner. Halfway through the evening, it turned into a multilevel marketing pitch. Never one to disguise how he feels, my dad got up from the dinner table and walked out. Can you blame him?

DO YOUR HOMEWORK:

1. Analyze whether the product can stand alone. Would it be competitive if it were being sold in a regular retail setting rather than

EMPLOYMENT

through multilevel marketing? Does the product have staying power, or is it tied to fleeting trends? Is it priced competitively?

2. Consider how you were approached. Was it deceptive? Did the company emphasize how great the *product* is, or how great the *business opportunity* is?

3. Ask the company if it allows unlimited numbers of distributors to work in the same territory. If it does, the marketplace could be saturated.

4. Figure out whether you can make good money just by selling the product, without recruiting other distributors.

5. Analyze whether *you* make the bulk of the commission when you sell a product, or whether people above you in the hierarchy make just as much off *your* work. If they do, that's not a healthy business model, and the company may be an illegal pyramid scheme.

6. Ask existing distributors how long it took them to turn a profit after joining the company. (Make sure they deduct operating expenses and product purchases when they do the math for you.)

7. Ask the company to break down its distributors' average income (after product purchases) by percentile. How much money do the top 1 percent make? How much money do the bottom 1 percent make? And so on, for every percentile in between. You're scrutinizing the company to see if the vast majority of distributors make little or no money. Also, compare these earnings figures to the minimum wage. If the company won't provide this information, don't get involved.

8. Ask longtime distributors when they last took a vacation. Ask them if they know anybody who no longer works actively in the business but still makes money from it. This is a test of the company's claims that you can make a good living and have more time for yourself through multilevel marketing.

WHERE TO COMPLAIN:

EMPLOYMENT

If you want to alert other consumers that an MLM is bad news, complain to the BBB and your county and state consumer protection offices. If you think the MLM is doing something illegal, try your state attorney general and the Federal Trade Commission.

SEE ALSO:

SCAMS: **Pyramid Schemes**

Trade Schools

In 1991, a U.S. Senate subcommittee found that "unscrupulous, inept and dishonest" trade schools had left hundreds of thousands of students with "little or no training, no jobs and significant debts that they cannot possibly repay." That's why you need to study a trade school before you study *at* a trade school. It's a shame that bad trade schools give the rest of the technical education community a bad name. I've always believed that people who don't flourish in academia often have other, more practical talents. So don't write off the idea of a trade school, just don't rush into it.

Unlike colleges and universities, trade schools are for-profit enterprises, so they have a motive to enroll as many students as possible and educate them as cheaply as possible. To entice potential students, some trade schools advertise that you're guaranteed to get a job if you go through their program. That's highly suspicious. The school may act like you're lucky to be admitted. Some trade schools even give entrance exams (which they don't bother scoring!) to give the appearance of exclusivity. Pushy schools may claim, "there's only one space left in the class, so you have to hurry." Baloney. Educate yourself first.

Many trade schools are eager to help potential students obtain federal loans. When there's a pot of government money lying around, there's always some private company angling to dip into it. Here's the problem: Plenty of people have obtained student loans and paid their tuition only to have the trade school go bankrupt on them—a double whammy. You don't get the education you paid for, but you still have to pay off the student loan. Alternatively, you get a student loan and pay your tuition, then discover the school's training is a joke. Some unscrupulous trade schools make it very hard to get a refund. So, once again, you're stuck owing something and getting nothing.

EMPLOYMENT

QUESTIONS TO ASK:

1. How long has the school been in business? (Confirm this with your state government.)
2. What is the program completion rate? The dropout rate?
3. Ask the school what its placement record is. If the school says, "100 percent," don't believe it. Ask for names of firms that have hired the school's graduates and call to confirm.
4. What kind of equipment does the school have, and what kind of access will you have to it? Can you use it outside of classes to practice?
5. What is the school's refund policy? Some states require trade schools to issue refunds on a prorated basis. Learn the law.

DO YOUR HOMEWORK:

1. Talk to people in the field you're interested in to find out what kind of training you need and what equipment you should learn to use.
2. Check the reputation of each and every school with the BBB and your county and state consumer protection offices.
3. If you're interested in a school, try to sit in on classes for a day. How big is the class? Does the instructor have recent experience in the field?
4. Talk to past and present students of the school and ask about their experience.
5. Carefully read any application before signing it. Some applications are actually binding contracts. Keep a copy of your application, contract, and any other documentation and ask for receipts for payments.
6. If you decide to withdraw from a trade school, request a refund in writing and keep a copy of your request.

WHERE TO COMPLAIN:

EMPLOYMENT

If you have a bad experience with a trade school, complain to the Better Business Bureau to give future students fair warning. Also lodge a complaint with your county and state consumer protection offices and your state office of higher education. If you took out a federal student loan to pay the school, make sure the U.S. Department of Education knows the school isn't worth the money.

SEE ALSO:

EMPLOYMENT: **Government Jobs**

Work-at-Home Schemes

You've seen the ads. Work at home! Set your own hours! Make thousands! Sound like a fantasy job? It's a fantasy, all right—a figment of somebody's scheming imagination. Work-at-home opportunities advertised on telephone poles and in the classifieds are a scam. There are two main variations: arts and crafts and envelope stuffing.

The arts and crafts scam is a crafty way to take advantage of people who are crafters. The ads claim you can make money assembling jewelry, knickknacks, and decorations at home. You pay money up front for a kit full of raw materials. When you get the raw materials, you discover the finished product is almost impossible to make. Plus, the promoter will only pay you if you make a specified number of products. If by some miracle you *do* manage to make your quota, the con artists have an answer for that, too: They tell you your finished products are substandard and they refuse to pay.

Danielle W. wanted something she could do at home while on maternity leave. She paid $50 for a kit to make twenty-four necklaces. When she got the kit, she discovered the string was too big to fit through the beads. Undeterred, she bought her own replacement string. But the beads were so tiny that Danielle started getting headaches trying to see the holes. You'd have to have the eyes of an eagle and the patience of a saint to complete even one necklace.

My station once ordered one of these kits to prove the point. We chose a woodworking project in which we were supposed to assemble teeny, tiny little wooden boxes. We took the kit to a pro-

EMPLOYMENT

fessional wood shop and asked the experts to give it a try. After three painstaking hours, the pros gave up. Besides, who would want to buy a wooden box the size of a pack of gum?

Envelope stuffing is the other classic work-at-home scheme. You've seen the want ads: "Make an extra $200 a week stuffing envelopes." The ads ask you to send money for more information. When you mail in your check, you get a packet that explains how to get into the envelope-stuffing business. But there *is* no legitimate business! The packet teaches you how to take advantage of the next set of suckers. You're told to place your own classified ad, then photocopy the very packet you're reading and send it to anybody who responds. *That's* the only envelope stuffing involved. If you follow this advice, you could be prosecuted for mail fraud. The postal inspector's office considers envelope stuffing offers to be elaborate, illegal chain letters.

Often envelope-stuffing ads imply that there are big corporate clients eager to pay people to prepare their mailings for them. Just to show how ludicrous that is, I once did a little experiment. On live TV, I folded, stuffed, and licked as many envelopes as I could in one minute. My total? Seven envelopes. That's 420 envelopes an hour— *if* I don't get a paper cut on my tongue. Ouch! By contrast, professional mailing companies have machines that can easily collate, fold, stuff, and seal five thousand envelopes an hour.

DO YOUR HOMEWORK:

1. Personally, I would never believe any work-at-home offer advertised in the classified section of the newspaper. If you want to work from home, find a legitimate, well-known company and see if it offers telecommuting positions.
2. If you insist on pursuing a work-at-home offer you see advertised, find out the name and phone number of the company and check out its reputation with the Better Business Bureau and your county and state consumer protection offices.

EMPLOYMENT

WHERE TO COMPLAIN:

The U.S. Postal inspector investigates many work-at-home scams because the kits are usually sent through the mail. If your kit is delivered by some other method, contact your county and state consumer protection offices and your state attorney general for help. File a complaint with the Better Business Bureau to warn other consumers that you had a bad experience.

SEE ALSO:

EMPLOYMENT: **Business Opportunities**

EMPLOYMENT

CHAPTER 10

Shopping

Auctions

There's something about an auction that gets people's blood flowing. Gets their cash flowing, too. People part with thousands of dollars because they feel like they've "won" something rather than "bought" something. Often they overpay. You *can* bid your way to a bargain at an auction, as long as you remember an old warning with a new twist: *Bidder* beware.

Think of government auctions as legal revenge! The government busts bad guys, then sells their belongings to make money for law enforcement. I covered a government auction once and was dazzled by the dizzying array of merchandise. Luxury cars. Diamonds. Gold bars. Persian rugs. Golf clubs. Ramen noodles. Yes, several tons of ramen noodles! If the government seizes it, the government can sell it. And you can buy it. Contrary to legend, you won't find a sports car for fifty bucks or a vacation home for $500. Government auctioneers set minimums and withdraw items from the auction if they fail to fetch a reasonable price.

The feds publish lists of government sales and auctions and make them available for free or for a small charge to cover postage. If you'd like to find out about government auctions, go to **www.pueblo.gsa.gov** and click on "Federal Programs." There are several brochures you can print out about government auctions. The Treasury Department holds auctions every nine weeks. For information on those, call **(703) 273-7373** or go to **www.ustreas.gov.**

Be aware that opportunists will try to sell you information about government auctions that you can get by yourself for free. The scam works like this: You see an ad about government or other glamorous auctions. You call the number. The operator asks you for your credit card or checking account number. The company charges you $50 to $75 dollars for a list of auctions. Maybe the operator offers to "throw in" a couple of extra auction books. You end up being charged for those as well.

Government auctions are so popular that copycats try to make their auctions seem like government auctions to lure customers. This is just one of many sleazy tactics used by traveling auctions held in hotel rooms and other rotating sites. Traveling auctions usually advertise in newspapers or send out direct mail. Beware of ads with statements like this: "AUCTION of goods previously held, sold and released by GOVERNMENT AGENCIES and POLICE DEPARTMENTS!" Unschooled readers may miss the fine print and mistake this for a government auction. It's a ploy. All it means is that the auctioneer himself attended a government auction and bought one or two things that he or she is now going to try to resell at a huge markup. That's if the auctioneer attended a government auction at all.

Fake estate sales are another favorite ploy of traveling auctions. The auctioneers persuade realtors to let them hold auctions on the grounds of mansions that are for sale. They imply that the merchandise for sale has a connection to the grand house, when really it's just cut-rate c-r-a-p trucked in for the auction. I went undercover to one such sale, where the auctioneer was selling off "the entire estate of Dr. Percy, leading figure in sports medicine." I asked the auctioneer whether it was the estate of *the* Dr. Percy, a professor at a near-by university. He said yes! So I called Professor Percy, who was very much alive and startled to hear his name was being used to sell art and antiques. He laughed and said he didn't know much about either one.

I attended another traveling auction where fake bidders were planted in the audience. These "shills" repeatedly bid up the prices so the real customers would end up paying more. How do I know? It was right in the auction contract, only they were called "house bidders." The contract said the auctioneer reserved the right to employ house bidders to ensure that he or she made a certain amount of money on each item. Customers had to sign the contract to get a bidder card, but apparently I was the only one who actually read it. Shills are illegal in some states, but many states don't regulate auctions or auctioneers at all.

These schemes seem pretty transparent—but they work. I attended one traveling auction in which the auctioneer raked in $93,000 in a single hour. The auctioneer claimed one diamond ring was of excellent quality and was worth $15,000. In twenty-one years, Mike D. had never been able to afford an engagement ring for his wife. He bought the diamond ring for $7,500. I approached Mike and offered to get the ring appraised for him. The appraiser said the ring was poorly cut, yellowish in color, and had imperfections so bad they were visible to the naked eye. The value? Just $6,500—a thousand less than Mike paid. Mike was so caught up in the auction that he also bought five oriental rugs, some furniture, and a painting. His grand total? Twenty thousand dollars. The poor man actually planned to delay his retirement to pay for the purchases.

Another traveling auction advertised "original signed Chagall lithographs." A bidder named Albertine V. bought one for $981. Again, I had it appraised. The piece turned out to be a fancy color copy. With the help of a magnifying glass, you could see the cheap dot matrix printing. And get this! It wasn't a Chagall. It wasn't even a *copy* of a Chagall. It was a composite of images from *other* Chagall works. So, if you raise your hand at a traveling auction, make sure your "bargain" doesn't turn out to be bogus.

DO YOUR HOMEWORK:

SHOPPING

1. The reputation of the auction house is crucial. Call the Better Business Bureau and your county and state consumer protection offices to do a background check. If your state licenses auctioneers, find out which department is in charge and do a background check with that department, too. Check under the name of the auction house and the auctioneer, in case the business has changed names.

2. Even if the company comes up clean, be wary if the auction is being held at a hotel or some other nonpermanent location. How will you track the company down if you have a dispute?

3. If you hear about a government auction thirdhand, contact the government agency directly to confirm that it really is holding an auction.

4. Call ahead and get a copy of the auction rules in advance, so you'll know how to proceed on the big day.

5. Try to find out what is being auctioned and research the value before you attend the auction. Set a limit on what you're willing to spend based on the actual value.

6. Figure out in advance how you plan to pay for items you buy at auction, especially if you're in the market for a big-ticket item.

7. Plan ahead how you'll get your merchandise home. Some auctions require you to take your purchases right away; others make you wait three or four days.

8. Attend auction previews to examine the merchandise. Take an expert with you if possible. Be wary of auctions that don't hold previews.

WHERE TO COMPLAIN:

If your state licenses auctioneers, complain to the department that handles licensing. If not, contact your county and state consumer protection offices and the Better Business Bureau.

Gift Cards

When you give somebody flowers, fruit, or food, you know your gift is perishable. But did you know some gift cards expire, too? It's the gift that *doesn't* keep on giving. When gift cards first came out, I bought a bunch from a bookstore. I thought I was sooooooo smart. I figured I would just keep a few on hand, and when a friend had a birthday, had a baby—or anything in between—I would be ready with an instant gift. You can imagine how embarrassed I was when I did a news story on gift cards a year later and learned they lose value over time or expire altogether. None of my very classy friends ever brought it up, and I was too mortified to ask, so if any of them are reading this book (which they didn't buy with the gift card I gave them!), this will serve as my confession.

Let me help you avoid a similar mea culpa. First of all, I'm talking about those plastic cards that have replaced gift certificates in many stores. They sell for standard amounts, or you can choose how much money you want to put on them. The recipient spends the credit on the card until it's used up.

Virtually all of these cards come with a catch. For example, some hold their full value for eighteen months, then drop off by $1.50. They continue to fall from there at set increments over time. Other cards have a hard expiration date. I got a call from a mom once whose children were devastated when they got to the cash register with their purchases only to learn that their two-week-old gift card was already worthless.

DO YOUR HOMEWORK:

1. Read the fine print before you purchase a gift card to make sure it's not a rip-off.
2. If you give a card that lasts, say, eighteen months, jot a note to let the recipient know about the deadline.
3. If you receive a gift card, for goodness' sake, hurry up and spend it!

WHERE TO COMPLAIN:

Take your gripe straight to the retailer in question. Consumer pressure recently prompted some big stores to start replacing lost, damaged, or stolen gift cards rather than treating them like cash. Maybe savvy consumers can pressure stores to get rid of expiration dates, too.

Going Out of Business

For some stores, going *out* of business is a business. Many jurisdictions now recognize this, so they require stores to get a permit to hold a going-out-of-business sale and they limit how long that sale can last. The store is typically required to file an inventory list when it applies for the permit. Bringing in brand-new inventory just for the sake of the sale is not allowed. Often the law also governs all the alternative ways of saying, "going-out-of-business sale"—like "closeout sale," "liquidation sale," and "lost lease sale."

Remarkable. Usually the government's the last to know. The fact that government regulators have clued in should be a clue to you. Don't assume you're going to bag a bargain at a going-out-of-business sale. Professional liquidators often run these sales and milk them for every possible penny. That's especially true for furniture stores and electronics stores that go out of business. Liquidators have been known to mark the prices up just so they can then mark them down and make you think you're getting a deep discount.

Going-out-of-business sales at oriental rug stores are legendary. I monitored one store for months as it "went out of business." The owner took out teary ads on local radio stations claiming he was shutting down because his beloved father, the founder, had died. Meanwhile, he moved the store into a much larger space to make room for all of the additional inventory he brought in for the "going-out-of-business" sale. After all the extra rugs were gone, he moved back to the smaller space and changed the store's name slightly. When I confronted him, he claimed he was just storing the rugs in the building and that they weren't for sale. If that's the case, it was the most elaborate "storage room" I've ever seen, with displays in the windows and an "open" sign on the door!

Stores that really *do* go out of business are an even bigger problem for consumers. What if your purchase is defective? What if the store goes belly-up before you even *get* your merchandise? Try not to buy ultra-expensive things from stores that aren't well established. If you have to make a down payment on something you're not going to receive until later, negotiate for the smallest possible payment. Don't let the store tell you that a minimum deposit is required by law. If anything, most states set a maximum deposit that stores are allowed to charge. Here's the best tip of all: Pay with a credit card. If the store folds before you get your merchandise, under the Fair Credit Billing Act, you can ask your card company for a refund.

If you've *already* been stiffed by a store that shut its doors (and you didn't pay with plastic), it's tough—but not impossible—to get your money back. If the company filed for bankruptcy, file a claim with the bankruptcy court. Personal claims like yours often get precedence over corporate creditors that are also trying to get paid. You can also sue the owner of the company in small-claims court, although it's hard to collect if it's a corporation. One other idea: some companies are required to post bonds to do business. Try to find out if there's a bond; then make a claim against it.

DO YOUR HOMEWORK:

1. Check the quality carefully in case a liquidator is breaking the rules and trucking in substandard merchandise.
2. If you want, you can check with your city or county to see if the business has a permit to run a going-out-of-business sale. It's an indication that at least the company is trying to do things by the book.
3. If you're considering a pricey purchase at a going-out-of-business sale, don't seal the deal until you've shopped around. You could end up paying more at the "sale." Plus, you'll have no recourse if the store closes and the item is defective.

4. Ask the store whether you have any protection if the merchandise is defective. If it's a name-brand item, there may be a manufacturer's warranty. If it's a store-brand item, the warranty may disappear with the store.

HOW TO COMPLAIN:

You may think it's hopeless to complain about a defunct company, but if enough consumers do, government watchdogs could see a pattern and decide to help. They might even pass a law that will protect people in the future. Try your county and state consumer protection offices and the state attorney general.

SEE ALSO:

BEFORE YOU BUY: How to Pay; SHOPPING: Sales

"No, No, No" Deals

"No money down! No interest! No payments until next year!" This is what's known as a "No, No, No" Deal. But, before you say "yes, yes, yes," you should know these deals can end up costing you a lot, lot, lot.

Here's the main problem: These offers are strictly structured so that if you don't pay off the full amount when the introductory period ends, you *do* owe interest. Worse yet, that interest is retroactive to the date of the original purchase. Worst of all, the interest rate is often sky high—about 20 percent. More than half of the consumers who participated in one such plan failed to follow the rules and ended up owing the retailer big bucks.

Another downfall is that the product price is often inflated to make up for the free financing. An electronics store offered a thirty-five-inch television for $999. But consumers who opted for free financing had to pay $1,499. A large appliance store advertised the following deal: no interest for six months *or* $150 off the purchase price. No, no, no deals are also sometimes limited to certain makes and models or require a minimum purchase.

Be alert to whether the offer is a "no, no, no" deal or just a "no interest" offer. If it's simply a free financing deal, you *will* have to make principal payments during the introductory period.

If you're required to use a store charge card to take advantage of a free financing offer, that can cause problems. Say you already carry a balance on that card or you buy other items that aren't part of the special offer. You may have to make two payments each month: your regular minimum payment, plus the payment required to satisfy the terms of the free financing offer.

SHOPPING

Some free financing offers actually require you to pay the interest up front. Then, if you make all your payments on time and pay the purchase off by the deadline, the company credits you back the interest payments. One false move by you and you don't get your rebate.

If you don't think you'll have the money to pay your purchase off in full at the end of the introductory period, you shouldn't sign up for a "no, no, no" deal or a "free financing" offer. You're better off paying with a low-interest credit card. These highly hyped deals only save you money if the product is competitively priced *and* you pay it off in time.

QUESTIONS TO ASK:

1. What size deposit is required? Sales tax only? More?
2. Will I have to make principal payments during the introductory period?
3. Does interest accrue during the introductory period?
4. Will I owe a large balloon payment at the end of the introductory period?
5. What happens if I can't pay off the full purchase price by the designated date?
6. If I end up having to pay interest because I can't pay off the item in time, what interest rate will I be charged, and when will the interest start accruing?
7. Am I required to use my store charge card? If so, how will other purchases on the card be kept separate?
8. Will I have to pay interest now and then get it refunded to me at a later date?

DO YOUR HOMEWORK:

1. Read and understand the fine print. If it's complicated, ask for a copy to take home so you can study it without a pushy salesperson breathing down your neck.
2. Give the salesperson or store manager the third degree!

WHERE TO COMPLAIN:

You can ask your county or state consumer protection office for general advice. With any luck, financing deals are regulated by your state's banking and finance division.

SEE ALSO:

CARS: Financing

Outlet Malls

One hundred fifty-two acres. Two hundred twenty stores. A mall a mile long. It's enough to make your head spin and your feet hurt. A big outlet mall can see thirty thousand shoppers in a single day. But will those shoppers find huge savings at a huge outlet mall? It depends.

Outlet malls claim they sell merchandise for 30 percent to 70 percent less than you'll find elsewhere. Some sell damaged or imperfect goods at cut rates. Some sell second-season merchandise that has already made the rounds at regular retail stores. And others claim they can cut prices by cutting out the middleman.

A producer and I systematically compared prices at an outlet mall and a regular mall. Sure enough, we found brand-name perfume for just $65 at the outlet. The same bottle was $105 at a regular mall. We discovered a jewelry outlet that was having a two-for-one sale on designer watches. The regular retail arm of the company was not. On the other hand, we saw major label sneakers for $16 *less* at a regular retail store that was having a killer sale.

Outlet malls are victims of their own success. Or, rather, *we're* victims of their own success. There just isn't enough imperfect and second-season merchandise to stock the outlet malls that now dot our nation's landscape. So some stores have started designing inexpensive lines *just* for their outlets. Others manufacture cheaper versions of their most popular merchandise. That can be a bargain—or a bummer. I once bought a pair of outlet store jeans that were tattered and torn after just ten weeks of wear.

Think of it this way. Since outlet prices are pretty good, and sales at standard stores are worth waiting for, then sales *at* outlet malls may be the ultimate! Just be sure to compare prices and assess quality.

DO YOUR HOMEWORK:

1. Wear comfortable shoes and never shop on an empty stomach! Those are two sure ways to make hasty choices.
2. Know how much you're willing to spend for a given item and base your buying decisions on that rather than on "compare at" price tags or overblown "sale" signs.
3. Don't buy things just because they're bargains. Make sure you really want and need them.
4. Outlet malls can be overwhelming, and some stores don't accept returns. Put items on hold as you go through the mall, then go back and buy the things you really want.
5. Examine articles to see if they're well made of quality materials.

WHERE TO COMPLAIN:

If outlet mall merchandise is substandard and it wasn't marked "as is," try returning to the store where you bought it. If you're pleasant but firm you may be able to get a refund, even at a store with a "no refunds" policy. If the store doesn't respond, try complaining to mall management.

SEE ALSO:

SHOPPING: **Sales**

Rent to Own

More than eleven million people a year use the "rent to own" method to furnish their homes. It can be convenient for people with poor credit, but in the long run, it's a lousy way to buy something. I once priced a twenty-five-inch television at a rental store and a regular retailer. The rental store wanted $86.25 a month for twelve months. That's a total of $1,035. The cash price for the same TV at the regular retailer was just $500! Plus, when you rent to own, it's possible that the TV is several years old and has been rented to countless other people before you.

Even paying by credit card and carrying a balance can be a better deal than renting to own. That's because if monthly rental fees were expressed as an annual percentage rate, or APR, they would range from about 100 percent to 350 percent. Credit card interest rates typically top out at 24 percent. (Then again, if you pay by credit card and carry the balance for years and years, you could eventually end up paying more *that* way.)

The best thing to do is take the same amount you would pay a rental company each month and put the money in a savings account instead. Take the twenty-five-inch television example, above. If you save $86.25 a month, after six months you would have enough to pay cash for the TV. The one disadvantage is that you have to wait.

If you need the item today, you might want to consider buying something at a garage sale or thrift store instead. After all, it's quite possible the rental store is going to provide you with used merchandise, so what's the difference?

QUESTIONS TO ASK:

1. How much would the item cost if I paid cash?
2. How many rental payments will I have to make to own the item?
3. How much will *each* payment be?
4. What will the *total* of all the payments be?
5. Will the item be new or used?
6. If you're late with a payment, will the store repossess the item?

7. If you have trouble making your payments, can you return the item without a penalty?
8. Are you allowed to pay off the item early to save money, or is there a penalty?

DO YOUR HOMEWORK:

1. Shop around. Compare the same item at different rental stores and retail stores.
2. Consider saving for the item or buying something used instead.
3. If you must rent to own, pay the item off early if you can to save money.
4. Make sure the rental store gives you a written contract and keep a copy of it.
5. Try to get the questions above answered in writing. Some states require it as part of your contract with the store.

WHERE TO COMPLAIN:

This is a case for the Better Business Bureau and your county and state consumer protection offices.

SEE ALSO:

CREDIT: Credit Cards

Returns

Stores can set their own return policies, and contrary to popular belief, they don't have to accept returns at all. As long as they post their policy, they can do whatever they want. Be sure to read the signs, read the receipt, or ask the cashier before you buy. Stores seem to be getting stricter about returns. Too many have been burned by customers who bring items back five years later or shoplift items, then try to return them for cash. All the more reason why you need to be prepared if you want many happy returns.

Of course, a receipt is your ticket to a successful return. I stuff all of mine into an accordion file organized by month. If you're buying a gift, more and more stores now offer gift receipts. Get in the habit of asking for one. If you lose your receipt and you paid by credit card, try taking your credit card statement to the store as proof of purchase.

If you don't have a receipt, you may have to settle for an exchange rather than a return. And be prepared to accept the lowest price at which the product has been sold in the past year. If the cashier claims the store doesn't carry the item, ask to see the department manager, who should be more familiar with the merchandise.

I once bought my husband about ten pairs of shorts to replace the ratty ones he insisted on wearing in public. I cut the price tags off because they were a gift for his birthday. Some of the shorts didn't fit (or were too nice for his tastes!). I had my receipt, but the store resisted giving me a refund because the tags were missing. These days I cut off just the price part of the tag and leave the product numbers and bar codes intact.

Be sure to save all original packaging until you know the product works. If the item doesn't work when you buy it, or it breaks down soon after, you should be able to take it back to the store rather than going through the rigmarole of contacting the manufacturer. Be pleasantly persistent.

If you have trouble returning something at the store level, and you're certain you are in the right, write to the company president and/or the customer relations department. If the item actually broke, tape a piece of the product to your letter, if possible. Visual aids help! If you don't get a response, write another letter to the Better Business Bureau and your county and state consumer protection offices.

Finally, try to make returns when the store won't be crowded. That way the cashier will be in a better mood and less likely to turn you down out of spite. The cashier may even be willing to give you the benefit of the doubt, because there won't be a whole line of people who are likely to overhear and demand the same favor.

DO YOUR HOMEWORK:

1. Find out the store's return policy before you buy.
2. Make a system for saving receipts or always pay by credit card and save your statements.

3. Keep the original packaging and the price tags until you're sure you won't need to make a return.

WHERE TO COMPLAIN:

The Better Business Bureau and your county and state consumer protection offices are a good start.

SEE ALSO:

BEFORE YOU BUY: **Cooling-Off Rule;** SHOPPING: **Warranties**

Sales

When I'm out shopping with friends, I'm a master at rationalizing almost any purchase. ("That's such a good deal, you would be *wasting* money by *not* buying it!") However, I will squelch my natural talent for "consumer therapy" just long enough to write this section. Here's the bottom line, sacrilegious as it may sound: Not every sale is a bargain and not every bargain is on sale.

Say you buy a gallon of milk every week for $2.50. Then, one day, you walk into the supermarket and see a huge sign: "Today only! Milk just $2.50!" You would know that's ridiculous because that's what you always pay for milk. But what about things you don't buy so often—like refrigerators, stereos, and winter coats? How will you know if the big sale claims are for real? To be a truly savvy consumer you need to be a good comparison shopper. (If it's any consolation, to be a good comparison shopper, you need to be a truly *frequent* shopper!)

Retailers play games to get our greedy little hearts going. What do you think those "compare at" price tags are all about? You know, the ones where the store states its price right underneath the "compare at" price, which is supposedly what some other retailer charges. I know of a popular clothing store that marks its classic lines "50% off!" one month, then, "buy one get one free," the next month—and continues this cycle year-round.

Sleazy retailers will actually mark merchandise up just so they can mark it *down*. That way, you think you're getting a great deal, but the store's charging the amount it always wanted in the first place. This practice is actually illegal in some jurisdictions, but it's hard to prove because consumer watchdogs can't monitor stores every day.

If you receive a coupon that offers $100 off, say, your next painting job, you can't tell if you're really getting a discount unless you know the painter's usual price. So call and get a quote and *then* reveal that you have a coupon. That way, you know the painter isn't marking the price *up* before applying the coupon.

Stores that offer a "low price guarantee" in which they promise to beat their competitors' prices can be crafty, too. Often these stores deliberately invent their own names and model numbers for their merchandise so it's difficult for you to comparison shop.

"Buy one, get the second at 50% off." Don't fall into this trap! If the extra item is something you really want, then great. But if you won't use it, then don't pay the extra money. The same goes for jumbo-size products that you buy in bulk. If the medicine will expire or the food will spoil before you can use it, it's not worth paying the extra money to "supersize" it.

DO YOUR HOMEWORK:

1. Let's revise the old rhyme. It should be *"comparison* shop 'til you drop."

HOW TO COMPLAIN:

If you have proof a store is marking prices up just so it can mark them down, report it to your county and state consumer protection agencies.

SEE ALSO:

SHOPPING: Outlet Malls, **Going Out of Business**

Warranties

I have this soft-sided leather briefcase that I absolutely love. I've had it for ten years—or at least one like it. You see, the briefcase came with a lifetime warranty. I've had it replaced twice. Once the strap broke under the massive weight of my files. The second time the stitching unraveled . . . under the massive weight of my files. Both times the manufacturer came through for me. And that's lucky, because a "lifetime warranty" is only as good as the company backing it.

You probably assumed "lifetime" means *your* lifetime, right? Not always. There's no set legal definition of "lifetime warranty." Some weasley companies choose to interpret it as the lifetime of the *product*. I know, it's ridiculous. That's like saying, "This product is warranted to last as long as it lasts." Companies that do it this way designate an amount of time they think their product should reasonably last. If your item breaks during that time, they'll repair or replace it. If it breaks later, you're out of luck.

Even if the product you buy doesn't come with a written warranty, you're still covered by some *unwritten* warranties guaranteed by the federal government. The first is called an "implied warranty of merchantability," which basically means that a product must do what it's supposed to do. In other words, a blender must blend and a car must drive. If the item you buy turns out to be defective, even if the seller has a "no returns" policy, you may be able to return it anyway. There's also an unwritten warranty, called a "warranty of fitness for a particular purpose," like when a salesperson says a sleeping bag is suitable for zero degree weather. These unwritten warranties apply unless the product is marked "as is" when you buy it.

If somebody tries to sell you an extended warranty, keep in mind it's not really a warranty. It's a service contract, often offered by an outside company. Less than 20 percent of consumers who buy service contracts ever use them.

QUESTIONS TO ASK:

1. Does it duplicate the protections offered by the manufacturer's warranty?
2. When does it start? The word "extended" implies that it extends the period of the manufacturer's warranty, but these contracts often kick in right away, which is a waste.
3. Is there a pricey deductible each time the item needs service?
4. Can you get service anywhere or only at the store where you bought the product?
5. Is the item you're buying even likely to break down?
6. If you do your homework and choose a good product, it probably won't.

DO YOUR HOMEWORK:

1. If you're buying something really expensive, you might want to contact company officials and ask them how they define the word "lifetime."
2. Save the receipt and file it with your warranty. That way you'll always have proof of the date of purchase and that you're the original purchaser.
3. Don't bother sending in the warranty postcard—unless you want to. The manufacturer's just fishing for names for its mailing list, and you're covered whether you send it in or not.
4. Perform any maintenance or inspections required by the warranty so you don't void it.
5. Before purchasing an extended warranty, find out the name of the company offering it and do a background check with the BBB.

HOW TO COMPLAIN:

Your county or state consumer protection office may be able to help. You can also file a lawsuit under the Magnuson-Moss act, the law that governs warranties.

SEE ALSO:

SHOPPING: Returns

CHAPTER 11

Services

Dating Services

There are no rules in love—and next to no rules in the *business* of love, either. There are about 88 million singles in America, and dating services are a $300-million-a-year industry. Hundreds of consumers complain about these services each and every year. That's why it's important to use your head in matters of the heart.

Frontline dating service representatives are often called "counselors," even though they have no psychological training. In reality, they are salespeople working on commission. These salespeople often meet with prospects for hours, deliberately asking depressing questions about relationship failures and loneliness. A salesperson at a major dating service told Sue W. she better hurry up and find somebody because her "biological clock was ticking." Once the salesperson has broken the individual down, he or she offers to build the individual back up again—through the dating service's expensive matching program, of course.

One dating service claimed to have a 75 percent success rate for placing people in long-term relationships or marriages. Former employees say the rate was more like 5 percent. Some dating services also lie about the number of members in your area or your age range. I once went undercover to test a dating service. The salesperson told me that most of the members lived in my county. When I confronted the company owner later, he admitted that very few of his clients lived there.

The company literature may be warm and fuzzy, but the company contract is cold, hard legalese. Phil R. paid $1,800 for the chance to go on a dozen dates. Unfortunately, he didn't read the fine print. The contract stated that once the dating service had gotten him just one referral, he was no longer entitled to a refund. That's pretty typical. After all, dating services make their money when they *sign* you up, not when they *set* you up. Once they've got your money, they have no more motivation to help you. Many dating company contracts are open-ended: they say they'll give you twelve referrals, but they don't say *when* they'll do it. You could be waiting forever.

DO YOUR HOMEWORK:

1. Do a background check on any dating service you are considering. Contact the Better Business Bureau and your county and state consumer protection offices. Find out the number and the nature of consumer complaints.
2. Choose a dating service that's been in business for a long time under the same owner.
3. Read and understand the dating company's contract. Take a copy home with you to read before putting any money down. Pay special attention to cancellation clauses and the company's minimum obligation to you.
4. If the salesperson makes verbal claims or promises, get them in writing.
5. Try not to pay too much money up front. Sign up for a couple of referrals, and if you're pleased, *then* pay for more.

WHERE TO COMPLAIN:

If a dating service breaks your heart, contact your state attorney general for help. File complaints with the Better Business Bureau and your county and state consumer protection offices to spread the word to other lonely hearts.

SEE ALSO:

BEFORE YOU BUY: **Contracts**

SERVICES

Funeral Homes and Cemeteries

It's depressing to think that you have to be a vigilant consumer when you're struggling to cope with the death of a loved one, but you do. For you, it's a life-changing event. For the funeral director and cemetery superintendent, it's a livelihood. Funerals are one of the most expensive purchases consumers ever make. A traditional funeral costs about $6,000, and fancier ones can easily top $10,000.

Your first task is to learn the law in your state. Perhaps a family friend can do the research for you. Find out whether your state requires funeral directors to be licensed and, if so, make sure yours is. Learn what services are required by state law. For example, some states require you to pay for refrigeration if the body is to remain unburied for more than 48 hours. Beware of unscrupulous funeral directors who claim additional services are *also* required.

There is also a *federal* law, called the Funeral Rule, that protects you. You have the right to choose the specific goods and services you want, instead of being pushed into a package deal. Funeral directors are required to give you an itemized price list that you can take home with you. Ask for one. They are also required to give you a list of casket prices before they show you any caskets. That's so

you'll know the full price range even if the funeral director is pushing pricier models. If you choose to buy a casket from someone
other than the funeral home, you can. Funeral homes are not
allowed to refuse an outside casket. You can also switch funeral
homes at any time, as long as you pay the original funeral home for
the goods and services you have already received.

SERVICES

You don't have to use a funeral home at all, but if you do, you are
required to pay the home's basic services fee, which includes the
services common to all funerals: securing permits and death certificates, preparing notices, sheltering the body, funeral planning, and
coordinating with third parties, like the cemetery. Funeral homes
often try to double-charge their customers for items that are included in the basic services fee.

Here are some other common schemes: charging extra for filing
the death certificate or getting it medically certified; charging a fee
to handle an outside casket; charging a commission for forwarding
payment to third parties; claiming embalming is required by law
when it's not; charging for goods and services the family did not
request; and charging for goods and services the family *did* request,
then not providing them.

When Patricia S. lost her son, Ronald, her grief was potent,
because parents never expect their children to die first. She paid the
funeral home for a concrete liner to protect Ronald's casket. Months
later, the cemetery reopened Ronald's grave because of a dispute
over burial plot locations. That's when she discovered that she had
not actually gotten the concrete liner. Patricia grieved anew. The
funeral home said it was the cemetery's fault. The cemetery blamed
the funeral home.

That's why it's important to have a separate business relationship
with each. Often funeral homes can sell you a cemetery plot, but I
don't recommend it. It's better to deal directly with the cemetery,
so you know what you're getting. Make sure you visit the cemetery
in advance and that you like it. Then sign a contract with the cemetery that includes the itemized cost of each burial service and the
location of the plot. Religious and nonprofit cemeteries often don't
have to be licensed; for-profit cemeteries often do. Find out whether
the cemetery you're considering is following the law.

Mary H. purchased a plot for a deceased family member through the funeral home instead of the cemetery. Weeks later, when she went to visit the grave, it seemed like it was in a different place from where it had been during the burial service. Mary demanded an explanation, but since she didn't have a contract with the cemetery, it was hard for her to claim that she had been wronged. I investigated, and the cemetery superintendent admitted the marker was misplaced and the grave was eight feet from where it should have been.

SERVICES

Lousy maintenance is the other troubling cemetery problem. It's understandable, yet disturbing. After all, when somebody dies, family and friends visit and keep a watchful eye on the cemetery. But when those family members and friends *themselves* die, the thread of family history is often lost, and there's nobody left to hold the cemetery accountable.

When Brenda M. buried her father at a cemetery, she never really thought about the future of his final resting place. Two years later, the owner abandoned the cemetery and it went to seed. Visiting families had to walk past open graves and wade through matted grass to pay their respects. Brenda began bringing a weed whacker with her just so she could find her father's tombstone.

It's a painful lesson. When you visit the cemetery, look for signs of deterioration. Consider whether you're buying one of the last plots. If so, the cemetery won't bring in new revenue for much longer and may face financial difficulties. Make sure your contract with the cemetery specifies the level of maintenance you can expect. Choose a cemetery with a perpetual care fund, which sets aside money for maintenance.

DO YOUR HOMEWORK:

1. If you choose to prepay for your own funeral, make sure your family knows. Leave instructions where your family can easily find them. Some families have paid twice for funeral services because they didn't realize their loved one had made arrangements.
2. Learn the law in your state.
3. Get itemized price lists from more than one funeral home and compare them. Make sure the funeral homes you check with are

not all owned by the same company. National chains now own many funeral homes, thus cutting down on competition.

4. Check the reputations of the funeral homes by contacting the BBB and your county and state consumer protection offices.

5. Find out what's included in the funeral home's basic services fee.

6. Get receipts for fees the funeral home will pay to third parties, like florists, limousine companies, and cemeteries, or pay these providers yourself.

7. Compare costs at different cemeteries.

8. Find out if the cemetery you're considering is required to have a license and whether it does.

9. Check out the cemetery's reputation with the BBB and county and state consumer protection offices.

10. Look for a cemetery with a perpetual care fund.

11. Visit the cemetery and the specific grave site before committing.

12. Sign a contract with the cemetery that specifies the price, where the plot is located, and the level of maintenance.

WHERE TO COMPLAIN:

You may find that your county and state governments don't readily know which department regulates "the death industry." It's a tricky area. It could be the health department or a board under the office of professional regulation. Contact your consumer protection offices and ask. It varies widely from state to state.

Gyms

'Til death do us part. It's a serious promise, associated with serious commitments like marriage and parenthood. But these days, some *gyms* want you to make the same commitment to *them*. You join a gym to exercise your body, but if you want to quit, you may find it hard to exercise your rights.

If you're hoping for buns of steel, then you'll probably be asked to sign an ironclad contract. Don't accuse gym managers of being dumb jocks. Their contracts are long, involved, and full of legalese.

If you sign one without reading it, *you're* the dummy. A contract's a contract. One national chain holds customers to their contracts unless they are gravely ill, badly injured, or move more than fifty miles from the nearest branch of the gym. Can you imagine driving fifty miles to work out?

Many gyms push three-year, five-year, or lifetime memberships. Customers go for it, because the longer the contract, the cheaper the monthly rate. But is it really a savings if you're dissatisfied with the gym and never go? As with all future services contracts in which you make a long-term commitment and pay in advance, there are risks. Some gyms have been known to sell memberships before they're open and then fail to open for months, if ever. Others have gone out of business, leaving prepaid members in the lurch.

Some states now require gyms to offer people the option of a brief introductory membership—typically ninety days. Here's the bad news: When I investigated the health club industry, none of the gym salespeople informed my undercover producer about the introductory membership option. Plus, when we went to cancel the various memberships we'd signed up for, some of the gyms sicced collection agents on us.

SERVICES

DO YOUR HOMEWORK:

1. Learn the law in the jurisdiction where you're thinking of joining a gym. Specifically, find out if gyms are required to offer a brief trial period before locking you into a long-term contract.
2. Check the gym's reputation by contacting the Better Business Bureau and your county and state consumer protection offices.
3. See if there's a good gym in your area that offers a month-to-month membership. Some gyms are starting to do this as a countermarketing strategy. Typically, you just have to give thirty days' notice and you're free as a bird!
4. Ask for free guest passes and visit the gym you're considering during the hours that you would normally work out. Some gyms set no limits on membership, so check for overcrowding.
5. Find out what is and isn't included in the gym contract. Will you have to pay extra for specialty courses like yoga and Pilates? Is your gym membership limited to certain hours?

6. Hold out. Gym salespeople have to make quotas. The longer you hem and haw, the more they'll drop the price or add incentives.
7. Read and understand the contract before you sign it. Take a copy home with you to study, if possible. Make sure all of the salesperson's verbal promises are included in the written contract.
8. Sign a short-term contract first, to see if you like the gym, even if it costs more. Then, if you're satisfied, you can enter into a longer agreement.
9. Pay monthly or quarterly so if the gym closes, you won't lose too much money.
10. Many gyms charge customers' credit cards or checking accounts each month. Use caution. When your contract ends and you go to quit, you could have trouble canceling that automatic debit. Some customers resort to cutting up their cards or closing their checking accounts just to ditch their gyms!

WHERE TO COMPLAIN:

This is a case for the Better Business Bureau and your county and state consumer protection offices. But, remember, if you signed a long-term contract, you may have no recourse.

SEE ALSO:

BEFORE YOU BUY: Contracts; SERVICES: **Personal Trainers**

Limousines

Renting a limousine can be the ride of your life or a very bumpy ride indeed. Every spring, which is prom season *and* peak wedding season, the limo complaints on my tip line rev up. It's sad, because most people hire a limo only for special occasions. And a lousy limousine company can really put the brakes on your big night.

Katie C. rented a limousine for her senior prom. After all, riding in a limo is sort of a rite of passage into adulthood. Unfortunately, Katie and her friends learned some especially grown-up lessons that night. While the teenagers danced, deputies arrested their driver and impounded his car. Authorities said the driver was unlicensed, and the vehicle was unsafe—and uninsured. Furthermore, the limousine company wasn't licensed to do business in that county. The high schoolers were stranded on their big night. The limousine company later offered them a free ride on another night, but that wasn't exactly appealing, given that the cops said the car wasn't safe. Katie's parents insisted on a refund, but months later the company still hadn't given them back their $500.

SERVICES

When I investigated the limo company in this case, it led to one of the most hilarious moments of my career. I discovered it wasn't really a "company" at all—just a lone guy with a stretch limo he kept parked at his apartment complex. So I called him. The man who answered the phone insisted he wasn't the owner. But because of the way he kept arguing and carrying on, I got the distinct impression that he *was*. So, finally, I asked him for his name for my records. The man was so tangled up in his lies, and so flustered by all my questions, that he blurted out the first fake name he could think of: "My name is Mary," he said. I nearly burst out laughing, but I kept my composure just long enough to ask him, "Okay, Mary, can I quote you on that?"

There's a point to this silly story. It's awfully easy for people like "Mary" to set themselves up in the limousine business—albeit illegally. After all, most people know how to drive, and all they have to do is rent or finance the car. Some limousine drivers do an all-cash business, so it's an area ripe for rip-offs. I also get a lot of complaints that property left in limousines is never returned. In fact, I myself lost a camera and a bunch of CDs years ago when I rented a limo for my twenty-first birthday. Recently, a driver told me that there's a lot of discrimination in the limousine business. He said minorities are often treated poorly and quoted higher prices. All the more reason to check out a limo company before you hand over your money.

DO YOUR HOMEWORK:

1. Book well in advance. The highest-quality limousine companies will fill up first. You don't want to be stuck with the fly-by-nighters.

2. Don't book a company just because it has a big ad in the yellow pages. That's how Katie found her limo. The people who print the phone book have no obligation to make sure a limousine company is properly licensed or has a good reputation.

3. Instead, get referrals from friends or take a *few* ads from the phone book and quickly do background checks. Contact your local Better Business Bureau and your county or state consumer protection office. Choose the company with the fewest complaints.

4. A few counties have elaborate licensing systems in place for limousines. If that's the case in your county, you can check with the department that does the licensing and get a list of approved carriers.

5. Ask the limousine company if it belongs to any professional associations. You could go a step further and call the association to confirm the company is a member in good standing.

6. When you make your reservation, ask the limo company to fax or e-mail you a confirmation stating the date and the price.

7. Try to pay with a credit card. (In fact, if the company *only* accepts cash, go elsewhere.) That way, if there's trouble later, you can dispute the charges through your credit card company.

8. Call to confirm your reservation the day before your event. Again, I speak from personal experience. I once hired a limo. When it didn't arrive on the appointed night, I called and learned the company had no record of my reservation.

SERVICES

WHERE TO COMPLAIN:

If you take all of these steps and you *still* have a bumpy ride, complain to the Better Business Bureau to create a paper trail for other consumers. Also complain to your county and state consumer protection offices. In some counties, police get involved in limousine licensing, so you may have to go a step further. If you're really angry, contact the DMV, too. That might make it harder for the company to register its vehicles next time.

Personal Trainers

"I am a personal trainer." Saying it is all you have to do to make it so. The government doesn't regulate personal trainers, so anybody can become one. You don't need a degree. You don't need a certification. For that matter, the government doesn't regulate the organizations that *provide* certification either. About fifteen different groups do so nationally; some respected, others not. Several organizations certify people as trainers after just one weekend of classes. Others just require an open-book test. When I investigated personal trainers, I even found a group that was willing to certify me by mail if I sent a videotape of myself exercising!

Personal training costs $50 to $100 an hour and up, so it *ought* to be a weighty decision. If you get the wrong trainer, you'll lose money and you *won't* lose weight. You could also seriously injure yourself. Don't choose a trainer just because he or she has a great body. Choose somebody who can help you achieve your fitness goals. Finding a good trainer should wear you out a little bit—just like a good workout.

Try to find a personal trainer who has a college degree in a relevant field, like kinesiology, biomechanics, exercise physiology, or health and fitness, plus a credible certification. The American College of Sports Medicine and the National Strength and Conditioning Association are the most well-respected certifying organizations. Knowing who trained the trainer really is key.

DO YOUR HOMEWORK:

1. If a trainer claims to be certified by a national agency, ask for the agency name, number, and Web site so you can confirm.
2. Also check to see that the trainer keeps up with continuing education.
3. Many certifying organizations keep grievance records, so you can find out if the trainer's background is clean.

4. Some trainers carry liability insurance, another thing you may want to consider.
5. Check the trainer's references and make sure his or her fitness philosophy is a good match for you.
6. Make sure your trainer is capable of performing CPR.
7. Get the trainer's cancellation policy in writing before you start working out.
8. If a trainer pushes you to use herbal supplements, resist. Personal trainers are not qualified to advise on supplements, and many of them are risky.
9. If a trainer pushes you to do exercises that hurt or make you uncomfortable, say no until you can get a second opinion.

WHERE TO COMPLAIN:

If the trainer works at a gym, complain to management. If the trainer is self-employed, file a complaint with the BBB and county and state consumer protection offices. Also lodge a complaint with the trainer's certifying organization.

SEE ALSO:

SERVICES: **Gyms**

Pharmacies

Medical mistakes are the eighth most common cause of death in the United States—ahead of car crashes, breast cancer, and AIDS. And a recent study showed that pharmacy foul-ups make up a big part of that number. A survey of patients checking into hospitals found that receiving the wrong medication is their number one fear. It's a rational worry, because even by conservative estimates, pharmacies make fifteen million medication mistakes every year.

Seven-year-old Zachary K. has a rare genetic disease that weakens his immune system. He takes a small dose of antibiotics every day to try to ward off illness. Recently, Zach's mom, Cynthia, noticed that his pills looked different. She was right. As it turns out, the pharmacy had dispensed the right pills in the wrong strength—*double-*strength. Cynthia complained to the pharmacy, turned in the bad bottle, and thought nothing more of it. Until it happened again a month later. The pharmacy had made the same mistake *twice*.

Spencer P. suffers from serious sinus problems. His doctor prescribed a new medication, and Spencer took it with high hopes. But he immediately suffered devastating side effects: dizziness, difficulty breathing, and tightness in his chest. He missed several shifts at his day job and had to quit his night job. Spencer kept taking the medication, hoping the side effects would wear off and desperate for the drug to work. After a month, he couldn't take it anymore and went to see his doctor. What a shock! The doctor had prescribed a nasal spray, called "Flonase." The pharmacy had dispensed a prostate drug, called "Flomax."

Why do medication mix-ups like this happen? For one thing, there are more prescription drugs on the market than ever before, a lot for a pharmacist to remember. To make matters worse, some of them have similar names—like Flonase and Flomax, Celebrex and Cerebyx, Lamisil and Lamictal. If a prescription is called in—or written in a doctor's famously messy handwriting—it's easy to see how a pharmacist could get it wrong. Plus, that pharmacist is probably overworked. Prescription drug use has doubled, while the number of pharmacists has remained the same.

The three most common mistakes are dispensing the wrong drug, dispensing the wrong dose, and giving the wrong instructions. It's hard to say how often pharmacy foul-ups happen, because many states don't require pharmacists to report their errors. When consumers complain, state pharmacy boards (made up of other pharmacists) often dole out light punishments. Ideally, pharmacists would serve as caring advisors and discuss medications with their patients, but the way things are now, they don't have time. Until pharmacists are able to spend less time putting pills in bottles, you'll have to pay more attention to what you're putting into your body.

DO YOUR HOMEWORK:

1. Know the size, shape, color, and strength of any pills you take routinely.

SERVICES

2. If you are trying a new medication, ask your doctor for a sample or ask to see a picture of the drug in the *Physician's Desk Reference.* You can also go to the **Physician's Desk Reference** Web site at **www.pdr.net.**

3. Many doctors now write prescriptions on a computer. If not, be sure your doctor writes neatly and ask him to identify the drug by both the generic and brand names.

4. Also ask your doctor what the medication is most commonly used for, how to take it, and what the side effects are.

5. Then ask the pharmacist those same questions and make sure the explanations match.

6. Finally, note the strength and instructions your doctor had in mind and make sure the pharmacist fills the order as intended.

WHERE TO COMPLAIN:

Voice your concerns to your state's board of pharmacy. Also file complaints with the BBB and county and state consumer protection offices.

Salons

Some ugly things go on in the beauty business. Salons perform some pretty intimate procedures, but how safe and sanitary are they? Beauty treatments *seem* glamorous, but they can be gross. They should be relaxing, but they can cause stress.

Kim S. is a licensed makeup artist herself, and she thought she knew what to look for in a salon. So when festering boils appeared on her calves, she didn't want to believe her twice-monthly pedicures could be the cause. Kim spent hundreds of hours and thousands of dollars trying to get better. She tried three different antibiotics. They made her sick and made her miss work, but they didn't cure her infection. It turns out the purplish sores on Kim's legs were caused by a bacteria related to tuberculosis. The throne-like footbaths that women consider so luxurious are hard to clean and harbor the bacteria.

Nail salons are number one when it comes to consumer complaints and disciplinary actions in the beauty business. Here are some other tidbits I uncovered during an investigation: One salon cut a customer's cuticle so deeply that it bled for days. A judge awarded another woman $150,000 because her nail salon used a hazardous chemical on her. Two other salons were suspended when health inspectors found rodent droppings on their nail implements. I sent a producer undercover, and she found violations at the first nail salon she visited. A technician filed her nails with a used emery board. That's a no-no. The tech also insisted on using a razor device on the producer's calluses, even though the devices are illegal in many jurisdictions.

SERVICES

Hair salons harbor their share of hazards too. The Food and Drug Administration says hair dyes and perm products are two of its top sources of complaint. Used improperly, the chemicals can make your hair break off or fall out; they can singe your scalp and even blind you. People with chemical allergies may go into shock or have trouble breathing. And it's no wonder. Take relaxers, for example. Many contain sodium hydroxide, the same chemical found in oven cleaner, car polish, and paint remover.

Hair salons are supposed to completely immerse combs and brushes in sterilizer solution. But I found salons that had been accused of watering down that solution or skipping it altogether. Worst case scenario? You could get lice along with your haircut and blow-dry.

We get our hair cut, colored, curled—and we get it removed. Many salons are not properly licensed to perform waxing. That's troubling because hot wax can cause serious burns if it's handled by an unskilled technician. I also found records of a woman whose face was permanently scarred when an unlicensed salon performed electrolysis with a needle that was too big. A young man died while undergoing laser hair removal because he was allergic to the anesthetic. The salon wasn't prepared to handle medical emergencies.

In many places, tanning salons aren't regulated at all. One woman had an allergic reaction to tanning accelerator cream and had to go to the emergency room. Another suffered first-degree burns when she fell asleep in a tanning bed without a timer. Nobody on the staff ever bothered to check on her.

Most jurisdictions only have a handful of health inspectors to monitor dozens of different industries, including salons. Typically, these inspectors don't do preventive spot checks of salons. They only respond to consumer complaints. So, if you see something suspicious, do yourself and other customers a favor: complain.

DO YOUR HOMEWORK:

1. Ask each cosmetologist to show you his or her license. Make sure it's current and issued by the correct jurisdiction. I've found that even the swankiest salons hire unlicensed workers.

2. Shop for a salon. Don't just drop in. Get referrals from friends and check the salon's reputation with county and state consumer authorities. If you're preparing for a major procedure, check health department records too.

3. Bring your own implements when you get your nails done.

4. Choose a nail salon with small portable pedicure baths instead of the giant "thrones." They're easier to clean.

5. Watch and make sure pedicure baths are completely drained and disinfected between customers.

6. Don't shave your legs before getting a pedicure. Tiny razor nicks provide a pathway for bacteria. Don't let nail technicians cut into your skin or cuticles.

7. Make sure all combs and brushes are completely immersed in sanitizer solution.

8. If you're trying a new hair treatment like hair color or straightener, ask the salon to do a patch test twenty-four hours in advance.

9. Make sure the salon—and the specific technician—is licensed to perform waxing. Watch to see if the technician does a temperature test on his or her own inner arm before applying wax to you.

10. Get laser hair removal done only in a doctor's office or a salon with a doctor on staff and present at the time of your procedure. Ask what emergency plans are in place should you have a serious reaction.

11. Make sure electrolysis needles are brand new for each customer. As in the medical field, dirty needles are a serious health concern.
12. Vigilantly file complaints to protect yourself and to show your local health department that salons need attention.

WHERE TO COMPLAIN:

Your county or state health department and/or the board of cosmetology.

CHAPTER 12

Travel

Airlines

In 1999, some members of Congress were all fired up and introduced the "airline passengers' bill of rights." They heard testimony on Capitol Hill from irate travelers with horror stories about the not-so-friendly skies. But then . . . they wimped out. The airlines pleaded that granting passengers certain rights would put them out of business. So, nothing much changed. However, you do have *some* rights. And if you've got gumption, you can *pretend* you've got others!

Unfortunately, if your flight is delayed or canceled, the airline is not obligated to do anything for you. Even if it's the airline's own darn fault. One nifty way to guard against this is to check the reliability of a given flight before you book. Ask the reservations agent to give you the on-time performance code for the flight you're considering. It's a one-digit code that tells you how often the flight has been within fifteen minutes of its scheduled arrival time over the past month. For example, if the code is "7," that means the flight was on time 70 percent to 79 percent of the time.

Of course, past performance is no guarantee of future success, so be ready to grab some extra rights for yourself through sheer will. If your flight is delayed or canceled, ask for stuff. Be that squeaky wheel! Ask the airline if it offers hotel rooms, meal vouchers, or telephone calling cards to stranded passengers. There is no law requiring airlines to do this, but many do. They are more sympathetic if the delay is their fault than if it is caused by severe weather. One study showed airlines respond best when passengers make specific requests. Don't just angrily ask to be "compensated." Instead, decide what you want and calmly and politely ask for it.

TRAVEL

A couple of years ago, my parents paid for our entire extended family of twenty-six to travel to Hawaii together. We got to the airport bright and early only to learn that our flight was canceled because the airplane door was jammed. We had to wait fifteen hours for the next flight. We missed our connection to Kauai. We had to stay in a scuzzy Oahu hotel that night. And we lost the money we'd paid for the first night in our *Kauai* hotel. Sound like a legitimate grievance? I thought so. I wrote a nice letter asking for free round-trip tickets for my parents to return to Hawaii at their leisure. The airline said yes (and was probably relieved that I didn't ask for more!).

If your flight is delayed or canceled and you decide to search for a flight on another airline, you may have better luck calling the toll-free number than going to the ticket counter. If you find a suitable flight but it's more expensive, ask your original airline to "endorse your ticket" to the new carrier. By doing this, you may not have to pay the higher fare. Airlines often honor each other's endorsements as a matter of goodwill, but they're not obligated to do so.

If the airline overbooks your flight and you are involuntarily bumped, that's another story. Then you do have specific rights that are guaranteed by federal law. First, the airline will try to find volunteers willing to give up their seats in exchange for compensation. If that doesn't work, typically the last passengers to check in are the first to get involuntarily bumped.

If you are bumped, and the airline manages to get you to your final destination within an hour of your originally scheduled arrival time, you get nothing. Sorry! But if the airline can't get you there until one to two hours (between one and four hours internationally) after your original arrival time, then it must reimburse you the cost of your one-way fare. This reimbursement is capped at $200. If the airline gets you where you're going more than two hours late (four hours internationally), you get double compensation—double the one-way fare, with a maximum of $400. You get the same compensation if the airline doesn't attempt to make any substitute travel arrangements for you at all. You also get to keep your original ticket and use it on another flight. Alternatively, you can make other travel arrangements of your own and demand an "involuntary refund."

If a flight is overbooked and you volunteer to give up your seat, how you're compensated is negotiable. If lots of people volunteer, the airline will choose the people who make the most modest demands. But if you can tell that the airline is having trouble getting enough volunteers, that's the time to go for the jugular! Most airlines offer a free round-trip ticket. Ask if you can have one without an expiration date. Without blackout dates. Without regional restrictions. Heck, ask for one that lets you fly to another country. For that matter, if you'd rather have cash, put on your poker face and demand money!

If an airline loses your luggage, don't immediately despair. Airlines are actually pretty good at finding people's suitcases even if "many bags look alike." Just think, you won't have to lug the thing, because most airlines deliver lost bags to your door. Years ago, when I was backpacking in Europe, an airline misplaced my big, grungy backpack in Zurich. I was on my way to a tiny town in the Alps that was hours away by train. Sure enough, the airline somehow arranged to drive my pack up the mountain and deliver it a couple of hours after I arrived at my hotel.

If you are not as fortunate, the airline is required to compensate you for the loss of your belongings. The domestic limit is $1,250; the international limit is $9.07 per pound, up to a total of $640 per bag. Be prepared to prove the value of the items you packed. Airlines compensate you for actual value only, not replacement value. If your suitcase is damaged in transit, most airlines will pay for repairs or pay to replace it. The same goes for the items inside, although the airline will balk if the contents broke and the suitcase itself appears unscathed. There *are* important exceptions you should know about. Most airlines post a list of excluded baggage they will not cover. "Electronic equipment" is a common exclusion and includes laptop computers.

DO YOUR HOMEWORK:

TRAVEL

1. Find out whether the flight you're considering is typically on time. Flights early in the day tend to have a better record because there's a domino effect in delays as the day goes on.
2. Ask for compensation if your flight is badly delayed or canceled, even though you have no legal right to it.
3. If you opt to change carriers, get the old carrier to "endorse" your ticket and try to get the new carrier to match the fare.
4. Arrive reasonably early so you won't be involuntarily bumped.
5. If you are bumped against your will, make sure you get the compensation guaranteed by federal law.
6. If you volunteer to give up your seat, negotiate the best possible compensation package for yourself.
7. Before going to the airport, see if the airline refuses to cover certain types of baggage. Either don't bring those items or carry them on.
8. If the airline loses your luggage, insist on filling out a written claim and keep a copy. Write down the names of each person you speak with.
9. If your luggage is never found, document the value of your belongings to receive the maximum compensation.

WHERE TO COMPLAIN:

You can write to the airline's own consumer affairs office. If that fails, address complaints about security to the Federal Aviation Administration and complaints about service to the U.S. Department of Transportation.

SEE ALSO:

TRAVEL: Frequent-Flier Miles

Frequent-Flier Miles

American Airlines introduced the first modern frequent-flier program in 1981. Since then the idea has taken off. All U.S. airlines and most foreign carriers now have programs. Technically, the airlines could end or cut back their mileage programs just as easily as they started them. There's no law protecting passenger's rights. Airlines can raise the number of miles required for a flight, lower the number of seats available, or cancel portions of their programs at will. That's why you should balance your desire to hoard miles for the priciest flights with the need to use miles up before the mileage program changes.

TRAVEL

Fortunately, even if your favorite airline goes out of business, your miles don't automatically crash and burn. For one thing, competitors are likely to honor your frequent-flier miles because they want your business. You'll probably have some warning before the airline goes belly up, so you can try to use up the miles first. If you can't squeeze in enough flights, you can use miles to shop, rent cars, or stay in hotels. You can donate miles to charity and take a tax deduction. If you're really worried, some companies now offer frequent-flier mile insurance.

The more immediate concern is how to get as many miles as possible and how to cash them in successfully. These days you can earn frequent-flier miles without ever actually flying anywhere. I love to travel, so I've signed up for every possible program. Long-distance service. Rental cars. Hotels. I even earned miles just for joining a wine-tasting association. Talk about a win-win! Every time my favorite airline offers an incentive, I snap it up. I got miles for going to Florida during a certain month. I got miles for trying the electronic check-in kiosk. I got *more* miles for checking my mileage statements online, where I gleefully noted just how many gazillion miles I have!

Now that I no longer carry a balance, I can also earn miles on my credit card. I charge everything! Groceries. Dry cleaning. I made the down payment on my car with a credit card. I charged my wedding reception and practically earned a second honeymoon. Many credit cards let you accrue miles on just one airline, but I prefer those that partner with multiple airlines and let you choose. American Express has a particularly generous program. If you don't have quite enough miles for a ticket, Amex will advance you the miles! Now *that's* service.

So, once you get piles of miles, the next challenge is *using* them. I actually know people who no longer sign up for frequent-flier programs because they've had trouble booking seats using miles. Pathetic! True, flying for free is not a sport for procrastinators. I usually have no problem because I plan all my vacations the first week of the year and book them by the end of January. That way you get to daydream about your vacations all year long. Airlines only give away 4 percent to 7 percent of their seats per flight. You *do* need to get a head start.

TRAVEL

If you still have trouble booking a trip, try avoiding hub cities. Consider flying to a nearby city and driving a little farther. If you're going to Disney World, fly to Tampa instead of Orlando. If you want to visit San Francisco, fly to Oakland or San Jose. I couldn't get frequent-flier seats to Rome one time, so I booked seats to Frankfurt instead. Then I bought tickets on a discount airline from Frankfurt to Rome for a grand total of $39 each way!

Other strategies: get on waiting lists. Airlines may release more frequent-flier seats at the last minute if they see that a flight's not going to fill up with paying passengers. You can also offer to cash in extra miles and see if that helps eliminate pesky blackout dates. Do that and you'll probably get an upgrade, too! Here's a spontaneous idea: Ask the airline what cities you *can* still get frequent-flier seats for—and just go! Try something new. Other ways to fly free: travel in the winter (which often requires fewer miles), overnight, or in the middle of the week.

As for international travel, see if you can fly on a foreign partner airline known for exquisite service, instead of flying on the same old U.S. airline. Here's a new one I just learned: You may be able to travel for free to two destinations instead of just one. I'm planning to go to Asia. I figured I would use miles to fly to Hong Kong, then I'd buy tickets to go to a couple of other cities. I found out I'm allowed to fly to Hong Kong, lay over for a week, then continue on to Bangkok— all for free! I saved myself a few hundred dollars just by asking.

DO YOUR HOMEWORK:

1. Sign up for as many frequent-flier miles as you can, including when you travel for job interviews or business trips.
2. Make sure the airline has your frequent-flier account number each time you book a ticket and board a flight.
3. Keep your ticket stubs until you receive your statement and see that you've been credited for each trip.
4. Sign up with frequent-flier partners.
5. Book free seats early (and often!).

SEE ALSO:

TRAVEL: **Airlines**

Hotels

If you want to learn about bargain travel, buy, borrow, or steal a travel book. If you want to know how to avoid travel rip-offs, I've got you covered. Hotels are full of them. I'm not talking about schemes or scams here; I'm talking about perfectly legal charges that you can avoid with perfectly legal strategies.

For example, when you call the toll-free number to make a hotel reservation, the hotel typically quotes you the "rack rate" for the room. This is an inflated price similar to the sticker price on a car. It's negotiable. Instead, try calling the hotel's direct, local number and asking for the best rate available. It often works!

Also ask about discounts. Business hotels offer special weekend rates, or you may be able to get a "group" discount, no matter how gigantic or nonexclusive the group. AA, AAA, AARP. Maybe a professional association you belong to. Whatever. Give it a try. Inquire about corporate discounts, too. Okay, so maybe you're not a corporate muckety-

TRAVEL

muck, but you probably work for a corporation, right? Swallow your pride and ask. Surely you could qualify for a family discount. You're somebody's family member, right? See if the hotel offers one.

Room service is typically 10 percent to 20 percent more expensive than the same meal eaten right in the hotel dining room. Now, personally, I *love* room service, but if you're pinching pennies, why not walk into the restaurant without revealing you're a hotel guest and order food to go? Then take it to your room and enjoy! Alternatively, have food delivered to your room by a local restaurant. Need a beverage with your meal? Minibars are notoriously pricey . . . double or triple store prices. Me, I like strolling to stores in new neighborhoods. Find the closest convenience store and stock up on what you need.

TRAVEL

If you have clothes cleaned at your hotel, you're probably paying about five times as much as you have to. Drop your things off at a local laundry instead. Some dry cleaners even pick up and deliver. Why not to a hotel? If you need clothes pressed, and there's no iron in your room, don't assume you have to pay a premium for somebody else to do the work. Call the front desk and ask for an iron. Chances are, you'll get what you need.

Here's a consumer quiz for you: When is a toll-free call *not* free? At a hotel. Most hotels add a surcharge of a dollar or more to each phone call, even local and toll-free calls. Find out how much your cell phone charges for roaming and use that instead. If you don't have a cell phone, use the pay phone in the hotel lobby. (Just be sure to read the pay phone section in the chapter on telephones first!)

Some hotels offer a free preview of in-room movies. But beware. If you watch for more than five minutes, you could be charged automatically. If you're traveling with children, it's wise to ask the hotel to block the pay channels in your room.

DO YOUR HOMEWORK:

1. Decide which is more valuable, your money or your time, then use the tips above to save one or the other.
2. Travel books are full of small but luxurious hotels that cost less than big, luxurious hotels. You often can save money and have a more personalized experience staying in one. Consider it!

Rental Cars

Some people use and abuse rental cars. I use and abuse rental car *companies.* When we take road trips, my husband calls me the "navigatrix." Ahem, anyway . . . you, too, can dominate your rental car company. First, call and check prices by phone. Then go online and compare. You'll be amazed at the difference. I typically find it's cheaper to book online, because the travel industry is trying to encourage customers to spend money without ever speaking to a human. Finally, when you get to your destination, walk into the rental office and ask about rates. Customers often get a better deal on the spot. If not, or if all the cars are taken, *then* reveal that you already have a reservation. The other way to save money is to learn the lingo and know how it applies to you.

TRAVEL

A **collision damage waiver,** or CDW, is an optional charge allowed in some states. It is not technically collision insurance. It's a guarantee that the rental car company will pay for damage to the car you rent. If you decline the waiver, you're accepting responsibility for any damage. That's fine if your personal car insurance policy covers rental cars or if you have good coverage through a credit card or motor club. But make sure, because, if you don't have any other coverage, you could be liable for the full value of the car. When I travel in a foreign country, I always accept all the rental company insurance, just to avoid potential headaches and hassles.

Personal accident insurance, PAI, pays a death benefit and/or a portion of your medical bills if you're in an accident while driving the rental car. If you have a good life insurance policy and good health care coverage, you shouldn't need this.

Personal effects coverage, or "PEC," is insurance for your luggage while you travel. Many homeowner's and renter's policies cover this. Find out, and if they do, don't waste your money.

Fuel charges are handled a couple of different ways. You can prepay for the right to return the car empty, or you can opt to refuel the car yourself. If you prepay, the rental car company will refuel for you and charge a price higher than what you'd find at an off-airport gas station. If you choose the option of refueling yourself, then fail to fill up, the rental car company will charge you a price *way* higher than what you'd find at an off-airport gas station. The gamble is yours.

Mileage charges are another thing to watch out for. It seems like most rental car companies offer unlimited mileage these days, but don't take that for granted. Some companies charge a few cents per mile, others charge a flat fee if you go over your mileage allowance. On the other hand, you may be able to get a lower overall rate if you know you won't be driving far and ask for a low mileage cap.

DO YOUR HOMEWORK:

TRAVEL

1. If you're planning to rent a car for four or five days, ask about the weekly rate, which is often actually lower than paying the daily rate for several days. Also inquire about special weekend rates.
2. Ask about fees that will raise the base rate, so you'll know the true price. Airport taxes are one example. Fees to drop the car off somewhere other than where you rented it are another.
3. Some rental car companies check your driving record when you arrive to pick up your car. Even if you have a confirmed reservation, they may reject you on the spot if you don't meet their safety standards. Check the company's policy when you book.
4. Ask whether the rental car company will block funds on your credit card while you drive the car. Companies do this in case you go on a joyride and never return. They don't actually complete the charge, but it does reduce the spending limit on your card. Keep that in mind if you plan to use the same card for all your other travel expenses.

WHERE TO COMPLAIN:

Rental car companies are largely unregulated. Address complaints to the state consumer protection office where you rented the car or where the rental car company is based.

SEE ALSO:

INSURANCE: Car Insurance

Travel Offers

Tricky travel offers are consistently among the top five consumer complaints. Americans lose $12 billion a year to travel fraud. I think it happens because we're so hungry for rest and relaxation that we're vulnerable to promises of paradise. The most common come-on makes it seem like you've won a free vacation. I fell for this once myself back in my college days. If you pay attention, you'll notice that the trick is in the wording. Just remember, YOU SHOULDN'T HAVE TO *PAY* FOR A "FREE" TRIP!

Clare E. thought she had won a free cruise to the Bahamas. After all, she received a "certificate of authenticity" in the mail—complete with a confirmation number. Luckily, Clare contacted me at the station to ask if she should pack her bags. I read her offer and noticed that it didn't say she had received a "fabulous vacation." It said she had received a "fabulous vacation *offer.*" This is the typical ploy. In other words, Clare was being given the chance to spend her *own* money on a cruise. Poor Clare. The company had gotten her hopes up, so she didn't want to believe me. She ignored my advice and called the salesman back. Sure enough, he asked her for $1,200 to pay for the trip she had "won." That's when Clare wised up.

What if she hadn't? What would have happened? Many travel offers are run by creative con artists who just take your money and run. But some do result in a trip for you—albeit a trip to hell and back. Some consumers report that their dream vacation turned out to be a week's stay in a crime-ridden neighborhood across a freeway from the beach in a cockroach-infested motel. Other travelers have complained that they got to their destination only to find that the travel promoter never made a reservation, and the hotel didn't have a room for them.

Some travel promoters make it almost impossible for you to book the trip you've paid for. They pile on the conditions and restrictions so you can't go anywhere, but then they refuse to give you a refund. Other vacation peddlers don't disclose up front that almost nothing is *included* in their offer. Then they nickel and dime you for every

TRAVEL

detail. Oh, you want a bed in your hotel room? That'll be an extra $200. Meals aboard the cruise ship? Five hundred dollars. You'll find that you could have booked a much nicer vacation on your own or through a travel agent of your choosing, rather than one who came after you.

If you pay a chunk of money now for the chance to vacation later, watch out. Time-shares. Travel clubs. Campground memberships. With deals like these, you may find that the package isn't worth what you paid or that you just won't want to use it in the future. One couple paid big bucks to a travel club, but when they got to one of the resorts, they learned they could have vacationed there for half as much if they had booked the trip directly instead of through a middleman. Salespeople sometimes claim that if you lose interest in something like a time-share, you can resell it at a profit. Very often that's not the case and you're stuck with it.

TRAVEL

KNOW THE SIGNS:

1. If the travel offer or "prize" comes in what seems like an urgent mail envelope, take a closer look. It's probably a bulk mailing designed to *look* important.
2. If the material inside the envelope looks like a certificate or voucher, that's another clue it's a con.
3. Study the wording. Have you won a fabulous vacation? Or a fabulous vacation *offer?*
4. If the offer is initially pitched as a prize but ends up costing money, that's vintage vacation baloney.
5. If the marketer says the offer's only good for one day, to pressure you into a quick decision, that's typical—and terrible.
6. If the travel *seller's* name is different from the travel *provider's* name, you may be dealing with a telemarketer who has no responsibility to you after the sale.
7. If the company sends a courier to pick up your payment, this may be an attempt to get around mail fraud laws.
8. If you get to your "free" vacation and the company tries to make you listen to a time-share sales pitch, that's a classic. Check local laws. In some states it's illegal to attach conditions to a prize.

DO YOUR HOMEWORK:

1. Check out any travel promoter with the Better Business Bureau and government consumer protection offices in your own state and the state where the company is based—*before* you buy.
2. For that matter, never give out your credit card number or checking account information unless *you* initiated the call.
3. Check out the offer with the hotels, airlines, or cruise lines that are named to verify they are a part of it.
4. Get the details of your trip—including the cancellation clause—IN WRITING *before* you pay.
5. Learn the law in the state where the promoter is based. In Florida, where many of these companies are located, you have thirty days to cancel a vacation contract.
6. Be the hunter, not the hunted! Buy a travel book or find your own travel agent and tailor the trip of your dreams instead of falling for some prepackaged schlock that's marketed to the masses.

TRAVEL

WHERE TO COMPLAIN:

Complain to the attorney general in the state where the travel promoter is located. If the offer came in the mail, you can also complain to your local U.S. postal inspector's office.

SEE ALSO:

Mail: **Sweepstakes**

CHAPTER 13

Mail

Junk Mail

Each American receives seventeen trees worth of junk mail per year. That's how many trees it takes to make one ton of paper. Uh-huh. Each American receives one *ton* of junk mail per year. In case that doesn't do it for you, two average-size horses weigh one ton. Two horses in your mailbox! But that's *nothing* compared to the elephants. Four typical elephants weigh 17.8 tons. And a letter carrier for the U.S. Postal Service carries all four in the course of a year on the job. Well, the carrier doesn't carry *elephants;* he or she carries 17.8 tons of junk mail.

Okay, so those numbers were tabulated by environmentalists (who send out billions of pieces of junk mail themselves, by the way), but if the stats are even half that bad, it's maddening. Of course, you didn't need me to lay out all those numbers to make you mad, did you? All you have to do is go open your mailbox. If you are jinxed with junk mail, if the envelopes seem endless, there is hope.

The Direct Marketing Association maintains a list of consumers who don't wish to receive what it insists on calling "direct mail" or "advertising mail." Write to the DMA and include every name—and every spelling of every name—under which you receive junk mail. Also make note if you are a "Jr.," "Sr.," "II," or "III." List your current address, your previous address, and your phone number. It'll take a couple months before you really notice a difference. (Plus, marketers that aren't members will still send you mail.) Keep the address somewhere safe, because the Direct Marketing Association honors each request for just five years. After that, you'll have to renew your request. Write to: **Mail Preference Service, c/o the Direct Marketing Association, P.O. Box 9008, Farmingdale, NY 11735-9008** or try **www.the-dma.org.**

MAIL

Credit card companies are the worst offenders in *my* mailbox. They obtain lists of consumers who meet their criteria and then deluge them with "prescreening offers." The big three credit bureaus have given you a way to block those, too. Just call **(888) 567-8688.** The first prompt you'll hear offers you the chance to opt out for the next two years. Don't jump the gun! A later prompt offers you the opportunity to opt out for good. Once you've made a choice, you *will* have to provide your Social Security number and some other basic information.

If you're still not satisfied, you'll have to contact other direct mailers, well, directly! When you receive a mailing from a group or company you don't want to hear from again, send it some direct mail! Make up a form letter on your computer, if you like. Enclose the envelope or the mailing label the group sent you, and ask it to stop.

DO YOUR HOMEWORK:

1. Send out *one* piece of mail and block *thousands* from coming *in*. Write to the Direct Marketing Association.
2. Call the big three credit bureaus and opt out of credit card offers.
3. Don't sign up for sweepstakes. Don't fill out warranty cards. Give a fake address when you apply for a grocery store discount card. All of these can be tools for busybody companies bent on building mailing lists.

4. If the people at your Department of Motor Vehicles give you the choice of keeping your name and address private, take the time to take them up on it.
5. Learn to recognize misleading junk mail designed to get you to open the envelope. Some of it is actually illegal! Junk mail is often disguised as overnight mail, government mail, a bill, or a personal letter.

WHERE TO COMPLAIN:

Address complaints about junk mail to the U.S. Postal Service or the company in question. To gripe about *misleading* junk mail, contact your local postal inspector.

SEE ALSO:

TELEPHONE: **Telemarketing**

MAIL

Speed

I once investigated whether First Class Mail is reliable and whether Priority Mail is worth the price. I sent two letters each to friends and family across the country. I mailed one First Class and the other Priority. Understanding the results could save you time and money.

First Class Mail is a class act. The U.S. Postal Service says half of First Class Mail gets to its destination overnight, the other half on the second or third business day. First Class travels by truck for up to five hundred miles and by plane for greater distances. As long as your letter weighs less than thirteen ounces, you can send it first class.

As for Priority Mail, it travels only short distances by truck, the rest by plane. The base rate in 2003 was $3.85—ten times that of First Class Mail. I found most people don't understand what they're getting for the price. I stopped people on the street and asked them how fast they thought Priority Mail is supposed to be. Three out of four thought it was an overnight service. *Not true!*

Priority Mail is a two- to three-day service—and it's not even guaranteed! That's only a goal. Unfortunately, it doesn't say anywhere on

the packaging or the paperwork that Priority Mail is not guaranteed.
It should. In 2001, a third of Priority Mail failed to get to its destination by the third day. The Office of the Consumer Advocate, a government board that represents the public in postal matters, says
First Class provides equal to or better delivery times than Priority.

So what did my own test find? I sent my letters from Washington,
D.C. Priority Mail won the race to Los Angeles, San Francisco,
Indianapolis, and Tampa. It arrived in two days, whereas the First
Class letters arrived in three days. Priority and First Class *both* took
just one day to get to the Washington suburbs, plus Philadelphia and
Chicago. But get this! Our First Class letter reached Duarte,
California, in just two days, but the pricier Priority letter took *four*
days. What can we learn from this? Consumer advocates suggest you
may not want to pay for Priority when you're sending things short
distances.

On the other hand, Priority Mail has one feature that may make
the higher price worthwhile: free packaging! One warning: during
my investigation, I found that not all Priority Mail packaging is created equal. The Postal Service makes two different kinds of Priority
envelopes. They're the exact same size and shape (about nine by
twelve inches), but with totally different price structures. One is a
"flat rate" envelope, so for $3.85 you can stuff it as full as you want
and send it wherever you want. The other is priced by weight and
zone *starting* at $3.85—*not* a good deal.

Now, about Express Mail, the U.S. Postal Service's premium service.
It's guaranteed to get there in one or two days. But, keep in mind,
"guaranteed" does not mean it'll definitely get there. It means you get
your money back if it doesn't. In 2001, Express Mail failed to meet its
deadline more than 11 percent of the time. Federal Express and
United Parcel Service have much more consistent records.

DO YOUR HOMEWORK:

1. If you want your mail to arrive speedily, don't use dark-colored
   envelopes. They camouflage postal bar codes and require extra
   processing time.

2. Colored inks also slow down the process. Blue and black are the fastest.

3. Typing or using mailing labels gets your mail there faster than handwriting addresses, because postal machines often have trouble reading your messy writing!

4. Putting the address too low on the envelope can also cause a delay, again because it makes the postal computers go haywire.

5. Leave the bottom right-hand corner of postcards blank, so the postal service can affix a bar code.

6. It's better to use no zip code than the wrong zip code, so if you're not sure, don't write one. It's easy to look up zip codes by going to **www.usps.com.** .

7. If you plan ahead, you can send packages "Parcel Post," which means they travel only by truck and train. It takes two to nine days, but it can save you money if you're sending a heavy package a long distance. Always check though, because Priority Mail is often just a few cents more than Parcel Post.

MAIL

WHERE TO COMPLAIN:

Direct complaints about postal service to the **Office of the Consumer Advocate,** a division of the **Postal Rate Authority, www.prc.gov.**

Sucker Lists

One false move and you can be branded a "sucker." If you buy a cheesy product or fall for even one scam, con artists will circle like vultures and try to get a piece of you. Like any businessperson, these clever crooks try to diversify their revenue streams. So they make their main money by scamming people. And they make *extra* money by selling lists of those they've scammed. The lists contain names, phone numbers, addresses, and how much money the "sucker" has paid in the past. Other criminals buy the lists. Think you're snowed under by junk mail? If you land on a sucker list, it'll come in hard and fast—more like hail. Cold calls can be a cold trail, but a pretested prospect warms a con man's greedy heart.

Diane V. ordered a strand of faux pearls from an ad in the back of a magazine. About a month later, she received a letter from a psychic who claimed to be "thinking about her." Creepy. What's more creepy, when I did some research, I learned the psychic had a lengthy fraud record. Perhaps that psychic could have foretold how many bizarre and bogus offers Diane would receive next. Diane could tell the pearl company sold her name because it butchered the spelling— and so did all the other hucksters. Suddenly her mailbox seemed more like Pandora's box!

Years ago, before Jerry F. was old and wise, he wrote a check to participate in a sweepstakes. All he won was a mailbox full of other fraudulent contest offers. He had landed on a sucker list. One letter promised "rewards, friends and a new life." Another said, "This is to certify that our special cyber-automated thinking computer has you successfully beating a state lottery very soon." Jerry was so outraged that he started saving his scam mail. By the time he contacted me to do a story, he had saved up dozens of garbage bags full of the stuff. To my dismay, he started sending the offers on to me after that! My mail slot at the station overflowed until I begged him to stop!

MAIL

KNOW THE SIGNS:

1. Answering ads in dicey places like the backs of magazines and the tops of telephone poles could land you on a sucker list.
2. Also beware of over-the-top catch phrases like "guaranteed," "fabulous," "valuable," "one in a million," and "specially selected."
3. The types of businesses most likely to work from sucker lists are fake foreign lotteries, questionable contests, travel promoters, credit repair companies, and manufacturers of cheesy products. These are also the types of businesses most likely to *sell* your name on a sucker list.

DO YOUR HOMEWORK:

1. Before responding to an offer or purchasing a product, make sure the company's name and address are clearly identified in the advertisement. If not, skip it.
2. If the company is identified, check it out with the Better

Business Bureau and your county and state consumer protection offices before buying.

WHERE TO COMPLAIN:

Your local postal inspector or state attorney general may be able to help.

SEE ALSO:

MAIL: **Junk Mail, Sweepstakes;** SCAMS: **Foreign Lotteries,** Nigerian Letter, **Reloading**

Sweepstakes

In a national survey, more than half of all American adults said they had entered a sweepstakes in the past year. That depresses me, because most sweepstakes are come-ons, and most adults should know better. Every day, consumers lose thousands of dollars to phony prize offers in which they're asked to "pay to play." Fair's fair and free's free. If you have to pay, it's *not* a prize. PURCHASING A PRODUCT DOES *NOT* INCREASE YOUR CHANCES OF WINNING. In fact, it's illegal for prize promoters to make you pay money or buy something to enter a contest.

The brown paper packages were relentless, and eighty-two-year-old Mary M. thought she had won. Here's what the letters whispered: "If you have and return the grand-prize winning number we can announce ..." Here's what they screamed: "... **MARY M. IS THE NEW $1,666,675 WINNER!!!**" Mary survives on Social Security. Her vision is poor, so she can't even *read* glossy magazines. But she thought subscribing would increase her chances of winning the sweepstakes. So she bought one magazine after another.

Mary finally came to her senses when a close friend died and Mary helped to clear out the woman's condominium. Inside she found stacks of unread magazines and big brown envelopes. She also found an $18,000 organ. Evidently, Mary's friend thought she was going to pay for the organ with her sweepstakes winnings.

Magazine and book publishers are some of the biggest prize pushers. Next in line are travel promoters, vitamin companies, and cosmetics firms. Even some nonprofits have been known to play the sweepstakes game.

No matter who approaches you, there are certain things they're *not allowed* to say. If you respond to a sweepstakes mailing and reach a telemarketer, it's against the law for that marketer to describe a fabulous prize and *then* make a sales pitch. The sales pitch must come first. Prize promoters are not allowed to claim you've won a prize unless you really have. They're not allowed to tell you that you have to pay an entry fee or buy something to participate in the sweepstakes. They can't use seals or names that make them sound like government agencies.

There are also certain things prize promoters *must* say. They must tell you the retail value of all prizes. They have to disclose your odds of winning, how many prizes are available, and when those prizes will be awarded, plus how to get a list of winners. They must alert you if there are any conditions you have to meet to win (like being at least eighteen years old.) If sweepstakes promoters send imitation checks, they must be clearly marked as non-negotiable. Sweepstakes are required to tell you that you don't have to buy anything. They must explain how to participate without making a purchase.

MAIL

KNOW THE SIGNS:

1. Sweepstakes mail often comes in official-looking envelopes that make it seem like an urgent letter or a government document.

2. Take a closer look. Fraudulent prize promotions are usually sent via bulk mail.

3. Sometimes the ruse continues with official-sounding names or "sound-alike" names that mimic a well-known organization.

4. Once you open the mail, you may find a fake check designed to pique your interest.

5. Some prize promoters include yellow sticky notes with what look like handwritten notes on them.

6. Silvery bars that you scratch off are another common sight in these misleading mailings.

7. Businesses that run reputable contests want you to know who they are. Fraudulent prize promoters downplay their identities.

8. Fraudulent sweepstakes ask you to pay to play. They often claim the payment is to cover taxes, shipping and handling, or processing fees or judging fees.

9. Some prize promoters ask participants to answer ridiculously easy quiz questions. They have you send a small "judging fee," along with your answers. Then they send you another set of questions and ask for more money. Participants want to quit but continue playing—and paying—because they believe they're getting close to the grand prize and they don't want to lose the money they've sunk into the game so far.

10. Some sweepstakes ask you to call a 900 number to claim your prize. Operators then keep you on the phone as long as possible to rack up expensive pay-per-call charges.

11. Sleazy sweepstakes may try to send a courier to pick up your entry fee. They do this to avoid mail fraud laws and to get your money before you think better of it.

MAIL

DO YOUR HOMEWORK:

1. Ask direct mailers to put you on their "do not mail" list. If the direct mail refers you on to a telemarketer, ask the telemarketer to put you on his or her "do not call" list.

2. If you are the caregiver for a family member, you can ask that the family member's name be put on these lists, too.

3. Do a background check before sending money or participating in any contest. Check with the BBB, county and state consumer protection offices, and, possibly, your secretary of state.

4. Never give out your credit card or bank account information unless you know the reputation of the company.

WHERE TO COMPLAIN:

In many states, sweepstakes are regulated by the secretary of state, so that's a good place to start. If the offer came in the mail, try your local postal inspector. Your state attorney general can prosecute fraudulent telemarketers, even if they operate across state lines.

SEE ALSO:

MAIL: Sucker Lists; SCAMS: Foreign Lotteries, Reloading

Unordered Merchandise

Have you ever opened your mailbox and found merchandise you didn't order? Next time, consider it an unexpected birthday present— even if it's nowhere *near* your birthday! Federal law makes it illegal for companies to send you something you didn't order and then bill you for it. You are allowed to keep the items as free gifts.

Winnie H. answered her door and found a deliveryman there with a big box for her—a box she hadn't ordered. Inside were books and a bill for $80. Winnie mostly reads magazines, so there's no way she would have ordered four big leather-bound volumes. She was wise enough not to pay for the books, but she did spend her time and energy lugging the heavy box down three flights of stairs and to the post office. And, of course, she paid for postage to send the books back. She didn't have to do all that. She could have rejected the books, kept them, given them to a friend, or donated them (and taken a tax deduction!).

You have no legal obligation to let the seller know you plan to keep the merchandise as a free gift, but you probably should. I know, I know, even having to write a letter is an imposition. The thing is, alerting the company that you know the law should put a stop to any collection notices headed your way. You may even want to send your letter certified mail to create a paper trail. Sigh . . .

DO YOUR HOMEWORK:

1. If you order goods that are supposed to be "free" or "trial" offers, scrutinize the fine print to make sure you're not signing up for future shipments you'll have to pay for.
2. If you learn that unordered merchandise was shipped to you through an honest error, write a letter giving the seller a reason-

able amount of time to send a courier to pick up the items. Alert the seller that, if this doesn't happen in the designated time frame, you reserve the right to keep the merchandise or get rid of it.

WHERE TO COMPLAIN:

If a company sends you unordered merchandise and won't back off about billing you, contact your local postal inspector's office for help.

MAIL

CHAPTER 14

Telephone

Fat Finger Dialing

Are you absent-minded? A poor speller? Do you have big hands? These traits could cost you. If you use a pay phone or make a collect call and accidentally dial a number that's one digit off from the number you meant to dial, your call may still go through. Some clever companies have snatched up the rights to numbers that are a digit or two off from those of popular services. Say you're trying to call 1-800-COLLECT, but you dial 1-800-COLECCT instead. Rather than reaching Ma Bell, you could reach a company you've never heard of, one that could charge you *prices* like you've never heard of—two to three times more than average.

DO YOUR HOMEWORK:

1. Slow down and dial carefully. Make sure you hit each number only once.

2. Listen carefully. If the company identifies itself with a name you've never heard or one that sounds "off," use caution.
3. If you're calling from a pay phone, the company is required to identify itself and give you a rate quote on request.
4. Don't accept collect calls either until you know what company you're dealing with.

WHERE TO COMPLAIN:

The Federal Communications Commission wants consumers to help it identify fat finger dialing scams. That's one call you *do* want to make!

SEE ALSO:

TELEPHONE: Pay Phones.

Pay-per-Call Scams

TELEPHONE

We all know what a 900 number is, right? You dial it, and the company it belongs to charges you megabucks by the minute for as long as you stay on the line. Old hat, right? OK, smarty-pants. What's an 809 number? A 758 number? An 813 number? Okay, that last one is actually the area code for Tampa, Florida. But the point is, you don't necessarily know, do you? And not knowing can be hazardous to your wallet.

Con artists call, page, fax, or e-mail unsuspecting consumers and leave messages asking them to call back. These strangers come up with various excuses to persuade you to call: You've won a prize, you need to straighten out a credit problem, or a relative of yours is injured, to name a few. The callback numbers they leave are pay-per-call numbers. If you call, the con artist will keep you on the line as long as possible to rack up charges. "809" is the same as a 900 number in the Caribbean; so are "758" and "664."

There are at least nineteen other such area codes in the Caribbean as well. No international code is required to dial the Caribbean from the United States, just a three-digit number that looks like an

American area code. In the United States, 900 pay-per-call numbers are required to play a message immediately warning you that the call will cost money. In other countries, there is no such rule, nor is there a limit on the charge per minute. Some Caribbean pay-per-call services charge $25 a minute. And since you're dealing with a foreign phone company, you'll have a tough time fighting the charges.

Don't assume toll-free 800 numbers are safe either. Occasionally, unscrupulous companies advertise 800 numbers, but when consumers call, they are then transferred to a 900 number without the required warning message.

KNOW THE SIGNS:

The following area codes are designated for pay-per-call services in the Caribbean:

264 Anguilla	473 Grenada
268 Antigua and Barbuda	876 Jamaica
242 Bahamas	664 Montserrat
246 Barbados	869 St. Kitts and Nevis
441 Bermuda	758 St. Lucia
284 British Virgin Islands	784 St. Vincent/Grenadines
245 Cayman Islands	868 Trinidad and Tobago
767 Dominica	809 Dominican Republic

TELEPHONE

DO YOUR HOMEWORK:

1. If you receive a page or message from a stranger with a strange area code, don't dial right away. Take a few moments to call 411 and ask the operator where the area code is located.
2. If you are the victim of a pay-per-call scam, call your phone company and ask to have the charge dropped. The phone company is not obligated to do this for you, but may as a courtesy.

WHERE TO COMPLAIN:

Contact the Federal Communications Commission, which regulates phone service in the United States and may be able to intercede with its foreign counterparts. Also complain to your state attorney general.

SEE ALSO:

SCAMS: Nigerian Letter

Pay Phones

If you can't remember the last time you used a pay phone, then the *next* time you do, you could be in for a shock. The same call could cost fifty cents or fifty bucks, depending on how you dial. Think nobody uses pay phones anymore? Think again. Pay phones are still big business.

In 1996, Congress and the Federal Communications Commission took steps to deregulate pay phones. These days, the pay phone business is open to anybody, and the companies can charge anything. One out of every four pay phones is owned by an independent. Unfortunately, consumers haven't really benefited from deregulation, because when you need a pay phone, you're not exactly in a position to shop around.

I tested pay phone prices for an investigation. What I found was so stunning that people stopped me on the street for weeks after the story aired to ask questions. At the airport, I tried dialing zero plus the number I was calling on a pay phone operated by a big long-distance company. The cost? Eight dollars and eighty-five cents for a four-minute call from Virginia to Florida. Travelers typically pay sixty times more than they should to make a call from an airport pay phone.

Next, I tried calling three different ways from a pay phone operated by an independent. When I used coins, a four-minute call to Florida cost just a dollar. When I dialed the 800 number on my phone company credit card, that same call came to $4.51. But when I dialed the operator and asked *her* to place the call, the total was $15.35. You see, when you place a call through the pay phone company's operator, some of the money goes to that company, some goes to the long-distance provider, and some goes to the business where the pay phone is located.

But that wasn't the most expensive call in my test. Another independently operated pay phone charged me $23.42 for the first three minutes of my call to Florida and $5.72 for every minute after that. A pay phone just a hundred feet away, operated by a different company, charged only a dollar for the exact same call.

And pay phone *prices* aren't the only issue. Megan C. got lost on her way to an appointment. She pulled over at a hotel and used the pay phone in the lobby. There was no slot for coins and the pay phone wasn't labeled, so she charged the call to her credit card. The total? Twenty-one dollars and seventy-three cents for a three-minute local call. I later tested that same phone and found it wouldn't let me dial the 800 number on my phone company calling card. Next, I dialed the operator and asked *her* to put me through to my phone company. She claimed my card wasn't working. That was a lie, and the phone was a fraud. By law, pay phone owners must post their names and addresses on their phones. They must provide a rate quote before you place a call. And they must let you access the long-distance provider of your choice.

DO YOUR HOMEWORK:

TELEPHONE

1. If you use pay phones often, stock up on name-brand prepaid calling cards. Some are as cheap as five cents a minute.
2. If you must use your phone company calling card, be sure to dial the 800 number on the back for direct access to your own phone company.
3. When using a phone company calling card at a pay phone, beware of "shoulder surfers" who watch you dial, write down your card number and PIN, then sell the information to strangers. Those strangers then use your account to make expensive calls, usually to foreign countries.
4. *Never* dial just "0" plus the number you are calling. When you do that, you end up with the pay phone company's long-distance provider—usually grossly overpriced.
5. If you have a cell phone, check to see if your provider imposes roaming fees. If it doesn't, you're in luck and that may be the cheapest option of all.

WHERE TO COMPLAIN:

If you spot an illegal pay phone without the required disclosures, report it to the Federal Communications Commission. The FCC depends on consumers to help it enforce the law.

SEE ALSO:

TELEPHONE: Fat Finger Dialing, **Prepaid Calling Cards**

Prepaid Calling Cards

Here's a riddle for you: When is a minute not a minute? When it's on a prepaid calling card! These cards are typically labeled "30 minutes," "60 minutes," and so on. But what you're really paying for is "units" of time on the phone. Usually a calling card minute will buy you a one-minute local phone call. International calls cost more, and there are all sorts of other exceptions that can make your "30-minute" card last for much less than a half-hour.

TELEPHONE

Hidden service fees are the most common complaint. Some card companies charge a connection fee, plus taxes and surcharges, which eat into your time. Others charge a minimum number of minutes each time you use the card. Maybe your phone call only lasts thirty seconds, but the card company charges you for its minimum of three minutes. Some companies debit your card even if your call doesn't go through. You should also know that many prepaid calling cards expire—usually a year after the initial use.

In addition to the above rip-offs, some prepaid calling cards are out and out scams. You may find that the access number is always busy or the PIN doesn't work. When you go to call the company to complain, you discover the customer service number is a 900 number or it's always busy or it isn't in service. Cards with unbelievably cheap prices often give you unbelievably bad connections, so you can't even hear the person you're trying to talk to. Finally, many consumers have found that the calling card company went out of business before they could use up their card.

QUESTIONS TO ASK:

If you plan to use a prepaid calling card often, call the company before you buy.

1. Will I be charged when I call somebody and the person doesn't answer?
2. Is there a minimum charge per call? How much?
3. Are there any service fees I should know about?
4. Can I add time to my card or trade it in for a refund when there's too little credit left to make a call?
5. Will the company replace my card if it's lost or stolen?
6. Does the card expire?

DO YOUR HOMEWORK:

1. Consider buying only name-brand prepaid calling cards from companies that are well established, like major phone companies.
2. If you must buy a calling card from an unknown company, dial the company's customer service number before you buy and see if you can get through. If not, take your business elsewhere.
3. Ask the store where you purchase the card whether you can get a refund if the calling card service is unsatisfactory.
4. The first time you use a company's calling card, purchase only a limited number of minutes so you can decide whether you're satisfied with the service.
5. Shop around for the calling card with the best rates for your needs. Some cards have good domestic rates, others offer attractive international plans.
6. Try to find a card company that issues you a replacement number (usually printed on a separate piece of paper). If your card is lost or stolen, you use that number to get a new card.

TELEPHONE

WHERE TO COMPLAIN:

Your county and state consumer protection offices and your state attorney general may be able to help.

SEE ALSO:

TELEPHONE: Pay Phones

Slamming and Cramming

Like a lot of wicked things, it started in the eighties. There was competition in the telephone industry for the first time, and nobody knew quite what would happen, so there weren't many rules. Long-distance companies didn't even have to get your permission to switch you to their service! So they just did it. "Slamming" was born. After a while, the FCC caught on and started requiring long-distance companies to get written or verbal agreement from consumers before switching them. So the companies—and their rogue employees—got more creative.

They started sponsoring contests and drawings at fairs and home shows. Consumers thought they were entering to win a prize and didn't read the fine print, which said their long-distance service would be switched. (Hmmm, why did the entry form require your phone number? To notify you when you won, silly!) Long-distance companies also started writing checks to consumers. Endorse and cash the check and you've got yourself a brand new long-distance company.

Of course, some telemarketing thugs weren't so subtle. They would call you and pitch their company's products, and even if you said no, they'd switch you anyway. Or they would forge peoples' signatures on written authorization forms. Here's my favorite: A few enterprising companies gave themselves names like "No Thanks Long Distance" and "Don't Call Back Long Distance." If a consumer gave a telemarketer the brush-off with one of these lines, the company took that as permission to switch the person's service!

When *local* phone service opened up to competition, I got a whole new round of slamming complaints at the station. I don't hear about slamming as much as I used to, but when one door closes, another opens. Say hello to a newer scam, called *cramming*. That's where companies cram your phone bill with all sorts of spe-

TELEPHONE

cialty services that you never ordered or used. Once again, the crammers are real scammers, with all sorts of creative tactics.

Some companies get people to call an 800 number to test out a "free" service like a dating line or a psychic connection. When you call, the company captures your phone number, then bills you for monthly services or subscriptions. Or maybe you receive a sweepstakes promotion in the mail that tells you to call an 800 number to claim your prize. When you call, you're asked to give your phone number to verify your entry in the contest. Once again, they've got your number.

Local phone companies provide billing for all sorts of other businesses. In addition to dating lines, psychic services, and adult entertainment, unscrupulous companies may try to cram fancy voice mail services, personal 800 numbers, or paging options onto your bill.

DO YOUR HOMEWORK:

1. If you like the local and long-distance companies you're with and the extras you currently have, call and ask that your account be "locked" so that your signature is required for any changes in service.

TELEPHONE

2. If a long-distance company calls and pitches its service, get the name and number of the telemarketer who's calling, even if you're not interested. If you *are* interested, ask the company to send you literature to review before you make a decision.
3. If you are slammed or crammed, immediately contact the company listed on your bill.
4. Also contact the company in charge of your phone bills (usually your local phone company) and ask that your account be switched back to the way it was. Your account should be set straight within 24 hours, with all switching fees waived. Ask to be credited for any difference in rates for calls you made while your account was hijacked.
5. Carefully read the fine print before entering contests. Avoid those that require your signature, a sign that you're being asked to agree to something.

6. Use caution when dialing unfamiliar 800 numbers. Be extra careful if you're asked to enter codes or answer "yes" to prompts.
7. Check your phone bill every month for unfamiliar companies and mysterious charges. Pay attention even to small charges. Some companies bill you a minuscule amount every month that adds up over time. It's often listed under "miscellaneous charges and credits." Look for catch words like "enhanced services," "minimum use fee," "activation," and "member fee."

WHERE TO COMPLAIN:

The Federal Communications Commission regulates phone companies. For help closer to home, try your public service commission or public utilities commission. Your state attorney general should also be able to help.

SEE ALSO:

HOUSEHOLD: Shocking

TELEPHONE

Telemarketing

If cold calls give you a hot head, I've got good news. There are now multiple ways to hang up on telemarketers. Telemarketing brings in more than $400 billion a year, so somebody out there is buying. Most sales calls are maddening but legitimate; however, consumers lose an estimated $40 billion a year to telemarketing *fraud*. By limiting the calls you receive from *legitimate* telemarketers, you'll be better able to spot the *illegitimate* ones.

To freeze out cold calls, use a multilayered approach, starting with yourself. Many consumers make the mistake of shrieking "take me off your list," when a telemarketer interrupts them in the middle of dinner. WRONG! That request has no legal teeth. Instead, ask to be put *ON* the list. The company's do-not-call list. Telemarketers are required to keep a list of people who do not wish to be contacted. If they call you again after you have made this request, you can sue them and collect compensation. The company could also face government fines of $10,000 or more. Keep in mind, big companies have multiple divisions. For example, if you tell the long-distance department not to call you anymore, you may still receive cold calls from the cellular division. If you receive automated calls with recorded messages, the company is required to give you its name and address so you can request that the calls stop.

Contacting the Direct Marketing Association is your next layer of defense. For years, the DMA has kept a list of consumers who do not want to receive sales calls. Companies that are members of the DMA—generally large national corporations—honor this list. Your request is good for five years or until you change phone numbers. Send your name, address and phone number to: **Telephone Preference Service, c/o Direct Marketing Association, P.O. Box 9014, Farmingdale, NY 11735-9014,** or, for five dollars you can register online at **www.the-dma.org.**

As I write this, thirty-three states have their own "do-not-call" laws in place, and the others are considering legislation. Many of these laws require telemarketers to obtain a license from the state. Some include a state do-not-call registry that consumers can join if they want to block telemarketers. Find out if your state has a registry. If so, sign up. Some registries are free; others cost a small amount, like $10. Joining your state registry will protect you against telemarketers who are calling from within your state.

The highly anticipated *national* registry is expected to shut down unwanted sales calls coming from *other* states. The Federal Trade Commission launched the National Do Not Call Registry in July 2003. The direct marketing industry filed multiple lawsuits against the registry, and the FTC appealed. You can register by going to **www.donotcall.gov.** You can also call **(888) 382-1222** from the number you wish to register. Assuming the registry survives, it will take a couple of months for your request to kick in, but then it will last for five years. The National Do Not Call Registry will not eliminate calls from politicians (go figure!), people conducting opinion polls, charities and nonprofits, or companies that you already have a business relationship with.

TELEPHONE

If, after doing all of this, you still receive obnoxious telephone come-ons, chances are the callers are crooks. Telemarketing fraud is devastating. Some people lose their life savings. The most common fraudulent phone pitches are prizes that cost money, cheesy travel packages, untested health care products, illegal investments, and fake charities.

KNOW THE SIGNS:

1. By law, telemarketers are not allowed to call before 8 A.M. or after 9 P.M. They must state immediately that it's a sales call. They cannot lie about prizes, investment returns, or the price of what they're selling. If a caller violates any of these rules, you may be dealing with a fraudulent telemarketer.
2. If a telemarketer asks for your credit card number, don't give it out unless *you* initiated the call.
3. Sleazy solicitors often ask for your checking account number or other numbers printed on your checks. *Never* give those numbers out over the phone.
4. Cold callers may ask for your personal information. Don't give out medical information, your driver's license number, or your Social Security number. Don't reveal your children's names or other family details.
5. Never pay for a prize. If you've really won, you don't owe a cent. Free is free.
6. Tricky telemarketers try to get people to make hasty decisions. Don't do it. Ask the caller to send you written information.
7. Telemarketers target older people. If you're over sixty-five, lots of hucksters could come a-calling. Single elderly women are a con artist's favorite "clients."
8. Currently, telemarketers' phone numbers come up on caller ID devices as "unknown" or "out of area." A new rule will require telemarketers to identify themselves to customers with caller ID.

DO YOUR HOMEWORK:

1. Tell telemarketers to put you on their company's do-not-call list.
2. Write to the Direct Marketing Association and ask to join the telephone preference service.

TELEPHONE

3. See if your state has a do-not-call registry and sign up.
4. Monitor the progress of the national do-not-call registry and sign up for that, too.
5. Never buy anything from anybody over the phone, unless you initiated the call and you know the company's reputation.
6. Ask for written materials before responding to a telemarketer's pitch.
7. Contact the BBB and your county and state consumer protection offices to check the reputations of companies that call you.

WHERE TO COMPLAIN:

To gripe about telemarketers that break the rules or the law, contact your state attorney general and the FTC. If the telemarketer is a telecommunications company, complain to the Federal Communications Commission.

SEE ALSO:

MAIL: Sucker Lists, Sweepstakes, SCAMS: **Police and Fire Fund, Reloading**

TELEPHONE

CHAPTER 15

Scams

Bank Examiner

A well-dressed, well-spoken man approaches you. He may walk up to you as you leave your bank. He may come to your door. He may call. He identifies himself as a detective and says he needs your help to catch a crooked bank teller. He explains that the teller has been laundering counterfeit money or stealing from customers. He asks you to withdraw money from your bank account so he can look it over. Then he switches your money with counterfeit cash. Or he says he needs to take your money with him to confront the teller. He gives you a receipt and says he'll call you when you can collect the cash. Of course, you never see him again.

It's the age-old bank examiner scam. The con men always claim they're FDIC (Federal Deposit Insurance Corporation) bank examiners or police officers trying to flush out a crooked bank employee. They often use names of actual police officers in the local department. Typically, they approach senior citizens. They make the target feel needed, then they make their move. Over the years, crooks have come up with thousands of variations. Here's one of them.

The con artists approached Meredith W. by phone. She knew seniors like herself are often the targets of scams, so she showed some moxie. She demanded that the caller prove he was actually a cop. Unfortunately, he was ready for her. "No problem," he said. "Hang up right now and call 9-1-1. Ask for Detective Darwin, and the operator will put you through to me." Meredith hung up, but the con artist did not. Instead, he kept the line open and handed the phone to a female accomplice. When Meredith dialed 9-1-1, the crooks were still on the line. The woman answered in an official tone, then "transferred" the call to her partner. "Detective Darwin" persuaded Meredith to withdraw $3,400 from her checking account and she handed it over to him later that day.

DO YOUR HOMEWORK:

1. If somebody asks you to withdraw money from your account and hand it over, carefully consider whether this could be a version of the bank examiner scam.
2. Keep in mind that no police department or government agency would ask you to provide money from your account to help foil a bad bank employee.
3. Look up the number for the bank and the police yourself. Call and ask questions.
4. Share this information with elderly friends and loved ones.

WHERE TO COMPLAIN:

If you are a victim of the bank examiner scam, contact your police department's financial crimes unit.

SEE ALSO:

SCAMS: Nigerian Letter

SCAMS

Candy Kids

You see them downtown, on the subway, at your own front door. They are the "candy kids," selling chocolate for a cause—or so they say. These kids often claim they're peddling candy so they won't have to peddle drugs. Sound familiar? Fifty thousand children nationwide are involved. They're often underprivileged and under-age. The U.S. Department of Labor says they're being exploited.

They sell sweets, but bite in deep enough and you'll taste the truth. That's what I learned when I spent a summer on the streets following candy kids. One boy told me he was selling candy for the Just Say No program at his school. When I called his school, I learned there was no such program. A girl said she was selling boxed candy for her basketball team. That was a lie. Another group of kids said they were with a nonprofit organization founded to keep kids off the street. The organization didn't exist.

But the kids aren't the ones at fault. Crooked adults, called candy "crew leaders," run these candy rings. The two crew leaders I investigated both had criminal records. One had been arrested for battery, possession of heroin, and receiving stolen property. The other had convictions for firearms violations, cruelty to animals, drug dealing, and shoplifting. Crew leaders recruit candy kids near schools, in public housing complexes— even homeless shelters. Parents go along with it because they don't care or don't know better.

The crew leaders tell the kids what to say and sometimes give them laminated identification cards to show customers. They pick the kids up by van early in the morning and drop them off in malls or neighborhoods far from home. The van returns for the kids after they've worked a twelve-hour day. Often, the children go without food, water, or a bathroom break during their shift. They are unsupervised. Authorities are aware of cases in which candy kids were mugged or raped while working.

So, is the work worth it? NO. One of the groups I investigated gave the children forty cents for each $2.50 candy bar they sold. The bars wholesaled for thirty-five cents, so the crew leaders made a

SCAMS

tasty profit. If the children showed up late to meet the van or goofed off on the ride home, the crew leader docked their meager pay. Many candy crews tout the fact that they reward the children with excursions to water slides and theme parks. My investigation showed those excursions either didn't happen or the kids had to pay their own way using their candy earnings.

So what's the law, and how can this happen? Each state has its own child labor laws. Typically, states allow children to begin working between ages twelve and sixteen, but there's little enforcement. I met kids on the street as young as seven. The problem is, police departments aren't trained or equipped to tackle this problem, and labor departments are chronically understaffed. Plus, if authorities do crack down, candy crew leaders often just move across state lines. So when will this cruel scam end? When customers stop buying.

DO YOUR HOMEWORK:

1. Ask questions. Ask the kids how much money they make from each candy bar or box they sell. Find out how they got to the spot where they approached you. If they say they're with a school, call the school on your cell phone and check.

2. Be vigilant. If you see candy kids going door-to-door in your neighborhood, call the police and ask your neighbors to call, too. When police realize citizens are upset about this child exploitation, they'll learn how to work with labor departments to stop it.

3. Don't buy from candy kids. If you feel you *must* help them, you could consider giving them a "donation" instead. I have mixed feelings about this. Many candy kids actually *ask* for donations, which is tantamount to organized begging.

WHERE TO COMPLAIN:

Your local police department and your state labor department.

Foreign Lotteries

They say you can't win if you don't play, but when it comes to foreign lotteries, you'll definitely lose. In fact, Americans lose tens of millions of dollars this way each year. The crooks claim you've won but then say you need to pay the taxes on your jackpot before they can forward it to you. Of course, they ask that you send the check to them. And what about the pesky fact that you never actually *entered* any foreign lottery? In their eagerness and greed, most victims never even consider that.

At all hours of the day, when Eva and Ken S. were minding their own business, strangers would interrupt them. It happened for five years. The callers claimed they'd won a big foreign lottery. Canada, Australia, China, Germany, Japan—a different country every day. Eva and Ken also received lottery come-ons in the mail. They had entered sweepstakes in the past (and that's probably how the foreign lottery hucksters got their names), but they brushed aside the foreign lottery offers. They just didn't feel right. This couple was lucky.

Not only could they have lost money, they could have lost their freedom as well. It's actually illegal to enter a lottery by phone or by mail, but most Americans don't realize that. So many people fall for it when con artists call or write claiming they have won a foreign lottery. The majority of these foreign lotteries don't even exist. If a foreign lottery *is* for real and you participate, you can be charged with mail fraud and violating customs laws.

Postal inspectors and customs officials try to intercept foreign lottery mailings, but the volume is overwhelming. Several years ago the government started recycling foreign lottery mail—to make toilet paper. What symbolism! It's the perfect use.

SCAMS

DO YOUR HOMEWORK:

1. To avoid foreign lottery come-ons, don't enter sweepstakes and don't buy products from the backs of magazines or other questionable sources. Your name could be sold on a "sucker list."

2. If you receive a letter saying you've won a lottery, think through whether you've ever *entered* a lottery and consider whether this could be a foreign lottery scam.

WHERE TO COMPLAIN:

If the lottery pitch comes in the mail, complain to the U.S. Postal Inspector. If the con men contact you by phone, report the incident to your state attorney general.

SEE ALSO:

MAIL: **Sweepstakes**

Nigerian Letter

You receive a letter or e-mail from somebody claiming to be an official with the Nigerian government or a Nigerian company. The writer explains that a government contract has just been fulfilled and there is a surplus left over—usually between $10 million and $65 million. You're asked to provide a bank account into which the surplus can be deposited. In exchange, you will receive a commission.

The Nigerian scammers typically ask targets for their bank name and address, account number, and Social Security number "in order to complete the transaction." Those who provide the information soon find that their bank accounts have been emptied and their identities stolen.

Sharp-eyed Dorothy H. was too smart for the scammers. She received a Nigerian letter and called me at the station. For this sweet retiree living in a mobile home park, at first the letter was a shock, then it was a hoot! Here's the *actual* text of the letter Dorothy received.

> Dear Sir:
> Request for urgent business transaction
> Transfer of $35 million American Dollars
>   I am the financial comptroller of the Nigerian National Petroleum corporation. This is money we got from gratification of contracts we

SCAMS

awarded toward technical assistance analysis supervision and behaviour or the components of the optimized system.

The contract has been completed and the contractor has since been paid remaining the balance of the $35 million American dollars which is our 10% commission for numerous assistance. This money is now ready for payment by transfer to an account that would be provided through the machinery's of the Central Bank of Nigeria through our foreign exchange reserve in New York within (48) banking hours.

Now our problem lies that we do not have a foreign account as such an account is against the civil service bureaucracy in Nigeria. We therefore decided to seek your assistance for a hitch-free transfer of this fund to an account you will provide. You would be entitled to 35% for providing an account where the funds would be lodged while 10% is mapped for contingencies/expenses and 55% will be for myself and my colleagues.

If you can assist in this regards, fax to us 234-1-5851214. Your company's account or personal account with the bank name, physical address with telephone, fax and telex lines/numbers and your company's name and physical address with phone and fax numbers.

This business will be carried out on the following terms: You will maintain absolute sincerity and confidentiality. Our share of the fund remitted into your account will be disbursed as we so desire immediately your account is credited.

We got your contact through our National Association Chamber of Commerce, Industries, Mines and Agriculture. If you are satisfied with the above conditions, send me a reply immediately by fax.

Salutations,

Mr. Isa Ahmed.

SCAMS

It's a scam so outlandish, it's hard to believe anybody falls for it, but people do. Let me get this straight. You receive a letter from Nigeria. You don't *know* anyone in Nigeria. You're asked to help *launder* money. And you actually believe you're going to *make* money?

Believe it or not, Americans lose hundreds of millions of dollars to the Nigerian letter scam every year. It's hard to pinpoint the precise dollar amount because many victims are too embarrassed to come forward. One man lost $400,000 before he reported it to the authorities. Another actually traveled to Nigeria in search of his portion of the money.

The trouble is, U.S. authorities can't prosecute the Nigerian perpetrators unless they travel to the United States. The Secret Service, which investigates many financial crimes, did establish a task force at the U.S. embassy in Lagos, Nigeria. In 1996, Secret Service agents helped Nigerian police nab forty-three people. They seized telephones, faxes, and fake letterhead. During the raid, authorities found files on victims from around the world.

KNOW THE SIGNS:

1. The letter is from Nigeria or another African country or it's from an African living elsewhere, like Europe. The Nigerian letter scam has been passed down through the generations and across borders.
2. The letter arrives in a brownish envelope. That's very typical.
3. The envelope or e-mail is addressed to "President" or "CEO" or another flattering term as if the writer believes you run a company.
4. The writer urges you to keep the matter confidential.
5. The letter is written in over-the-top "officialese," yet words and punctuation are used incorrectly.
6. Proceed with caution any time you are contacted by a stranger from Africa. The Nigerian letter scam has mutated into other schemes. For example, if you advertise a car for sale online, you may receive a generous offer from somebody in Africa. The person will send you a check for more than the amount you've agreed upon and ask you to send a check for the difference. The scammer is hoping you will send the money before you discover that *his or her* check is no good.

DO YOUR HOMEWORK:

1. Speak to friends, family, and police before responding to any stranger who asks for your personal financial information.

WHERE TO COMPLAIN:

The U.S. Secret Service investigates outbreaks of the Nigerian letter

SCAMS

scam. Go to **www.secretservice.gov.** If your letter arrived via U.S. mail, you can also contact the postal inspector for help.

SEE ALSO:

SCAMS: Bank Examiner

Police and Fire Funds

In the emotional days after September 11th, my next door neighbor gave in. She had gotten calls from people asking her to donate to police and firefighter funds before. This time she said yes. It's understandable. We all feel grateful when police officers and firefighters put their lives on the line to help us. That's exactly why con artists pose as police officers and firefighters and ask for money.

Recently I got some insider insights from a guy who had just quit working at one of these dishonest boiler rooms. He told me all the scammers use fake names when they call people on the phone. He said he and his colleagues regularly ignored laws that make it illegal to pose as a police officer or firefighter. He said the head of his operation routinely paid off the receptionist at the local fire department so she would lie and say the group was for real. And he explained that whenever he got a donation by claiming to be collecting money for the *police,* he would then give the number to a coworker who would call back and try to get another donation for the *fire* department.

Just to make matters more confusing, *real* police and fire organizations typically hire paid professional fundraisers to raise money for them. Even though these professionals are representing the real deal, it can still be a raw deal for you. Whenever there's a middleman less money goes to the actual cause. Here's another problem: Sometimes legitimate public safety organizations collect money without guaranteeing that the funds will be used *locally.* Don't assume your donation will help the police or firefighters down the street unless you ask.

KNOW THE SIGNS:

1. Keep in mind that groups that have nothing to do with police or firefighters can put those words in their names to gain your sympathy. Plus, the fakers often use names very similar to those of real organizations to confuse you.
2. Scam artists posing as police or firefighters may tell you that you'll receive special treatment if you donate. For example, they may say posting the group's decal in the window of your car will help ward off traffic tickets. Utterly unscrupulous—and untrue.
3. If you donate once, you will be bombarded with calls and letters asking you to donate again. The same group may claim it's been a year since you last gave (even though it hasn't). Or a different group may come calling, claiming you've donated in the past. That's because con artists sell their sucker lists to each other.

DO YOUR HOMEWORK:

1. Always ask fund-raisers to identify themselves. Ask whether they are paid solicitors. Some states require solicitors to provide this information immediately.
2. Ask what percentage of your donation goes to professional solicitors versus what percentage goes to the cause.
3. Find out whether your money will be used locally. If it's important to you, get that guarantee in writing.
4. Ask the caller for a number you can call back after you've thought about it. Again, shady groups won't want to provide this.
5. Ask solicitors to provide detailed written information explaining how your money will be used. If the group is illegitimate, you'll never receive it and you'll have saved some money.
6. Keep in mind, just because a group is tax *exempt* (like a fraternal organization) doesn't mean your contribution is tax *deductible*. Ask if it is. If so, get the group's tax ID number and make your check out to the official name of the organization—not a go-between.
7. Contact your local BBB and ask if there are complaints on file about the group.
8. Before you give, contact your local police or fire department or

SCAMS

the police or fire union to verify that the solicitors who approached you really are raising money for them. Try to speak to somebody other than the person who picks up the phone.

WHERE TO COMPLAIN:

Local police usually get all fired up about con artists using their name in vain. Give them a call. You can also contact your state attorney general. Put your complaint on record with the BBB.

SEE ALSO:

FINANCES: **Charity;** CARS: Donations

Pyramid Schemes

A pyramid is a sound structure for a building, but not for a business. Yet, thousands of people have lost millions of dollars to pyramid schemes. The most basic pyramid scheme is the old chain letter. You know, you receive a letter (or e-mail) containing a list of names. You're asked to send a dollar to the name at the top of the list. Then you're supposed to cross that name off, add your own name to the bottom of the list, and send the letter on to ten friends. Theoretically, if your friends do their part and pass the letter (and cash) along, eventually your name will be at the top of the list and you'll receive all sorts of money from strangers.

SCAMS

Bull! First of all, these chains usually break after just a couple of rounds. Second, they are just transfer schemes to move money from the bottom to the top of the pyramid. Third, they're illegal! Chain letters are easy to spot, but many illegal pyramid schemes disguise themselves as businesses, especially multilevel-marketing businesses.

Here's the key. In legitimate multilevel marketing, sales reps make money when they sell products and when reps they've recruited sell products. In an illegal pyramid scheme, sales reps make money when they recruit new reps and when the reps they've recruited recruit still *more* reps. Now here's the rub: Today more and more pyramids *trick* people by coming up with a product to use as a false front.

I investigated one company that claimed to be a multilevel-marketing business selling Internet service. I arranged for an undercover producer—and three hidden cameras—to hear the pitch. The salesman didn't *know* much about the Internet service he was supposed to be selling, and that was our first clue. He couldn't remember how much it cost per year! Next, the salesman told our producer he would have to pay $295 to come work for the company. That was red flag number two. Legitimate companies don't *charge* you to go to work for them.

The salesman said it was possible to make money gradually by selling the Internet service, but he made it clear that the *real* money was in recruiting and training *other* sales reps. That's the hallmark of a pyramid scheme: making money through recruitment. Furthermore, the company structured that recruitment rigidly. Each new rep had to recruit two more reps who, in turn, had to recruit two more, and so on. If you draw a diagram of the recruiting structure, guess what it looks like. A pyramid. That telltale structure is one of the things investigators look for.

The salesman claimed some of his colleagues were making $25,000 a week, and the company was making $500,000 a month. Grandiose claims about earnings potential are another classic pyramid tactic. And get this! When I confronted the company and asked if the Internet service was up and running yet, the salesman admitted it was not. If there was no *product* to generate all that *profit,* where was the money coming from? Well, it was coming from the poor recruits. Remember, each one paid $295 to join the company. It was a pyramid scheme, and it collapsed soon after my investigation.

The government has struggled to define pyramid schemes and prosecute their perpetrators. Here are two tests investigators *have* come up with. The sales reps must make substantially more money from selling the product than they do from recruiting new reps, and they must sell the product to people *outside* the company who actually *use* it. Here's the most insidious thing about a pyramid scheme: Even though you are a victim of the people *above* you in the pyramid, you can be prosecuted for taking advantage of the people *below* you.

Here's another way of thinking of it: Pyramid-shaped business plans are mathematically doomed to failure. It's called exponential

SCAMS

expansion and it's impossible to sustain. Let's take a "two by two" scheme like the one I investigated. Every rep has to recruit two more reps, who have to recruit two more, and so on. After just thirty-three levels of recruitment, they will have used up the entire population of the planet earth! There won't be anybody left to recruit!

KNOW THE SIGNS:

1. If an acquaintance lures you to a recruiting meeting without saying what it's about, that's a classic approach.

2. At that meeting you're likely to hear incredible claims about how much money you can make and how you can retire young. The person presenting may even show up in a fancy car to drive home the point.

3. You'll hear very little about the product. In fact, if you examine the "pyramid pitch" carefully, you'll probably find there is no demand for the product outside the company. Illegal pyramid schemes often require their sales reps to buy a huge inventory of the product that they later find they can't sell.

4. You will be asked to pay money to join the company. Sometimes this fee is disguised as a payment to stock up on the product.

5. Pyramid operators often pressure you to get in now or miss a golden opportunity. They push "fast track" and "quick start" programs to try to rush you into making a decision.

6. If you analyze the payment plan (which is hard to do because it's rarely in writing), you'll find that the company promises more money for recruiting than for selling the product.

7. That recruitment will follow a rigid structure. To make money, you must recruit a certain number of reps who, in turn, must recruit the same number. A legitimate business would be happy to let you recruit as many sales reps as you can or would be happy if you recruited none and focused on selling the product.

SCAMS

DO YOUR HOMEWORK:

1. If somebody offers you a "business opportunity," insist on getting details in writing. Study the written offer at home, at length. Never join a company at a rally-style recruitment meeting.

2. Consider whether the product is high-quality and whether there's a demand for it outside the company.
3. Study the payment plan and figure out what it's based on: recruitment or product sales.
4. Pyramid schemes use slippery language to confuse you. If you're still unsure, consult authorities before joining the company.
5. Do an Internet search of the company's name. If it's an established pyramid, you'll find all sorts of online rants from disgruntled sales reps who've already realized they were conned.
6. Check out the Web site, **www.pyramidschemealert.org.** See if the company is listed. Read more about telltale signs of a pyramid pitch.

WHERE TO COMPLAIN:

This is a job for your state attorney general. Also complain to the BBB to put other consumers on notice and write to the Federal Trade Commission. The FTC can't solve your individual case, but may take legal action if enough consumers complain; go to **www.ftc.gov.**

SEE ALSO:

EMPLOYMENT: Business Opportunities, **Multilevel Marketing, Work-at-Home Schemes;** FINANCES: Investment Fraud

Reloading

Every year Americans lose $40 billion to telemarketing scams. You'd think if you're one of the victims, you'd be less likely to fall for future schemes. But nothing could be further from the truth. Con artists target the same people over and over again—with startling success. It's called "reloading." Fraudulent telemarketers have learned that only 10 percent of the population will respond to a conniving cold call, but 80 percent of people who've been victimized *before* will fall for it again.

Every week Deanna A. received reams of junk mail—enough

come-ons to fill a garbage bag. Foreign lotteries to enter. Sweep-stakes prizes to claim. She began sending small checks, thinking it would increase her chances of winning. Soon she had spent $1,500. She didn't know that foreign lotteries are usually fake, and they're illegal in the United States. She didn't understand that legitimate sweepstakes have to let you enter for free.

Deanna didn't win a thing, but the con artists did. They got her money, but more important, they got her *name*. Crooks often start with junk mail because it's a cheap way to identify a soft target. Then they start calling. One man called Deanna morning, noon, and night. He told her she was on the verge of winning $31 million. Deanna's Hungarian family had endured terrible times in the 1940s between the Nazis and the communists. She allowed herself to dream of a better life now. She told the telemarketer he could charge $12.99 to her credit card. He charged $1,299 instead. At last, she swore off sweepstakes and lotteries.

But then Deanna received a different kind of call. A soft-spoken man called and claimed he was with a law firm. He said he under-stood a telemarketer had victimized her, and his firm could help. The man said he had negotiated a settlement for Deanna: $110,000 in compensation because she was cheated by the lottery and sweep-stakes industry. He explained that she would just have to send a check for $3,000 to cover the taxes on her settlement. Deanna did it. Next, he made the excuse that he needed $11,000 to get Deanna's settle-ment through customs. This seventy-five-year-old woman cashed in a CD, got a cash advance on her credit card, and sent the money.

It was the classic reloading scheme. The original con artist has an associate pose as a lawyer or cop who offers to help the victim. Deanna lost $17,000 in all—her life savings. FBI investigators say some reloaders make as much as $500,000 a year. Unfortunately, many are based in Canada—our neighbor to the North has looser laws. The FBI and Canadian authorities are beginning to work together to short-circuit reloaders. Not long ago, investigators infil-trated a reloading operation by pretending to sell a device that would save the telemarketers money! They've also had some suc-cess operating reverse boiler rooms where volunteers call likely vic-tims and warn them about reloading.

SCAMS

DO YOUR HOMEWORK:

1. Don't respond to sweepstakes and lottery offers you receive in the mail.
2. If somebody tries to sell you something over the phone, refuse to be rushed. Ask questions and request written information.
3. Buy only things you really want. Don't get suckered into buying one product for a chance at winning some prize. By law, contests must let you enter for free.
4. If you do decide to buy something by phone, pay with a credit card. If it turns out to be a scam, you can dispute the charges through your credit card company. If it's a case of fraud, there is no time limit for making a claim. The credit card company will credit your account, then pursue the crook's bank to get the money back.
5. If you've already been scammed, carefully consider whether subsequent callers are for real. Could a con man be trying to pull off a reloading scheme? Share this information with your senior citizen friends.

WHERE TO COMPLAIN:

Contact every law enforcement agency you can think of. That way you'll increase the chances that your case will cross the desk of an investigator who understands this tricky topic. Try the FBI, the Secret Service, your local police department's financial crimes unit, the state attorney general, and your county and state consumer protection offices.

SCAMS

SEE ALSO:

MAIL: **Sucker Lists,** Sweepstakes; TELEPHONE: Telemarketing; SCAMS: Foreign Lotteries

CHAPTER 16

Fighting Back

Better Business Bureau

Pop quiz: (Hint: this is an open-book test. If you read chapter 1, you'll know the answers!)

Is the Better Business Bureau a government agency?

Does it have the power to *make* businesses do the right thing?

Answers:

No! It's a private, nonprofit company funded by member businesses.

No! The BBB can *ask* companies to respond to consumers, but it doesn't have the power to *tell* them what to do.

The Better Business Bureau has phenomenal name recognition— partly because it does good work and partly because it has a catchy name. When consumers call me at the station to complain about a business, typically the *one* step they have taken on their own is to contact the BBB. They don't realize that the BBB's power is limited and that there are government watchdogs they can call on for help, too.

When you complain to the Better Business Bureau, here's what happens: The BBB forwards your letter to the business and asks for a response or resolution. If the company feels your complaint is unfounded, it can write a response explaining its side of the story. The BBB writes you back and offers you the chance to make a rebuttal. On the other hand, if the company feels your complaint has merit, it can offer to resolve it. In that case, the BBB writes you back with the company's offer. Many BBB branches also offer more formal mediation and arbitration programs.

The Better Business Bureau says its success rate for resolving consumer complaints is more than 70 percent. That's impressive, since the only leverage the BBB can use to influence the outcome is its rating system. Failure to respond to just one consumer complaint automatically earns a company an "unsatisfactory" rating. If the company *responds* to complaints but fails to *resolve* two or more of them, that's also grounds for an unsatisfactory rating. An unsatisfactory rating hurts the business when prospective customers do a background check with the BBB and decide to take their business elsewhere. In my opinion, the BBB is most successful with *good* companies that want to do the right thing.

If the BBB identifies a troubling *pattern* of complaints against a company, it alerts authorities. The Better Business Bureau and a few other grassroots groups take the pulse of the people and pass that information on to law enforcement. If you're feuding with one of the bad boys of the business, and you don't want to wait for the level of complaints to reach critical mass, you may have to take stronger steps on your own.

FIGHTING BACK

DO YOUR HOMEWORK:

1. Do a background check through the Better Business Bureau *before* you do business with a company. The BBB is still the single best source of information on companies' reputations because so many consumers know about it.
2. Find out whether the company you're feuding with is a Better Business Bureau member. If so, the BBB has additional programs to help smooth relations between customer and company.

3. File a formal written complaint with the Better Business Bureau by going to **www.bbb.org**. The national Web site will link you with the nearest local BBB. Do this because it may help you and because it will *definitely* help other consumers, by leaving a complaint trail.
4. If the Better Business Bureau cannot resolve your dispute, it may be able to help you identify which government agencies to turn to for additional help. Read the articles on the BBB Web site or call and ask for guidance.

SEE ALSO:

BEFORE YOU BUY: **Checking Out a Company;** FIGHTING BACK: **Government Watchdogs**

Complain Effectively

The first secret to complaining effectively is to complain in the first place. Only about 4 percent of dissatisfied consumers bother. The rest assume their complaints will go nowhere, so that self-fulfilling prophecy comes to pass. Studies show it's cheaper for a company to keep an existing customer than to attract a brand-new one. Use that statistic to your advantage. The second secret to complaining effectively is to be effective when you complain!

When you have a problem with a product or service, first gather your evidence. Collect price tags, receipts, warranties, manuals. Photograph or videotape the product or evidence, if applicable.

Next, adopt the right attitude. No matter how irate you are, set aside your anger. It's called acting! Be polite but firm. Avoid displays of temper, which will only get you labeled as a crank. People instinctively go on guard and resist your requests when you're overly aggressive. They may even say no just to spite you. The best approach is to say that you have a problem and ask for help. Most people have trouble turning away somebody who humbly asks for assistance.

FIGHTING BACK

Years ago, I wanted to exchange a defective portable stereo at the store rather than going through the manufacturer. I was in a mellow mood, so I pleasantly asked the sales guy if that might be possible. Even though the store had no obligation to help me because the exchange period was long over, he did it. He explained that he helped me because I wasn't shrill and obnoxious like so many of his customers. (He caught me on a good day ... and I learned a good lesson!)

I got lucky with that salesman, and that's where you should start, too: at the bottom. Contrary to popular belief, "taking it straight to the top" is not always best. The company president will only hand your complaint off to the customer service department anyway. Corporations often establish complex complaint procedures to discourage casual gripers. Demonstrate your seriousness by going through the process. As you proceed, keep a written record of who you spoke with, what the person promised and when. If possible, visit the business in person. It's harder for employees to dismiss somebody who's standing right in front of them. As you pass through each level of the hierarchy, thank each person, tell them you appreciate how helpful they've been (even if they haven't), and move on. The person at the next level is likely to consult with the underling you just dealt with, so leave a good impression.

Verbal requests only go so far. At some point, you may need to make your complaint official by putting it in writing. Keep your letter concise—one page if possible. List the product or service you had trouble with, giving details like makes, model numbers, names, and dates. DO NOT ramble about other things that bugged you about the sales experience. Stick with the core facts. Enclose *copies* of your documentation, *never* the originals. State the specific solution you would be satisfied with: a refund, exchange, repair, etc. Specify a reasonable time limit, maybe two weeks, and explain that after that you will have to seek assistance from a third party. Note that you've always liked the business or it came recommended (to imply that it's possible to keep you as a customer if the company does the right thing). Include your day and evening phone numbers. Make a copy of the letter for your files and send it certified mail, return receipt requested.

FIGHTING BACK

If the business agrees to help you, write a confirmation letter and send that certified also. It can double as a thank-you letter. The sign of a good business is not whether it makes mistakes, but how it addresses those mistakes.

DO YOUR HOMEWORK:

1. Keep receipts, price tags, contracts, warranties, instructions, and owner's manuals for everything you buy.
2. Do some deep breathing or something to adopt the right attitude before you complain. In with the positive, out with the negative!
3. Work your way up the food chain, refining your argument as you go.
4. Keep a record of each person you speak with, the date, and what the person said.
5. Research which government watchdog oversees the business— but don't file a complaint with that watchdog yet. Instead, name that third party in your letter.
6. Think about what outcome will satisfy you and ask for it in a firm, concise letter.
7. If you paid with a credit card, consider disputing the charge through your credit card company, too. You generally have sixty days to do this after the charge is made.
8. If you financed the item, you can get the finance company involved as well.

WHERE TO COMPLAIN:

FIGHTING
BACK

If the business fails to meet your deadline, then complain to the Better Business Bureau and the relevant government watchdog.

SEE ALSO:

FIGHTING BACK: **Better Business Bureau, Government Watchdogs,** Lawyers, Small-Claims Court

Government Watchdogs

I'm always amazed how many unhappy consumers contact the Better Business Bureau and consult a lawyer but do nothing in between. Where's the anger? The outrage? If you can keep your righteous indignation going long enough to find the government watchdog that has authority over the business you're mad at, you might actually see justice done. The Rolling Stones told you, you "can't get no satisfaction." I prefer the Jimmy Cliff song: "You can get it if you really want. But you must try. Try and try." Sometimes you *do* have to "try and try" to find the one government agency that can help you. Finding the one government bureaucrat at that government agency who can help you is even harder.

Here's what I suggest: Start by finding out whether your city or county has a consumer protection office. It could be part of the Department of Housing, Fair Housing, Licensing, Regulation, or some other bizarre, irrational, and unpredictable government umbrella agency. It may be called Consumer Affairs, Consumer Services, or Consumer Protection. Look online or flip through the blue government pages in the phone book. If you have trouble finding it, contact your elected county representative and ask. Not all local governments have the budget for consumer protection. If yours does, consider yourself lucky. Contact the department and ask for help with your dispute. Also ask whether there are other, more specific county agencies you can contact for help.

If your city or county does not have a consumer protection office, then you'll have to search at the state level. State consumer protection usually falls under the attorney general or the department of agriculture, but not always. Once again, go online, try the blue pages, or skip straight to the governor's office, which should be able to tell you which state agency looks out for consumers. Once you find the right place to complain to, file a complaint with your state consumer protection agency. Consumer protection statutes cover unfair and deceptive practices in general. But don't stop there! Ask whether the business you're complaining about is regulated by any *other* state agencies.

FIGHTING BACK

Here are some examples: The Department of Motor Vehicles may license car dealers. The Insurance Commission has authority over insurance companies. The licensing board could oversee contractors. The Public Utilities Commission regulates power companies. The state comptroller might monitor stockbrokers. The list goes on and on. Government consumer agencies are far from perfect. They're overworked, understaffed, and sometimes they get too cozy with the businesses they oversee. Increase your odds of success by asking multiple watchdogs for help. If you "try and try," you might just get some "satisfaction."

DO YOUR HOMEWORK:

1. Find out whether your city or county has a consumer protection office. If it does, file a complaint and ask for referrals to other government agencies.
2. Figure out which state agency protects consumers. File a complaint and ask for referrals to other agencies that may have the power to yank the company's license or shut it down.
3. Keep in touch with the government investigators assigned to your case. Let them know you are still waiting and wondering whether they can help you.
4. If the government watchdogs fail you, but you're convinced you're in the right, consider going to small-claims court or hiring a lawyer.

SEE ALSO:

FIGHTING BACK: **Better Business Bureau,** Small-Claims Court, Lawyers

FIGHTING BACK

Lawyers

If you've just lost hundreds or thousands of dollars to a crooked company, the idea of shelling out more money to a lawyer may be daunting—but don't despair. You may not have to pay the lawyer! Most consumer protection statutes require the business to pay the consumer's legal fees—*if* the consumer wins. So, if you feel confident you've got a good case—and an attorney agrees with you—you could be in luck. So how do you find a lawyer who handles consumer cases? It can be tricky, because these aren't usually big-dollar disputes, so not all attorneys are interested in taking them on.

There's an organization called the **National Association of Consumer Advocates**, or NACA, which is made up of consumer lawyers. If you go to the NACA Web site at **www.naca.net,** you will find the names of hundreds of attorneys across the country, with a description of their expertise. If you don't find what you need there, try contacting your local bar association. Ask the bar whether it has a consumer affairs committee. If it does, get the name of the chairman and contact that person. Ask for a referral to a consumer lawyer who handles your type of case. Another option is to go to the Web site, **www.martindale.com,** and look up lawyers in your area.

Now, I would be remiss if I didn't tell you how to check out the lawyer who's going to sue the company that you should have checked out in the first place, right? It's not as easy to do a background check on an attorney as it is to do one on, say, a used-car dealer. (Gee, I wonder who all the lawmakers are? Former lawyers!) But here's what you *can* do. Local bar associations *do* keep records of complaints against lawyers. The bar association should also be able to tell you if the lawyer has ever been disciplined or disbarred.

Once you've found a lawyer you like, you'll need to figure out how you're going to pay his or her fee. There are lots of options. Some attorneys want to be put on retainer. Others are paid hourly. Some keep track of their hours but don't charge you until the case is over. Others will take your case on contingency and ask for a percentage of the settlement. The lawyer is required to give you a written statement specifying how he or she expects to be paid and how much it will cost.

FIGHTING BACK

DO YOUR HOMEWORK:

1. Try some of the free options for fighting back before looking for a lawyer.
2. But don't wait too long. Find out what the statute of limitations

is for filing civil suits in your jurisdiction and make sure you find an attorney well before that.

3. Find a consumer lawyer through NACA, Martindale, or your local bar association or get referrals from friends.
4. Check the lawyer's reputation with the bar association.
5. Ask the lawyer how many cases of your type he or she has handled and what the results were.
6. Negotiate the best fee arrangement you can.
7. Sue the hell out of the company that wronged you!

WHERE TO COMPLAIN:

If you have a bad experience with your attorney, take your grievance to the local bar association.

SEE ALSO:

FIGHTING BACK: **Small-Claims Court**

Small-Claims Court

It's called *small*-claims court, but it can be a *big* relief if somebody owes you money. The dollar amount you can sue for in small-claims court varies depending on where you live. Some states limit small claims to $1,000. I've seen others that allow claims for $5,000. If your dispute is for slightly more than the limit, it may still be worth it to file a small-claims suit. You won't be able to sue for the full amount, but you'll avoid the expense of a regular lawsuit. The small-claims filing fee varies from state to state. It can be as cheap as $20, or as much as $200.

Generally, you have two to four years after the initial dispute to file a small-claims suit. Check the statute of limitations in your state. You can usually file in the county where the business is located or the county where you live. Check this out. Not all jurisdictions offer small-claims court, but if they don't, they often relax the rules in regular court for people trying to settle small arguments. To file your

FIGHTING BACK

suit, you usually fill out a form stating your name, the defendant's name, and the nature of the dispute.

You have to give the court the correct name and address of the defendant for your suit to go forward. If it's a company, you need the name of the owner. If it's a corporation, you need the name of one of the corporate officers. If the corporation uses a fictitious business name, you need the real corporate name. For example, you may know the business as "Mack's Towing," but the actual corporation may be called, "Mack Jones, Inc." Usually your secretary of state can give you information about a business and its owners. You will have to pay to have your lawsuit served on the defendant. Some states allow you to do this by certified mail, others require you to pay the sheriff's department to hand deliver your lawsuit.

To prepare for your day in court, you should write up a chronology of your dispute with the defendant. Also gather every piece of written evidence you have: contracts, receipts, leases, etc. Make two or three copies, so you'll be able to share your documentation with the court. If applicable, consider taking photographs that help prove your point, too. In addition, some states allow you to call witnesses to small-claims court. Finally, prepare your presentation by writing out bullet points that you want to cover and noting which documents or witnesses can help to illuminate each bullet point.

The great thing about small-claims court is that you don't have to pay a lawyer more money than your dispute involved in the first place. In fact, lawyers often aren't *allowed* in small-claims court. If you want to fine-tune your case, you could hire a lawyer for an hour or two to go over the case with you outside of court. Once you get to court, a judge or arbitrator will hear your case. You won't have to know the rules of court procedure and you'll be able to present your side in plain English.

If the defendant doesn't show up in court, often you win automatically. Keep in mind that if you lose your case, you do not have the right to sue again in a regular court. However, if the *defendant* loses, he or she *does* have the right to appeal to another court.

If you win, there's still no guarantee the defendant will pay the judgment. In some states, the court has no power to make the defen-

**FIGHTING
BACK**

dant hand over the money. Other states are more helpful. It's possible the defendant simply doesn't have the money to give you. At that point you can research whether the defendant owns any real estate and put a claim, called a "lien," against that real estate. When the defendant goes to sell the property, he or she will have to pay you out of the proceeds. If the defendant owns any valuables like a car or store inventory, you may be able to get the sheriff's department to seize those valuables and auction them off to satisfy your judgment. You may also be able to garnish the defendant's wages.

DO YOUR HOMEWORK:

1. Try free measures like complaining to the BBB and to government watchdogs before suing in small-claims court.
2. Determine the statute of limitations for your type of dispute in your jurisdiction. If you do want to sue, be sure you do it before the deadline.
3. Get an accurate name and address for the company or person you are suing; otherwise, your case will be dismissed.
4. Carefully prepare for your day in court. It's your only chance, so get organized and prepare to fight!
5. Follow all the steps allowed in your jurisdiction for collecting your judgment.

SEE ALSO:

FIGHTING BACK: **Lawyers**

FIGHTING
BACK

RESOURCES

AARP: Consumer services for people over age fifty.
www.aarp.org

The Better Business Bureau: Consumer advice, links to local BBB branches, and background checks on businesses.
www.bbb.org

Call For Action: Consumer assistance in partnership with local broadcasters.
www.callforaction.org

Consumer Federation of America: Consumer information, news of consumer issues before Congress.
www.consumerfed.org

Consumer Information Center: Order federal consumer publications or view them online *The Consumer's Resource Handbook* is free and lists corporate customer service contacts plus state consumer agencies.
www.pueblo.gsa.gov

Consumers' Checkbook: Publications rate local businesses on price and customer service.
www.checkbook.org

Consumer World: Privately run Web site lists local, state, national, and international consumer resources.

www.consumerworld.org

Federal Deposit Insurance Corporation: Rules and advice about banking and personal finance transactions.

www.fdic.gov

Federal Reserve Board: Information on banking, credit, loans; lists of low-interest credit cards.

www.federalreserve.gov

Federal Trade Commission: Articles on dozens of consumer topics, enforcement actions against bad businesses.

www.ftc.gov

Financial Planning Association: Find a Certified Financial Planner, or "CFP."

www.fpanet.org

First Gov for Consumers: Collection of consumer articles by various federal agencies.

www.consumer.gov

National Association of Attorneys General: Consumer news. Links to state attorneys general.

www.naag.org

National Association of Consumer Advocates: Consumer articles, referrals to consumer lawyers.

www.naca.net

National Consumers League: Consumer activism and information on dozens of consumer topics.

www.nclnet.org

RESOURCES

National Fraud Information Center: Advice about telephone and Internet fraud; clearinghouse for complaints.

www.fraud.org

Public Citizen: Consumer lobbying and education.
www.citizen.org

U.S. Public Interest Research Group: Consumer and environmental research and activism.
www.pirg.org

RESOURCES

INDEX

ABOUT THE AUTHOR

Elisabeth Leamy is the consumer and investigative reporter for Fox 5, WTTG in Washington, D.C. Elisabeth has won eleven Emmy awards, four regional Edward R. Murrow Awards, and an Associated Press award, among many others. Elisabeth's consumer and investigative stories have resulted in arrests, new city laws, and congressional inquiries.

Before joining WTTG, Elisabeth worked for WFLA, solving consumer problems in the Tampa Bay area. Elisabeth began her on-air career at KERO in Bakersfield, California and has also worked for ABC News in London. Elisabeth received her bachelor's degree in mass communications and rhetoric from the University of California, Berkeley. She earned her master's in journalism at Northwestern University's Medill School of Journalism.

Elisabeth grew up in Marin County, California, and now lives in the Washington, D.C., area, with her husband, Kris, and her dog, Buddha.

For more information, visit **www.thesavvyconsumer.com.**